S0-AGZ-111

Rowan
University

Native People of Southern New England, 1500–1650

The Civilization of the American Indian Series

Native People of Southern New England, 1500–1650

By Kathleen J. Bragdon

University of Oklahoma Press : Norman and London

Chapter ornaments are drawn by Kimberly Wagner. The ornaments for chapters 1–5 and 7–9 are based on drawings by William Fowler in the *Bulletin of the Massachusetts Archaeological Society*, vol. 27 (1992), p. 44, figs. 1, 4, 5, 6, 7, and 8, 10, 11, respectively. The ornament for chapter 6 is based on a drawing at the Peabody Museum of Archaeology and Ethnology, Harvard University. The ornament for chapter 10 is based on a photograph at the Peabody Essex Museum, Salem, Massachusetts.

Bragdon, Kathleen Joan.
Native people of southern New England, 1500–1650 / by Kathleen J. Bragdon.
p. cm. — (The civilization of the American Indian series; v. 221)
Includes bibliographical references and index.
ISBN 0-8061-2803-8 (alk. paper)
1. Indians of North America—New England—History—16th century. 2. Indians of North America—New England—History—17th century. 3. Indians of North America—New England—Social life and customs.
I. Title II. Series
E78.N5B73 1996
974.01—dc20 95-42067
CIP

Text design by Cathy Carney Imboden. Text typeface is Baskerville II.

Native People of Southern New England, 1500–1650 is Volume 221 in The Civilization of the American Indian Series.

The paper in this book meets the guidelines for permanence and durability of the Committee on Production Guidelines for Book Longevity of the Council on Library Resources, Inc. ∞

1 2 3 4 5 6 7 8 9 10

To Marley III and Marley IV;
past, present, and future

Contents

Illustrations

Figures

Illustrations

Maps

Preface

In this book I portray the indigenous people of the region now called southern New England as they lived in the sixteenth and seventeenth centuries. These people include the Pawtucket, Massachusett, Nipmuck, Pocumtuck, Narragansett, Pokanoket, Niantic, Mohegan, and Pequot, as well as the peoples of western Connecticut and Long Island (Map 1). My goal is to provide an account that is, as far as possible, consistent with the Native point of view and with Native voice. Hence, I often make use of the indigenous term, *Ninnimissinuok*, to refer generally to people of the region. This term, a variation of the Narragansett word *Ninnimissinnûwock*, which means roughly 'people,' connotes familiarity and shared identity (Williams 1936:A3; Trumbull 1903:306), and thus avoids not only the awkwardness and inaccuracy of the use of multiple "tribal" labels, but also the troublesome fact that these names were sometimes tags applied to the inhabitants of this region by others, including non-Natives.[1]

The use of the term *Ninnimissinuok* does not imply, however, a homogeneity of social forms or motivations among the various groups so labeled. The region now known as southern New England

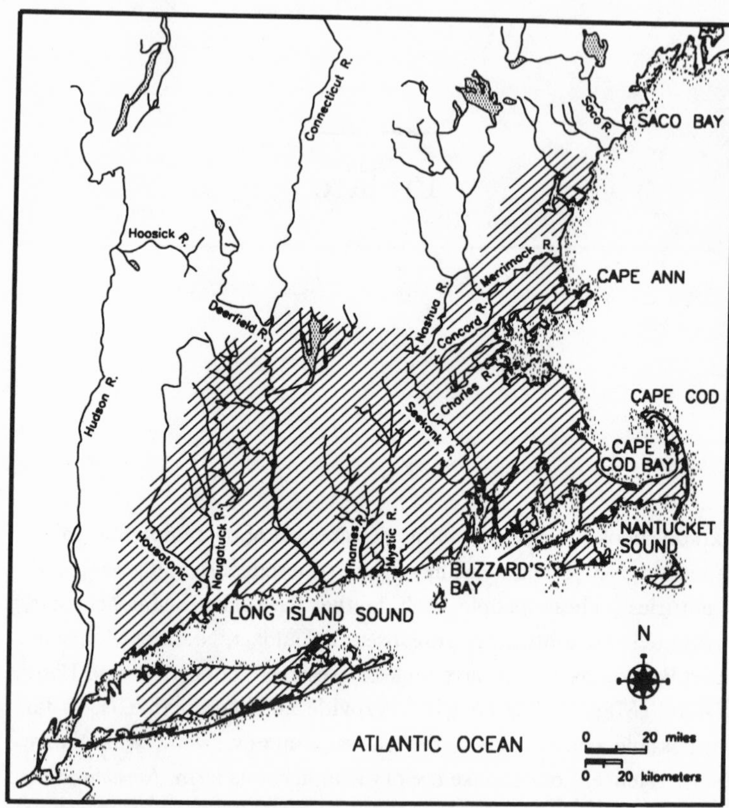

Map 1. Southern New England, with emphasis on the regions occupied by the Ninnimissinuok in the early seventeenth century. (Artist: Sondra Jarvis.)

was home to a complex variety of communities, sometimes grouped into larger polities, which can be divided into at least three basic ecological subregions: the coastal, the riverine, and the uplands. Although sharing an underlying cosmology, similar languages, and a long history, the peoples living in each of these regions developed distinctive social and economic adaptations. Of southern New England, we can use a Narragansett phrase, *yo chippachâusin*, "there, the way divides"(R. Williams 1936:69). The interactions between these peoples and the outcome of such interactions can be understood at least in part in light of this regional socio-ecological complexity.

This is a book about Native people, and only secondarily a book about their interactions with Europeans. Following Ortner (1984:143), I am attempting to write about the Ninnimissinuok of southern New England, and not "the impact of our history" on those people. While many scholars working in southern New England pay lip service to the admonition "to portray native people in their own right, acting for their own reasons in light of their own cultural norms and values" (Berkhofer 1987:36), the Ninnimissinuok of southern New England have not yet moved "to the front of their historical stage" (36)—in part because they continue to be monolithically defined in terms of western concepts of economic rationalism, most notably encompassing such generalized "Indian" qualities as reciprocity and egalitarianism (cf. A. Weiner 1992).

My position also departs from the "world systems" perspective, with its focus on the spread of capitalist systems (e.g., Wallerstein 1974); while acknowledging the impact of western economy, politics, and world view, I believe that internally developed motivations, structural relations, and cultural perceptions account for much Native action within the early contact period, and in any case require separate treatment. As an anthropologist, I further reject the assumption, common among historians of southern New England, that indigenous people are (were) essentially similar to descendants of the western tradition, that they share(d) the same emotional, physical, and psychological responses to the world, and thus can be understood in light of any deeply considered life experience (e.g., Axtell 1985:14). This is an ethnohistory, in the sense of a historical ethnography or a historical anthropology, of the Ninnimissinuok; it is not a portrait of their relations with others.

The first detailed word pictures of the Ninnimissinuok are from a time when they were undergoing tremendous change. Developments in the late fifteenth and sixteenth centuries toward greater population concentration and sociocultural complexity throughout the region are as yet poorly understood. The complexity of aboriginal developmental trends was of course magnified manyfold by the effects of European exploration, trade, and settlement in the sixteenth and seventeenth centuries. The cultural modalities outlined in the chapters to follow, and the underlying ideological systems on which these rested, are composities, depicting systems at arbitrary points along what must have been a mosaic-like spectrum of adaptations, some precontact and others reflecting at least some degree of postcontact adjustment. I do not claim that the cultural systems described here are "aboriginal," whatever that might mean, but only that they represent those configurations that seem most consistent with one another, and with archaeological, ecological, and cross-cultural studies of people with similar languages and/or economic adaptations.

Theoretical Framework

The enduring fascination of anthropology stems in part from its perpetual failure to reconcile "competing" paradigms, most of which still find voice in contemporary ethnography, archaeology, and ethnohistory. I believe that the essentially Boasian respect for the history and integrity of each cultural order characteristic of ethnohistory is also compatible with perspectives that seek regularities in behavior cross-culturally. Among these, I have paid special attention to phenomenological approaches that emphasize the role of habitual action in the creation and maintenance of cultural patterns. Such a perspective, among other things, permits a detailed culturalist understanding of economic behavior, with an emphasis on the metaphors with which people conceptualize their world (Gudeman 1986). In addition, a phenomenological approach argues that social relations link what has traditionally been known as society's "base," those institutions and behaviors most directly related to subsistence, and "superstructure," that is, ideology, cosmology, belief systems, and symbol systems in general. Such an approach obviates the necessity to separate out the economic from the ideological; it in fact sees them as part of the same, seamless whole. The habitual actions of collecting, farming, and hunting among peoples of coastal southern New England, for example, appear to have been constituative of the sexual division of labor, gender relations, social hierarchy, and understandings of the supernatural.

When the ecological is also firmly connected to the behavioral and the cognitive, it comprises what Anthony Giddens calls "locale" (1990:220). The physical world is at once the "frame" within which actions take place, the basis for a metaphorical model of social relations, and a "record" of the symbolic and ethical principles characteristic of a people (e.g., Basso 1984). At least since Bronislaw Malinowski's careful descriptions of the Kula route (1984), it has been clear that actors are fully aware of the context in which their actions take place, and that full understanding of utterances and behavior depends on the awareness of all participants in a communicative event of the landscape in which it is enacted. The symbolic weight that landscape has is well documented in indigenous societies worldwide. Among the Ninnimissinuok such a consciousness was marked in the careful siting of ritual activities, and in sacred stories, stories still told among their descendants today (Simmons 1986).

Locale might also be said to include social actors, actors whose motives must be carefully and critically scrutinized. Marxist and feminist concerns with inequality, its origins, and its relationship to gender roles, family structure, and to other social modalities also inform my discussion of the status of women, of kinship, and of governance. It is difficult not to conclude, for example, when examining descriptions of women's habitual work among the Ninnimissinuok, that their status was not commensurate with their important contributions to the indigenous economy. Much of the literature on southern New England Native society has obscured the nature of gender relations by focusing instead on assumed differences between its "egalitarian" social organization in contrast to that of Europeans.

The anthropological and historical literature on southern New England has also been obscured by the use of various sociopolitical labels, most notably the term *tribe*, to characterize the nature of governance and sociopolitical organization in that region. Some writers, such as Frank Speck, used the term interchangeably with *band* or *village* (e.g., 1928). Others use the term as a convenient gloss for otherwise nondifferentiated people (e.g., Vaughan 1965). Elman Service's definition of a tribe as transitional between band and state (1962) has also been applied to the polities of southern New England, particularly by Thomas (1979), Snow (1980), and Salwen (1978). The reality of this vaguely conceived entity in "prehistoric" North America has been vigorously questioned by numerous scholars, and its applicability in southern New England is likewise questionable. In part because previous discussions of the nature of governance in southern New England have been couched in terms of a dichotomy between "kin-based" social orders and those of the "rational/legal" state (e.g., Thomas 1979), many scholars have hesitated to attribute "evolutionary" complexity to Ninnimissinuok sociopolitical organization, in spite of solid evidence in its favor. One further complication in southern New England is the likely distinction between coastal, riverine, and uplands modes of political organization, which have not been adequately recognized. The interchangeable use of sources derived from different regions and peoples has led to a great deal of confusing argumentation and to a false impression of homogeneity and stasis among the Native people of southern New England.

The seemingly static character of indigenous societies increasingly appears to be an artifact of the perspectives of the observer, rather than being inherent in so-called "cold" or traditional cultures, for each has its own unique history, a history that colors contemporary events and actions. It has long been the contention of Boasian anthropology that, as Karl Marx put it, "Human beings make their own history . . . not under circumstances chosen by themselves . . . but directly encountered, given, and transmitted from the past" (Marx and Engels 1968:97). Structural continuities, evident in the archaeological and historical record, are also continually tested against contingent events. It is in fact the attempt to reproduce such historically grounded modalities, which, in contact situations, sometimes results in their transformation (Sahlins 1985). The dearth of first-hand accounts of Native reactions to European presence makes cultural adjustments difficult to detect, but Ninnimissinuok ritual in particular demonstrates ways in which structures and symbols were transformed in the crucible that was southern New England in the early seventeenth century.

Another such transformation was an increasing appreciation for tradition among southern New England's Native people, particularly as expressed in ritual. Giddens has pointed out that two casts of thought characterize western societies: historicity and deroutinization (1979:220–22). Historicity, or the consciousness of the progressive (and linear) passing of time, although not the exclusive province of western societies, frequently emerges as a category of local discourse in situations of developing "ethnicity" or in periods of cultural contact. It is with the appearance of such historicity among the Ninnimissinuok that I leave off my analysis—not as a tacit admission of the failure of those people to survive the invasion of their homelands, but as a marking of the emergence of a constellation of cultural premises and practices more characteristic of the late seventeenth and eighteenth centuries (e.g., Bragdon 1981, 1987a; Goddard and Bragdon 1988).

Ethnohistory and the Ambiguities of Archaeology

A question that confronts all researchers who study the historical record in southern New England is the contrast between what the documents describe and what archaeological data imply. The late Lynn Ceci, in particular, has been influential in urging archaeologists and ethnohistorians to re-examine their assumptions about late prehistoric settlement and subsistence in the Northeast, arguing that many patterns presumed to have been aboriginal were in fact artifacts of European contact (1975, 1977, 1979–80). Many scholars have suggested, for example, based on the descriptions of early explorers and settlers, that the Natives of southern New England occupied settled village sites, dependent on maize horticulture. In opposition to this "ethnohistorical" model, Ceci and others have more recently argued that maize horticulture and settled village life in coastal regions were in fact a response by Native people with a band-like sociopolitical organization to the development of trading relations with Europeans, but that prehistorically such Natives were part of mobile groups with egalitarian social structures. The archaeological evidence does not support the ethnohistorical model, but at the same time, recorded Native traditions, early descriptions of Native social order, and linguistic data imply a complex system, one that seems unlikely to have evolved in the period commonly called *protohistoric*, that period during which European trade goods entered Native trade networks, and knowledge of brief exploratory visits by Europeans began to filter through Native societies.

It appears, as Bruce G. Trigger has argued, that ethnohistorians must ally themselves with archaeologists in forging their own theories about societies in the past (1987:28–29). The growth of contract archaeology since the 1970s in the wake of federal and state historic preservation legislation has added a tremendous quantity of new information to the literature on southern New England prehistory, much of it at odds with previous findings. At the same time, archaeologists in New England and elsewhere have been forerunners in the development of new theories of sociocultural evolution, the origins of complex societies and the state, and the interrelations of ecological, social, and ideological factors that have been influential in the writing of this book (e.g., Upham 1990; Earle 1987). Can stratification exist without sedentism? Can complex sociopolitical entities be formed without a permanent village focus? How do we understand such complexity, and what are its parameters? Can sedentism exist without agriculture? What would such a sedentism look like? Such questions, still largely unexplored in the ethnographic literature, must be addressed before we can turn to the study of sustained interaction between the Natives of North America and Europeans.

Methods and Sources

The Ninnimissinuok of the early seventeenth century are known to us primarily through documents written by Europeans and to a lesser extent through archaeology. The terrible population losses experienced by these people in 1616–1619, and again in 1633, have undoubtedly led to confusion in the records about ethnic boundaries, modes of succession, and other political and economic matters considered important by English observers. This, added to the well-known bias, inaccuracy, and lacunae of most documentary sources, makes the cultural portrayal of these Natives approaching even the "near approximation" of contemporary ethnographic description a formidable task.

Two additonal sources of information can in part compensate for the problematic historical and archaeological record: cross-cultural models and examples, and ideas derived from the study of historic and modern eastern Algonquian languages. In addition to word lists and descriptions of Native languages supplied by early English observers, and contemporary analyses of the languages spoken in southern New England (all members of the eastern branch of the Algonquian language family), another unique source of linguistic information available for the Massachusett-speaking peoples of the region are documents written in that language by Native speakers, who adopted literacy in the 1650s. These records are slightly later in time than the period discussed in this book but constitute a unique source of firsthand information about Native languages that cannot be ignored by the ethnohistorian (Goddard and Bragdon 1988).

My methods have been to collect the earliest and most reliable sources of information on every topic, to carefully sort them by region, and to interpret these data in light of contemporary theories of cultural continuity and change. A tremendous amount of research on the backgrounds and motives of many historical figures who penned descriptions of Natives in the Northeast has been completed in recent years, all of which makes the evaluation of their observations a great deal easier. Many of these individuals, and the writings that survive them, are discussed in my introduction. In some cases I have sought descriptions that detailed the actions of specific individuals or groups, and from these compiled an "action inventory" in much the same way an ethnographer would record events, in order to determine what underlying structural or otherwise culturally determined principles might unify the actions so described. I have also attempted at every stage to go beyond the critical evaluation of sources required of any historical writer so as to be particularly sensitive to the presence of cultural and gender-based bias both in the historical sources and in previous interpretations of Native life in the Northeast written by historians and anthropologists.

It may be thought inconsistent that I occasionally use sources dating later than 1650, but my justification for this is that ethnohistory is inherently "deconstructive." By ordering early descriptions of "others" in ways that reflect longstanding patterns of behavior, the ethnohistorical perspective allows a more comprehensive picture of indigenous lifeways and perspectives to emerge than one tied to a strictly temporal arrangement of sources.

The most challenging effort in writing this book, however, has been to combine data successfully from archaeological, linguistic, historical, and ethnographic sources into a coherent picture of the Ninnimissinuok in the period 1500–1650. It is the combination of these sources, I believe, that allows the best understanding of the nuances and complexities of Native life in southern New England, gives the Native voice its greatest power, and best informs theoretical debates about cultural construction, maintenance, and change.

Previous Studies of the Ninnimissinuok

Historians have long written about the Ninnimissinuok, although not by that name, as have anthropologists and those working within the more recently developed field of ethnohistory. My study builds on the work of many of these writers, a body of scholarship with roots in the seventeenth century. The earliest histories of Native people written in New England reflect (as do all histories) the preoccupations and prejudices of their time, characterizing and "reinventing" the Natives as cunning, idolatrous savages (e.g., Mather 1702; Hubbard 1865), celebrating their providential removal by a just God (Salisbury 1982:4–5), and, by the early nineteenth century, depicting them as worthy but vanquished opponents of progress (Berkhofer 1978). As constructed as are any "inventions," these interpretations consistently failed to acknowledge the coherence, integrity, and equivalent humanity of Native cultures, and continued to employ the Natives as foils against which the actions of colonists, statesmen, and pioneers could be favorably judged. Not until Lewis Henry Morgan documented the symmetry of Iroquoian kinship and political systems did Native people begin to figure as rational actors in the drama of American history (1871). Even those historians who benefitted from Morgan's scholarship (and that of the newly developing field of ethnology) saw Native culture, regretfully, as fragile, vulnerable to western technological superiority, and irretrievably lost.

Anthropologists working with the descendants of historic Native people in southern New England likewise understood themselves to be doing "salvage ethnography," among people whose behavior and folklore were considered to be an unsystematic collection of remnant "traits." The influential studies of Speck (e.g., 1928), Tantaquidgeon (1930), Rainey (1936), Flannery (1939), and Butler (1948), although innovative in their use of primary sources to reconstruct past lifeways, suffer not only from the limitations of the "inventory" approach to cultural analysis characteristic of much of the culture-area school of anthropology, but also from their romanticized and mordant views of Native cultural disappearance.

The virtual explosion of writing on southern New England Native people since the sixties can be attributed at least in part to a renewed interest in frontiers (e.g., Bailey 1969) and to new orientations within the field of history, particularly the New Social History's emphasis on the experiences of previously understudied segments of society (Henretta 1979). At the same time, critical anthropological understanding of cultural representation and the impact of hegemonic constructions on perception led many to the restudy of cultural interaction in southern New England. Galvanized by Francis Jennings's *Invasion of America* (1975), historians and anthropologists, now often calling themselves ethnohistorians, turned again to seventeenth-century sources to discover Englishmen whose charters of religious freedom and missionary zeal masked a grim determination to possess both the land and its original owners, and Native people with "agendas" of their own (Burton 1974; Weinstein 1983; Grumet 1978). Recent scholarship has contributed immensely to our understanding of what are sometimes called "Indian-White" relations (e.g., Salisbury 1982; Axtell 1985) of cultural change (e.g., Simmons 1979; Ronda 1981; Von Lonkhuyzen 1989), as well as of cultural continuity (e.g., Simmons 1986; Goddard and Bragdon 1988). It has also served to fill in many of the gaps in our knowledge of Native life in the late sixteenth and seventeenth centuries.

Organization

This book builds on such scholarship, and relies on it heavily. Chapters 1 and 2 consider the "locale" of action, including the "prehistoric" setting reflected in archaeological remains. The patterns discernable in the archaeological record are related in turn in chapters 3 and 4 to early descriptions of subsistence and to the "relations of production" that made up the bulk of everyday experience for the Ninnimissinuok. The next three chapters describe social relations and the wider network of intergroup connections of which they were a part, and chapters 8 through 10 link the previous discussions to the cosmological and ritual practices that made sense of the lived world. Although frequent reference to Europeans is made, this is by no means meant to imply the subsuming of Native action within a European frame. Rather, such references acknowledge the significance of the English as sources of information about Native people and as goads to action within a Native context.

The description of Native lifeways ends with the 1640s—before the adoption of Christianity, the establishment of "praying towns" in many parts of southern New England, and the concatenation of events leading to King Phillip's War in 1675. The later seventeenth century was a period of complexity equal to that of the early contact period, and one that can only be understood in light of the events and structural relations emergent in the protohistoric period. It is these events and relations that form the subject of this book, a portrait of the Ninnimissinouk not on the verge of disappearance, but poised Janus-like between a "traditional" yet dynamic past and an equally challenging new reality created by the contingent events of southern New England's colonization by Europeans. There again, "the way divides."

Acknowledgments

The regional portrait I present here was drawn from a large variety of sources and benefitted from the scholarship of numerous people. I would especially like to thank my colleagues in archaeology, Kevin McBride, Steven Mrozowski, Constance Crosby, Brona Simon, Deborah Cox, James Bradley, Lucianne Lavin, Barbara Luedtke, James Petersen, Elizabeth Little, Frederick Dunford, Harold Juli, Eric Johnson, Nick Bellantoni, and Alan Leveille, for their patience with my questions and for sharing unpublished data with me. Nathan Altschuler, Brad Weiss, William Fisher, Elizabeth Little, David Bernstein, Barbara Luedtke, Jack Campisi, Neal Salisbury, and an anonymous reviewer read drafts of chapters or of the entire manuscript, and all made many helpful comments. The staffs of the Harvard Peabody Museum, the Rhode Island Historical Society, and the Haffenreffer Museum of Anthropology generously allowed me to examine and photograph items from their collections, and the Massachusetts Archaeological Society kindly gave me permission to reproduce drawings from their published proceedings.

I would also like to thank my research assistants, Neil Kennedy, Barbara Heaps, and especially Shannon Dawdy, who labored long over maps, archaeological reports, and nineteenth-century local histories. Artists Kimberly Wagner and Sondra Jarvis worked cheerfully to complete maps and illustrations. My parents, George and Patricia Bragdon, have provided, as always, unflagging support. Finally, my deepest gratitude goes to my husband and colleague Marley Brown, whose initial encouragement led me to write this book, and who has suffered many months as a result, and to my dear son Marley, who has patiently shared me with this work.

Native People of Southern New England, 1500–1650

Introduction

This account of the Ninnimissinuok is primarily an ethnography, an analysis of the principles on which life among these people was based, and to a lesser extent, how these principles were transformed after English colonies were established in southern New England. Like other ethnographies, this one relies on, and makes visible, ethnological theories, models, and data. Certain debates among scholars are discussed, not merely as an academic exercise, but to emphasize what is often hidden in narrative accounts: the hegemonic quality of both seventeenth-century primary data and twentieth-century analyses of that data. Following in the long tradition of ethnographic writing, this portrait of the Ninnimissinuok begins with an acount of arrival (Pratt 1986:40–43), in this case the arrival of European explorers and English settlers in the region. But although the Europeans speak first in this ethnography, they do not have the last word.

The "Observers" Observed: Europeans in New England, 1524–1650

[June (?), 1524] We . . . proceeded to another place, fifteen leagues distant from the island [Block Island], where we found a very excellent harbor. Before entering it, we saw about twenty small boats full of people, who came about our ship, uttering many cries of astonishment, but they would not approach nearer than within fifty paces; stopping, they looked at the structure of our ship, our persons and dress, afterwards they all raised a loud shout together, signifying that they were pleased. By imitating their signs, we inspired them in some measure with confidence, so that they came near enough for us to toss to them some little bells and glasses, and many toys, which they took and looked at, laughing, and then came on board without fear. Among them were two kings more beautiful in form and stature than can possibly be described; one was about forty years old, the other about twenty-four, and they were dressed in the following manner: The oldest had a deer's skin around his body, artificially wrought in damask figures, his head was without covering, his hair was tied back in various knots; around his neck he wore a large chain ornamented with many stones of different colors. The young man was similar in his general appearance. This is the finest looking tribe, the handsomest in their costumes, that we have found in our voyage. They exceed us in size, and they are of a very fair complexion; some of them incline more to a white, and others to a tawny color; their faces are sharp, and their hair long and black, upon the adorning of which they bestow great pains; their eyes are black and sharp, their expression mild and pleasant, greatly resembling the antique. (Verrazzano 1970:137–38)

So the residents at what is now Newport harbor appeared to Giovanni da Verrazzano in 1524 (Quinn 1975:154–56). This striking passage recorded by the Italian captain sailing with a commission from Francis I depicts a joyful paradise, an encounter between strangers unmarred by fear or violence. As participants in a literate tradition (the Ninnimissinuok, in contrast, were masters of the oral turn), Europeans have been awarded ascendancy in historical accounts partly because of the permanency of their written impressions, the most enduring artifacts of such early encounters. The Ninnimissinuok, however, also remembered, judged, and responded to those newcomers and their goods.

Nearly sixty years passed between the publication of Verrazzano's report and the appearance of accounts by later explorers, soldiers, and traders who sailed the New England coast. In the 1580s and 1590s promoters such as Richard Hakluyt the younger touted the idea of English enterprise in northern New England (Quinn 1975:390–91), and early in the seventeenth century several English expeditions reached the shores of New England, including those of Bartholomew Gosnold in 1602, Martin Pring in 1603, and George Waymouth in 1605 (Brereton 1968; Pring 1930; Rosier 1930). Meanwhile, the French, who had been concentrating their efforts in the Saint Lawrence, ordered Samuel de Champlain to investigate the New England coast, a mission he carried out in the summers of 1604 and 1606. Champlain's detailed descriptions and maps, and those of Marc Lescarbot, who accompanied Champlain on his later voyages, are a most important early source of information on the coastal cultures of New England (Champlain 1922; Lescarbot 1907).

The regions west and south of Buzzard's Bay were less well known in the early seventeenth century, until Dutch explorations began to add additional geographic detail. After an abortive search for the Northwest Passage,[1] Henry Hudson coasted south from Newfoundland as far as the Chesapeake in the summer of 1609. Doubling back, he began his renowned explorations of the Hudson river in September of that year (Juet 1912). Adrien Block's voyages, undertaken between 1612 and 1614, provided added cartographic data (Salwen 1978:168) and were the basis of the first account of the Natives living between Narragansett Bay and western Long Island, published by Johan de Laet in 1625 (Laet 1909).

The voyages of John Smith, who, after his successes with the Jamestown colony in Virginia, was eager to promote settlement in New England, took place in 1614. His descriptions, and in particular, his map of Native villages, are an additional important historical source for the southern New England region (Smith 1912), as is the brief letter of Thomas Dermer, who sailed to New England in 1619 accompanied by Tisquantum, otherwise known as Squanto, the Patuxet Native who was captured and taken to England by Thomas Hunt in 1614 (Dermer 1968; Salisbury 1981:234–35).

The descriptions written by these explorers, and the eye-witness verbal reports, rumors, and outright fabrications circulated in Europe, formed the body of knowledge brought with the earliest English settlers, whose actions most profoundly affected the Native inhabitants, and whose descriptions provide the bulk of information we now possess about the Ninnimissinuok in the seventeenth century. The Ninnimissinuok too relied on these early encounters in forming their impressions. As might be expected, the realities that came to expression in these encounters were not fully understood by either people.

Early Encounters

Encounters between the Ninnimissinuok and numerous European explorers served as prototypes for those that were to follow. For their part, Europeans found Natives ceremonious, eager to trade, hospitable, curious, and sometimes "thievish" (e.g., Brereton 1968:43). As the number of those encounters increased, however, explorers noted an increasing cynicism and suspicion, and a tendency to respond with violence in uncertain situations (e.g., Dermer 1968:251–52).

A chronicle of encounters might explain such a transformation, for Native people soon observed that certain European explorers were absolutely without conscience regarding Native property or persons. Dozens of people were captured and transported to Europe and especially England during the late sixteenth and early seventeenth centuries, and only a handful ever returned. Sailors looted Native graves, and stole their seed corn, tools, and household goods. Exploring parties deployed vicious dogs, discharged guns, and built forts, displaying their hostility with every gesture (Brasser 1978:80–83).

Indeed, by the time the first lengthy descriptions of the Ninnimissinuok were written in the 1620s, the idyllic portrait penned by Verrazzano was no longer (if it had ever been) an accurate depiction of European admiration or welcoming Native response. The Ninnimissinuok emerged into European literary consciousness debilitated by disease and disenchanted with encounters with all-too-human others. It is only in light of these aspects of the early contact period, that the later descriptions, on which the ethnography of the Ninnimissinuok is based, can be understood.

Englishmen Who Wrote about the Ninnimissinuok

The reports of early explorers regarding the Ninnimissinuok were necessarily cursory due to the shortness of their stays, and more importantly, the inadequacy of their knowledge of Native languages of the region.[2] The most complete descriptions of native life in the seventeenth century come from colonists who meant to make their homes in southern New England. Among the earliest of these was that written by Edward Winslow (1595–1655). Winslow was an urbane and clever ambassador, apologist, and statesman, whose presence in the infant Plymouth colony did much to ensure its survival. Together with the enigmatic Stephen Hopkins, Winslow served as liaison to the powerful Pokanokets—the Pilgrims' nearest neighbors and their most important Native allies. Winslow's account, written in 1624, is considered among the most complete and sympathetic of the early reports on Native life, but was nevertheless composed in order to justify colonization, the rout of the Weston colony and Thomas Morton's Ma-re Mount, the implementation of the wampum trade, and subsequent missionary efforts among the "subject" Natives of the Massachusetts Bay and Plymouth colonies.

Another resident of Plymouth was William Bradford, governor of the colony from 1627 to 1656. Bradford was born in 1590 in

Austerfield, Yorkshire. His early association with the Congregationalists at Scrooby led him first to the Low Countries, and ultimately to New Plymoth. A weaver by trade, he was self-educated in Latin and Hebrew, and widely read. He arrived in the New World on the Mayflower in 1620 and served as leader of the colony for most of the remainder of his life (Bradford 1970:xxv). Bradford's *Of Plymouth Plantation* provides full descriptions of encounters with the Pokanoket and the Massachusett in the early years of settlement, without Winslow's analytic talent or promotional zeal.

It was another apologist for colonization, William Wood, who published the best early description of the Ninnimissinuok living in the northern regions of the Massachusetts Bay. Very little is known about Wood (Kupperman 1980:25–26). He probably came to Massachusetts Bay in 1628 with the original settlers of Salem, and his writings indicate that he was well-educated. Karen Kupperman notes that several William Woods were students at Cambridge and that the New England writer was probably one of them (25). Wood stayed in New England for only four years but evidently spent a good deal of time with the Native people of the Naumkeag area. His volume *New England's Prospect* contains a lengthy description of the "Aberginians" of his locale, to which is appended a "small nomenclator," the first published word list in a southern New England Native language. Wood is especially voluble about gender relations and gender roles and uses the Indians as a mirror for his readers' understanding of those issues.

Additional information on the people of the Massachusetts Bay appeared in lawyer Thomas Morton's *New English Caanan*, written in 1637. With the support of Sir Ferdinando Gorges, Morton established himself at the tiny settlement at Mount Wollaston (now Quincy, Massachusetts), which he renamed *Ma-re Mount* and where he traded with the local Massachusett for furs and other commodities. Well-educated, and a royalist, Morton brought to his descriptions a deep contempt for the Pilgrim and Puritan settlers of the region. According to Kupperman, Morton "set himself up as the opposite of everything that his Puritan neighbors stood for" (26). For his pains, Morton was imprisoned three times by Puritan authorities. His lively descriptions of the Massachusett with whom he lived and traded are generally free of the moral outrage common in later accounts, and he saw much in their lives worthy of emulation, but was, perhaps because of his stubborn anti-Puritanism, strangely blind to Native spirituality, of which he claimed he could find no trace.

Not so Roger Williams (ca. 1603–1683), who was born in London, the son of a shopkeeper, and migrated to Massachusetts Bay in 1631. After serving as minister in Salem, Williams was banished from the colony in 1635 and in 1636 settled in Providence, Rhode Island. He later was the London agent for Rhode Island and president of that same colony. An orthodox Calvinist, Williams is best known to historians and anthropologists for his sensitive and informative *Key Into the Language of America* (1643), written while at sea on his way to London. Both the flaws and strengths of this work can be related to Williams's philosophy of noninterference, which permitted him to find much to respect in the ways of his Indian neighbors and yet forbade him to investigate those domains that he believed might imperil his own soul (P. Miller 1953:256).

John Josselyn's *New-Englands Rarities Discovered* (1672) and *An Account of Two Voyages to New England* (1674), although often cited in general discussions of the Ninnimissinuok, are probably derived from observations of ancestors of the Eastern Abenaki. Josselyn, the son of an impoverished nobleman, had an extensive and liberal education, and was well trained in the natural sciences. From 1638 through 1639, and again from 1663 to 1671, Josselyn resided with his brother Henry, an agent of Sir Ferdinando Gorges at Black Point, now Scarborough, Maine. Critical of the Puritan hegemony at Massachusetts Bay, John Josselyn's own writings were criticized in his time and by modern scholars for their occasional credulity.

Nevertheless, his work is a valuable source of information on local folklore and contemporary values and perceptions, and contains a relatively sympathetic description of Native life (Lindholdt 1988:xiii–xx).

A less humane, although useful account was written by John Winthrop, one of the founders of the Massachusetts Bay colony. Winthrop was son of an auditor of St. John's and Trinity Colleges, Cambridge, and from his youth was a copious writer and journalist. At the age of forty-two he was elected governor of the new colony to be established at Massachusetts Bay and arrived there in June of 1630. His *Journal* records events pertinent to the colony from 1630 to 1649 (Winthrop 1908). Most of his references to the Ninnimissinuok are included in accounts of diplomatic relations with the Massachusett, Narragansett, and Pequot. His comments are terse and impersonal, showing little interest or understanding of Native motivations and little appreciation for the Native point of view.

Winthrop's son, John Winthrop, Jr., became governor of the colony of Connecticut in 1635, arriving from England to settle lands "ceded" by the Pequots and building a garrison at Fort Saybrook at the mouth of the Connecticut River. His well-known description of Native horticultural practices (1889) is probably most accurate for those people living in the lower and middle reaches of the Connecticut River Valley.

Several crucial figures in the history of Christian missionization in southern New England wrote accounts of Native life, including John Eliot, Daniel Gookin, Thomas Mayhew, Jr., Thomas Mayhew, Sr., and Matthew Mayhew. Eliot (1604–1690) studied at Jesus College, Cambridge. He later served under the Reverend Thomas Hooker, a noted nonconformist, and determined to immigrate to New England. After his arrival in Massachusetts Bay in 1631, Eliot took up a position as lecturer, and later pastor, of the church at Roxbury (O. Winslow 1968). From there he began a largely self-motivated missionary effort that spanned the remainder of his long life. Eliot's pro-active campaign sought to alter all facets of Native culture; from government, to marital relations, to dress and comportment. He undertook the massive task of translating the Bible into Massachusett, a work completed in 1663. His knowledge of Massachusett was surpassed only by members of the Mayhew family, many of whom were probably native speakers of the island dialect of the language. Eliot's ethnographic writings were largely concerned with shamanism and with political organization.

Equally significant but less often identified in the missionary effort was Captain Daniel Gookin (1612–1687), who served as Superintendent of the Indians of Massachusetts Bay, and as Eliot's advisor, for more than thirty years (F. Gookin 1912:81ff, 114–16, 128ff, 177, 181). A soldier and veteran of English campaigns in Ireland and Virginia, Gookin arrived in Boston in 1644. He was appointed Superintendent in 1656, a position he retained for the remainder of his life. Gookin too regarded Native salvation as possible only through the total transformation of their culture, and worked toward that end throughout his career. His accounts, entitled *Historical Collections of the Indians of New England* and *An Historical Account of the Christian Indians in New England in the Years 1675, 1676, 1677,* were first published in 1792 and 1836 respectively. Both contain important information about the experiences of Christianized Natives, whose scattered frontier communities he visited regularly for decades. Unsympathetic to much of Native life, his intimacy with Nipmuck communities otherwise remote from English settlement allowed him glimpses of customs nowhere else recorded.

The island of Martha's Vineyard was settled in 1642, by families from Marshfield, Massachusetts, who were led by Thomas Mayhew, Jr. (1621–1657). During the latter half of the seventeenth century these settlers shared the island with more than three thousand Natives. Mayhew, Jr., began missionary work on Martha's Vineyard in 1643 and wrote several letters regarding his work that contain important information about the religious beliefs and political structure of the Natives of Martha's Vineyard. After his death at sea, his father, Thomas Mayhew, Sr., took up his work, and pursued it vigorously until his death in 1682 (Hare 1932). Matthew Mayhew (d. 1710), eldest son of Thomas Mayhew, Jr., was educated at the expense of the New England Company to carry on the work of his father and grandfather (Kellaway 1961:101). His accounts, published in 1694 and 1695, describe the social structure, shamanistic practices, and government of the Native people of Martha's Vineyard, and are very valuable, combining as they do his observations with those of his family and Native friends.

The journals and account books of the Pynchons, William and John, are of importance in reconstructing the experiences of the Natives of the interior Connecticut Valley, who were unseen or undescribed in the earliest contact sources. William Pynchon, the founder of Springfield, Massachusetts, was born into a respected family in Springfield, England in East Anglia in 1589 or 1590. Pynchon was one of twenty-six patentees in the charter for the Massachusetts Bay Company and a signer of the Cambridge Agreement (August 26, 1629), which committed his group of London merchants to emigration pending a royal charter. Pynchon, his son John, and his son-in-law Henry Smith were active in promoting settlement in the Connecticut Valley, and succeeded in establishing a plantation at Agawam, soon after the defeat of the Pequots opened the way for English entrepreneurship on the central Connecticut River. Pynchon wielded considerable power in the new settlement, both as magistrate and as Assistant to the General Court in Boston (Thomas 1979:132). Pynchon's interests included extensive landholdings in the Springfield area, a grist mill, and sole control of the Indian trade.

Like many of his contemporaries, Pynchon was not only a merchant and colonial official, but a man of deep theological conviction. His first monograph, *The Meritorious Price of our Redemption*, published in 1650, was burned for heresy in Boston. Apparently as a result of this, Pynchon transferred all his property to his son John and returned to England in 1651. John acted as an "agent" in the fur trade that his father mediated, at least by 1645. John's extensive notes on Indian customs indicate that he must have been well acquainted from his youth with the Native people of the middle Connecticut Valley. Yet he was fully identified with the colonial administration, serving as commissioner for the town of Springfield, Deputy to the General Court of the Massachusetts Bay, and later, as judge of the County Court of Hampshire. Pynchon was directly responsible for the purchase of Native lands at Northampton, Hadley, Westfield, Deerfield, Northfield, Enfield, and Suffield (Thomas 1978:273). Peter Thomas argues that "it is reasonable to assume . . . that John Pynchon's position as leading fur trader and part of the county judicial establishment allowed him to assume the role of 'patron' to a number of Indians in the middle Connecticut Valley." Thomas further suggests that Pynchon used this role to maintain peaceful relations with the local Indians during the period 1652–1665 (275).

Although the reports of these men, and of earlier explorers, have been used interchangeably in many analyses of southern New England Native life, they do not form a homogeneous body of information. The reports of Josselyn, Wood, and Gookin are most appropriately used to discuss the Native people of the northern Massachusetts Bay and its interior regions—an area occupied by the Pawtucket, Nipmuck, and possibly the Western Abenaki (Salwen 1978; Day 1978). Morton's and John Winthrop, Sr.'s descriptions are most relevant for the Massachusett, as are some of those of Eliot, who also worked with Nipmuck people and visited Martha's Vineyard. Winslow and Bradford were most knowledgeable about the Pokanoket but had some dealings with the Massachusett and Narragansett. Verrazzano described the people of Narragansett Bay region in 1524, and the Dutch explorer Adrien Block made similar observations there in 1614. Roger Williams was an authority on the same region after 1636. The Mayhews knew the islands best, while John Winthrop, Jr., was most familiar with the people who lived at the mouth of the Connecticut River. The Pynchons kept careful records of their transactions with the Pocumtuck who otherwise were best known to the Jesuits on the Saint Lawrence (Day 1978). Later seventeenth-century historians, to whom some ethnohistorians have referred, are, by virtue of their distance from the events and people of the early seventeenth century they describe, less reliable. Writers in this category include Edward Johnson (1910), Cotton Mather (1702), and William Hubbard (1677, 1865).

English Cultural Background

The presence of ethnocentrism and bias in the earliest descriptions of the Ninnimissinuok is a fact so often discussed, as to acquire a kind of obligatory status in ethnohistorical writings on southern New England. Rather than reviewing this issue again, what follows is a brief summary of what historians have written concerning the English world view of the early seventeenth century, a world view that dictated not only what was written about in the earliest descriptions of the Ninnimissinuok, but what was omitted as well.

Certain aspects of English thought are explicable in light of time-honored patterns of social relations, of traditional economic activities, and of ideological structures characteristic of the English during the centuries of nascent capitalist development prior to the colonization of the New World. Most important among these, according to historian Neal Salisbury, was the "family-oriented economic independence" of the gentry and "middling sort"—an independence itself threatened by wider trends of capitalist expansion and demographic growth (1982:10). This independence was especially manifest in the lives and writings of the Puritans, religious nonconformists whose theology "constituted the basis of a radical critique of the political, moral, and ecclesiastical status quo in England" (10). Expecting, in light of their conceived contractual relationship with the divine, to control all matters, both sacred and profane, many Puritans understood their "errand into the wilderness" as a covenant with God, one with prescribed rules for both human and divine behavior, and one that guaranteed Puritan ascendancy (P. Miller 1964). Although restless under the yoke of English government, the Puritans who eventually emigrated to the New World were interventionist and evangelical in practice. Although calling in their renowned "contracts" for communalism, their actions in England and in the colonies favored individuality, the nuclear family, and competitive acquisitiveness, justified by an ideology of hierarchy and meritocracy.

English actions have commonly been interpreted as the result of sociological and ideological factors, but ecology and economic practices also played a significant role in their motives, desires, and perceptions. The English farming complex, which revolved around the sowing of a fixed number of crops, a dependence on dairy products, and the maintenance of domesticated animals, was linked to other economic practices with profound ecological and social implications. The clearing and fencing of fields, the damming of mill streams, and the use of saltmarsh for grazing, among other things, radically altered the landscape the English occupied (Thomas 1979; Cronon 1983). Such an economy was labor intensive, often requiring the use of additional hired male labor, large families, and a complex system of barter, exchange, and mutual obligation (Bowen 1990).

Native subsistence, although requiring approximately the same amount of land per comparably sized community (Thomas 1979), contrasted with the English system in the way in which labor was organized and in its impact on the landscape. Women among the Ninnimissinuok were responsible for the bulk of farming and food collecting, while men hunted, fished, and performed other heavy but sporadic tasks. To the English, it appeared that Native women did the majority of the work. English eyes were also deceived by the landscape, which was formed by Native horticultural and hunting practices. Native gardens were small, unfenced, and multi-cropped. The outlines of the planting fields were irregular. Burning the undergrowth, a yearly activity designed to encourage game and semidomesticated berry and nut bushes and trees, created a "park-like" landscape, but one with a much less obvious stamp of human activity (Cronon 1983).

These different systems of labor and land-use in early colonial New England inevitably led to clashes in perceptions of property, wealth, and productivity. Among the Puritans, unceasing labor on the part of men and women was generally economically necessary as well as a mark of rectitude. Land itself was a sign of and contributor toward wealth, and was controlled physically through the establishment of strict boundaries, marked by fencing, and legally through taxation and a patrilineal system of inheritance. Land was an asset, to be bought and sold, and was employed to produce commodities, ideally through cultivation. The heavy labor of Indian women and the seasonal and sporadic activities of Indian men, the unbounded, "natural" appearing landscape, and the fluidity of Native concepts of land tenure all led English people to judge Native economy unbalanced and their lands underused (Cronon 1983:56).

As Thomas has also pointed out, the consequences of these contrasts were both ecological and social (1976). The two systems could not coexist, relying as they did on similar resources. The only role Indian people could play in the English system was in the lowest tier, as hired laborers, or as members of sovereign and separate polities. While the English sought the former, the Native people, when they could, grimly defended the latter.

Kupperman argues that although many contemporary historians assume that English perceptions of Indians were colored by racism, other considerations, notably the importance of status differences, and general perceptions about human nature, were more significant in their interaction (1980:2). From the first, she suggests, Indians were viewed by the English as possible subjects for exploitation because of their lower status as non-English, rather than because they were thought to be racially inferior. Kupperman also notes that English observers had much in common with the Ninnimissinuok (1980:2), particularly in their belief in the efficacy of witchcraft and in their acceptance of an established social hierarchy. For the English, law and hierarchy were signs of civilization and humanity, just as treachery was natural to the human condition. Kupperman notes that the English had "tests" for what constituted civil society, and these included complex language, government by hereditary hierarchy, organization of society in towns, tilling of the soil, and evidence for future planning—all of which the Indians passed (46, 132–33). Edward Winslow, whose accounts of the Pokanoket are among the most valuable seventeenth-century sources on that people, structured much of his narrative in order to illustrate just those facets of Native society.

Early accounts were also highly colored by the differing military tactics employed by the indigenous people and the "invading" English. The "skulking way of war" so deplored by early English writers (Malone 1990) soon evoked even harsher critiques as some Native warriors engaged in traditionally forbidden hostilities in response to European brutalities (Hirsh 1988:1201–203).

Religious differences likewise led to a great deal of misunderstanding. The lack of a regulated ritual in the Christian sense, the apparent absence of an established priesthood or of permanent structures for worship, led many observers to doubt the existence of religious principles among the Ninnimissinuok (e.g., Morton 1947). The embedded quality of religious belief, the spirituality that pervaded all Native action, went unappreciated by most early English observers (Shuffleton 1976). Ironically, they also failed to appreciate the links between curing and spirituality among the

Ninnimissinuok in spite of similar connections between healing and religion that were common in rural north and west England (Kupperman 1980:117–18).

Early descriptions also highlighted English ambivalencies about their own rapidly evolving society. In particular, they regretted the loss of simplicity in their own society while at the same time fearing its association with incivility (41). Descriptions such as those by Thomas Morton allude to these yearnings, even as they illustrate the brash enterprise of the seventeenth-century English entrepreneur. Likewise, the role of women was an ambivalent one in English society; many early observers, like William Wood, criticized the Ninnimissinuok for the heavy burden of work placed on their women, while at the same time English women were treated as dependents to be ruled and instructed (62).

As Jean and John Comaroff point out, much early contact literature was part of a "story" Europeans were telling each other about conquest (1991:33ff). The English believed that although savage, the Indians were not only educable, but also easily led to an appreciation of the superiority of English ways (Axtell 1985:131–32). Missionaries like Eliot, Gookin, and members of the Mayhew family sought the transformation of Native society, even as they became intimate with its strengths. For many of the earliest English settlers who were motivated to write about Indians, the human condition, reflected by outward signs, inward states of grace, redemption, or damnation, was of deep and abiding interest.

Human nature was also a wilderness to be tamed, and the discourse of colonization was thick with allusions to such wilderness, both physical and spiritual (P. Miller 1964). In particular, descriptions of the strength, health, and beauty of Native people can be seen as metaphors for the newly appropriated, but still uncontrolled land, with the earliest of these emphasizing the vigor, stature, and dignity of Native bodies, while deploring their nakedness, sexual promiscuity, and elaborate paint, hairstyles, and ornament. Since Native people "embodied" the perceived ambivalencies of nature, it is no accident that the first missionaries to the Ninnimissinuok insisted on sober English-style clothing and hairstyles and on monogamy for their converts (Salisbury 1974).

Another assumption common among the newly arrived English, one well known to students of American history, was the expectation that the lands and people of southern New England were there to be appropriated. The long tradition of travel and contact accounts, which includes, as others have pointed out, much early anthropological description, was underlain in part by a pervasive cognitive link between description and control (Clifford 1986). The categorization of human groups into discrete polities was a step on the way toward political and military domination, a lesson John Smith learned well in Virginia. The descriptions of Native trade and economy were an approach to the absorption of that economy. The analyses of Native languages, particularly Eliot's *Indian Grammar Begun* and Roger Williams's *Key into the Language of America*, likewise implied control over their speakers, an appropriation of that most intimate of cultural products, a cooption and transformation of a unique possession of the "other" (Bragdon n.d.).

At the same time, the content of such descriptions was both deliberately and unintentionally subversive and/or self-critical. The completeness of some of these early depictions implied an intimate knowledge of a people regarded by the majority as inferior, but portrayed in the main as human and even admirable. Descriptions of Native women in particular referred directly and indirectly to English women and constituted a commentary on the generally unquestioned restraints under which English women lived. Analyses of Native languages admitted the possibility of variation, of solutions different but workable, of valuable insights into nature and the human condition. It is worth repeating that English men and women who took on the task of describing Native people to their contemporaries contributed to the transformation of their own societies as well as of those who were the objects of their literary "gaze."

Later descriptions, penned by settlers and established traders such as William and John Pynchon, were motivated by an increasingly arrogant assumption of strength and superiority, a burgeoning entrepreneurial focus, and a regional chauvinism that pitted colony against colony. Native people, who once had figured as unspoiled inhabitants of a beautiful and bountiful land, increasingly became either barriers to economic expansion, if powerful, or pitiable heathens, if weak. The "middle ground" (White 1991) forged by early settlers and traders with powerful Indian groups such as the Pokanoket was later swept away by a "reinvention" of Indians as hostile and depraved (Mather 1977; E. Johnson 1910; Rowlandson 1913).

People and Places

From the decks of their ships, European explorers observed thickly settled coastal regions ranging from Long Island Sound to Cape Ann. Verrazzano reported encounters with extensive communities at Narragansett Bay, on Cape Cod, and in the Massachusetts Bay area. Champlain encountered large numbers of people somewhere north of Boston harbor (Champlain 1968:79–80). In 1614, John Smith explored and mapped the New England coast noting at least nine coastal and estuarine "towns" between Cape Ann and Cape Cod, each ruled by a sachem or sagamore, whom he named.[3] Smith also heard of "more than twentie severall habitations and rivers that stretch themselves farre into the Countrey, even to the Borders of divers great Lakes" (1912:661–62).

Contradictory and confusing ethnonyms for the Ninnimissinuok began to be collected. Champlain wrote of the "Almouchiquois," a term that seems to have designated those Natives from the Saco River to Narragansett Bay. William Wood of Naumkeag (now Salem, Massachusetts) used the term "Aberginian" to refer to the people of that region. John Smith labeled the coast stretching from

Cape Ann to the upper reaches of what is now Cape Cod Bay "the country of the Massachusits" (1614).

Smith also noted the location of "Pakanokick," the village of the chief sachem Massasoit, who became an ally of the Plymouth settlers (E. Winslow 1910:283). The term *Pokanoket* was later extended to refer to all the territories and people controlled by Massasoit and his descendants (Salwen 1978:174). *Wampanoag*, as an ethnonym, now used to designate the modern descendants of the Pokanokets, was probably derived from the name *Wapanoos*, first applied by Dutch explorers and map-makers to those Natives near Narragansett Bay, with whom they had no personal experience, based on information from the peoples of the lower Hudson. The term means 'easterner' in Delaware, and was probably not an original self-designation (175). The Jansson-Visscher map of this region called its residents the *Horican* (Map 2).

Both the Dutch and English were in contact with the Narragansett, who were noted on Block's map as *Nahicans* (Laet 1909:42), and referred to variously by the English as *Nanohigganset* (E. Winslow 1910:297), *Nanhigganeuck* (R. Williams 1936:A3), or *Narragansetts* (Wood 1977:80).

Johan de Laet, sailing with Adrien Block in 1614, met a group called the *Morhicans* (Mohegans) on what is now the Thames River, and they and the Pequots on the Mystic River first appear on Block's map of 1614. Block also encountered the Sequins, Nawaas, and Horikans on the middle Connecticut River (Laet 1614), while Wassenaer named a group living there the *Sickanames* (Wassenaer 1909:86).

People who occupied the southwestern corner of what is now Connecticut, long linked to the now discredited "Wappinger Confederacy," can be loosely grouped under the general designation *Paugussett*. These people occupied the lower Housatonic River area in the early historic period, and were distinct from the Mahican, the Connecticut River Indians, and those of the lower Hudson to the west (Wojciechowski 1985).

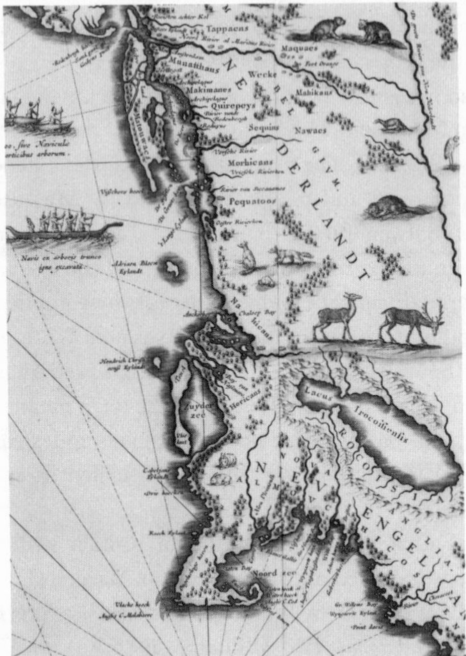

Map 2. Jansson-Visscher map of southern New England, circa 1635. Top of map is south. (Courtesy of the John Carter Brown Library, Brown University.)

An early Dutch description of the Native people of the Lower Hudson reads as follows:

Below the Maikans [Mahicans] are situated these tribes: Mechkentowoon, Tapants, on the West side; Wickagjock, Wyeck, on the East side. Two Nations lie there lower down at Klinckersberg. At the Fisher's hook are Pachany, Warenecker, Warrawannankonckx: in one place, Esopus, are two or three Tribes. The Manhates are situated at the mouth. (Wassenaer 1967:67–68)

Dutch explorers also visited the eastern end of Long Island, where they found people called *Souwenos* (Siwanoys) and the *Sinnecox* (Shinnecocks), and noted that they were "held in subjection" by the Pequots (De Rasieres 1909:103). Roger Williams later spoke of the *Munnawtawkit*, or *Montauk*, of Long Island, named, like many of the Ninnimissinuok, for the places where they lived (Salwen 1978:174).

The peoples of the interior regions of what is now central Massachusetts were designated *Nipnet* (Eliot 1834:170–71) or *Neepmuck* (Williams 1936:105). Their territories ranged from somewhere west and south of the Nashua, Concord, and Charles Rivers, and were bordered on the south by the Quinebaug and Blackstone rivers, land in Narragansett and Pequot/Mohegan control (Connole 1976; Salwen 1978:173).

The region between Northampton, Hadley, and Hatfield on the Connecticut River was referred to by local Natives as *Norwottuck*, as were its inhabitants. Other groups that lived near Agawam (Springfield, Massachusetts), were the Pocumtuck (Deerfield and Greenfield) and the Woronoco (Westfield). The Quabaug were located to the east, near Brookfields (DePaoli 1984). People of the middle Connecticut River, north of the community at Pocumtuck, were virtually unknown to English settlers before 1640 (Thomas 1979:79), but French missionaries were in contact with the Sokokis or Squakheages, residents of the region near present-day Northfield, Massachusetts, who were in turn linked to the residents of Amoskeag (now Concord, Massachusetts) sixty miles to the east and to the people of Norwottuck forty miles to the south (Day 1965:237–49;1975; Thomas 1979:80–81).

Modern scholars generally have accepted Gookin's summary of native territorial organization as the most complete of those written during the early colonial period (e.g., Salwen 1978). Gookin wrote:

> The principal nations of the Indians, that did, or do, inhabit within the confines of New-England, are five. 1. Pequots; 2. Narragansitts; 3. Pawkunnawkuts; 4. Massachusetts; and, 5. Pawtucketts. (1806:147)

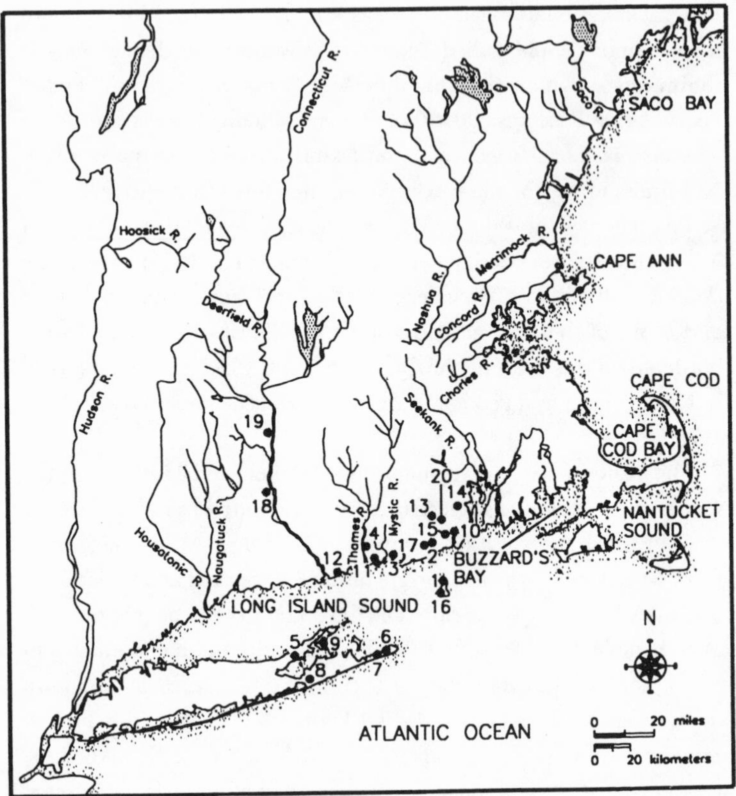

Map 3. Native people and polities in southern New England circa 1620. (After Salwen 1978. Artist: Sondra Jarvis.)

According to Gookin, these "nations" were made up of a number of subdivisions and were at times both at enmity and peace with their neighbors (147). For example, the Pokanokets comprised those people living in eastern Rhode Island and southeastern Massachusetts, but the Pilgrims at Plymoth hinted at alliances between the Pokanoket proper and the Natives of Cape Cod, including the territories of the sachems Totoson and Coneconam, which ranged from New Bedford to Sandwich, and the Nausets further east (Bradford 1970:87–88). Later sources also include Martha's Vineyard within the domains of the Pokanoket sachem Massasoit (Eliot and Mayhew 1834:209). William Simmons identifies the Niantic, Coweset, Pawtuxet, and Manissean (Block Island residents) as sachemships allied to but distinct from the Narragansett (1978:190). In the early seventeenth century, the Mohegans were not tributary to the Pequot sachem Sassacus, in spite of later seventeenth-century assertions to the contrary (e.g., Gookin 1806:147; Salisbury 1982:83; E. S. Johnson 1993). However, the Pequots did have influence among the Natives of Long Island, the Quinapeake (Quiripi) sachems, the Connecticut River sachemships, and the Nipmuck as far as Quinabaag (near Dudley, Massachusetts) (Gookin 1806:147). The locations of these and other territorial or political groups documented before 1650 are illustrated in Map 3.

Population Estimates and the Effects of European Epidemics

Population estimates for southeastern New England have been a source of much debate among historians and anthropologists (Thomas 1979:25–26; Snow and Lanphear 1988). Again, Gookin's estimates are now generally accepted, suggesting a pre-epidemic regional population of more than 90,000, of which 72,000 were distributed as follows:[4]

Group	Gookin's Estimates	Estimated Total Population
Pawtucket	ca. 3,000 fighting men	12,000
Massachusett	ca. 3,000 fighting men	12,000
Pokanoket	ca. 3,000 fighting men	12,000
Narragansett	ca. 5,000 fighting men	20,000
Pequot/Mohegan	ca. 4,000 fighting men	16,000
Total		72,000

Snow estimates an additional 8,000 for the people of the Pocumtuck region and 13,000 for the lower Connecticut and central Long Island peoples (1980:33). Population densities ranged from 190 to 250 people per 100 square kilometers in coastal areas and on the lower and middle Connecticut River, to 22 people per 100 square kilometers on the upper Connecticut and Merrimac Rivers (Snow 1980:33; Thomas 1979:28).

Losses of tragic proportions followed two epidemics: one centering in Massachusetts Bay in the years 1616–1619 and the other on the Connecticut River in 1633. The former, a virgin-soil epidemic of unknown origin, was referred to as the "plague" by several seventeenth-century writers (Salisbury 1982:101), and one eyewitness, Thomas Dermer, mentioned "the sores of some that escaped" (Dermer 1968). The major symptom elderly people described to Gookin fifty years later was yellowed skin, leading Spiess and Spiess to argue that a hepatitis virus was the most likely agent (1987). Whatever its nature and origin, this terrible epidemic reduced populations among the Ninnimissinuok of the northern and central Massachusetts Bay by as much as 90 percent. Following the epidemic, Native settlement in Massachusetts Bay was attenuated, particularly on the Merrimac, in the lower Bay itself, on upper Cape Cod, and within the drainage of the Taunton River. In 1630, the sachem Chickataubot, living near what is now Quincy, Massachusetts had only fifty to sixty subjects, while Wonohaquaham and Montowompate, sons of the great sachem Nanepashemet, who controlled lands surrounding what are now Chelsea, Saugus, and Marblehead, Massachusetts "command[ed] not above thirty or forty men" (Dudley 1970[1630]:305–307). The Pilgrims estimated that only about sixty men looked to Massasoit himself (Mourt 1963:52–64) (Map 4).

Although the Narragansett and Connecticut coastal and interior groups escaped the effects of the first wave of sickness, they were not so fortunate fourteen years later when a smallpox epidemic

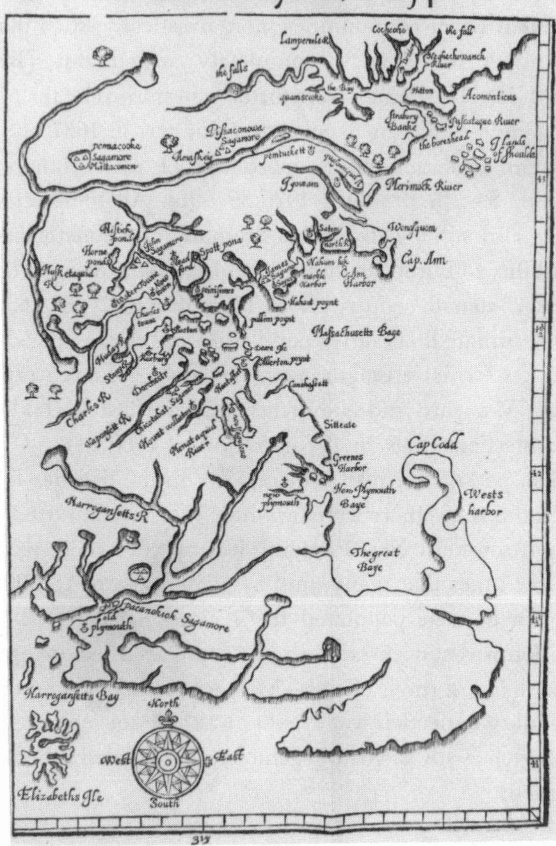

Map 4. William Wood's Map of southern New England, 1634. (Courtesy of the Manuscripts and Rare Books Department, Swem Library, College of William and Mary.)

wreaked havoc among them (Snow and Lanphear 1988:23). The epidemic robbed the Narragansett population of seven hundred souls (J. Winthrop 1959, 1:118) and affected the lower and middle Connecticut River communities more drastically, such that some communities there were completely wiped out (Bradford 1970:270–71). The Pequot were further diminished by the massacre of four hundred of their people at Mystic fort in 1637 and by the subsequent execution and deportation of many others (John Winthrop, Sr., in Bradford 1970:397–98). All the Native communities also suffered from less dramatic but nonetheless lethal susceptibility to European endemic and epidemic diseases throughout the seventeenth century (Cook 1976:36–37;44). By 1650, most scholars estimate that Native population was thus reduced to one-tenth of its former strength, with the highest concentrations on Martha's Vineyard and Nantucket, and in coastal Rhode Island and Connecticut (Salwen 1978:169; Snow 1980:34).

English population rose with rapidity in the decades following 1630. In the 1620s there were few more than five hundred English settlers in southern New England, but by 1630 there were more than three times that many, and by 1640, close to 18,500 people of English descent populated the region (Salisbury 1982:225). Population was concentrated in just those areas where epidemics had had the most tragic effects—Massachusetts Bay, and the lower and middle Connecticut valley—but was still unevenly distributed in the region, with English hegemony only partially, and locally, established.

The Languages of Southern New England

Early descriptions of European traders, settlers, and missionaries confirm that the Ninnimissinuok spoke a number of related languages of the eastern branch of the Algonquian language family and shared other features that further united them into a southeastern nucleus. These languages, known today as Western Abenaki, Massachusett, Loup A, Loup B, Narragansett, Mohegan-Pequot, and Quiripi-Unquachog (Goddard 1978), were spoken by peoples living in the regions south and west of the Saco River, including eastern Long Island. Evidence from a number of seventeenth-century sources also suggests that many people in coastal regions were multilingual in two or more related languages (Bragdon n.d.).

Native Views of the Newcomers

Native authorities on Europeans included Tisquantum (also called Squanto) of Patuxet, Hobbomok of the Pokanoket, and Epanew of Martha's Vineyard. Tisquantum and Hobbomok lived with the Pilgrims at Plymoth, the latter for nearly twenty years (Nanepashemet 1993). Both Tisquantum and Epanew, as captives of Thomas Hunt, had traveled in Europe and England, and spoke English (Dermer 1968). These men have left no written accounts, but their experiences and impressions formed part of the increasing body of lore upon which Native people drew in encounters with English settlers. Just as Europeans saw the Ninnimissinuok through the lens of their cultural background, so too the Native people interpreted early encounters in a manner consistent with their own ethos. Accounts of first encounters include one by Wood, who was told:

> They took the first ship they saw for a walking island, the mast to be a tree, the sail white clouds, and the discharging of ordnance for lightning and thunder, which did much trouble them, but this thunder being over and this moving-island steadied with an anchor, they manned out their canoes to go and pick strawberries there. But being saluted by the way with a broadside, they cried out, "What much hoggery, so big walk, and so big speak and by and by kill"; which caused them to turn back, not daring to approach till they were sent for. (1977:95–96)

Terms for various Europeans also give some clues as to their place in Native perception. The English were called *wautaconuaog* ,'coat men,' or *chauquaquock*, 'knife men,' by the Narragansett (R. Williams 1936), and "cut-throates" by the Massachusett (Morton 1947). Wood quoted the Aberginians on the differences between various Europeans:

The Spaniard they say is all one aramouse (viz., all one as a dog); the Frenchman hath a good tongue but a false heart; the Englishman all one speak, all one heart. (1977:92)

To the English eye, Native men were:

straight bodied, strongly composed, smooth-skinned, merry countenanced, of complexion something more swarthy than Spaniards, black haired, high foreheaded, black eyed, out-nosed, broad shouldered, brawny armed, long and slender handed, out breasted, small waisted, lank bellied, well thighed, flat kneed, handsome grown legs, and small feet. (Wood 1977:82)

Many European men considered the women of the Ninnimissinuok "very well favoured" (Brereton 1968:47) and "very graceful, of fine countenances and pleasing appearance in manners and modesty" (Winship 1968:15). For their part, the Ninnimissinuok considered European men to be unpleasantly hirsute and European women excessively voluble and prating (Wood 1977:83; 92). Other Native commentary on the English, generally took, and takes, a subtle form—in gesture, in the construction and definition of social space, in folklore, and in cultural style. Although unwritten and intangible, these forms of discourse are nonetheless "real" sources for understanding cultural interaction, all the more crucial for their longevity.

Such Native commentary has often been overlooked in the face of the magnitude of written reports of European origin, reports that represent varying perceptions of Native people and that are composed by individuals of mixed education, motivation, and experience. It is for this reason that archaeological and ethnological examples must be included, in an effort to "foreground" the enduring parameters of Native life and to document their integrity in the contest for "authenticity" that began when two such different peoples first encountered one another.

The Ninnimissinuok in Archaeological and Theoretical Context

Three related issues continue to occupy archaeologists and ethnohistorians studying the fifteenth through the seventeenth centuries A.D. in southern New England: the extent and onset of reliance on maize horticulture, the nature of settlement, and the level of sociopolitical integration there. Each of these has implications for the interpretation of Native ideology, cosmology, and social relations during the contact period, and of the Native people's response to European explorers and settlers as well. Although the Ninnimissinuok shared an underlying cosmology and a cultural tradition of considerable temporal depth, by the Late Woodland period, archaeological evidence suggests that they were participants in three distinct sociocultural patterns: northerly or uplands hunter-gatherers, whose organization was predicated on mobility; riverine village-based polities dependent on agriculture; and coastal communities best understood as a series of linked small-scale sedentary societies (Upham 1990:3), whose complex sociopolitical integration developed prior to widespread reliance on maize horticulture.

The archaeological record suggests that since about 1000 A.D. the Ninnimissinuok of the coastal regions of southern New England shared many characteristics typical of simple chiefdoms (Feinman and Neitzel 1984), which, because of their inherently unstable nature, appear to have "cycled" through periods of greater and lesser complexity in the succeeding five hundred years (cf. Earle 1987:297). Sites dating to the centuries immediately before sustained contact with Europeans indicate increasing political centralization in coastal regions, due to factors related to population increase, reliance on maize horticulture, the development of the wampum trade, the influence of the powerful but volatile Hopewellian state, and perhaps the effects of the presence of European trade goods that filtered into southern New England via indigenous trading networks possibly since 1000 A.D. (Fitzhugh 1985:28–29) and certainly by the fifteenth century A.D. (Bourque and Whitehead 1985).

The arrival of European diseases and of Europeans themselves further accelerated and ultimately subverted these trajectories. Confusion in the early contact accounts is no doubt attributable in part to the previously underappreciated links with specific adaptations, and to the local complexities of societies moving toward centralization. Archaeology and cross-cultural comparisons would appear to provide the best corrective to the lacunae and biases of these early reports. The theoretical issues that have emerged in recent analyses of southern New England Native society make this region one of intense interest, particularly to those concerned with the origins of, and relations between, agriculture, sedentism, and social inequality, and their ideological and cosmological correlates.

Prologue to the Late Woodland: Archaeology and Linguistic Prehistory 2700 B.C. to 1000 A.D.

The two-and-a-half millennia before present (B.P.) encompass three "periods" in New England prehistory: the Early and Middle Woodland (ca. 700 B.C.–1000 A.D.) and the Late Woodland (including the "contact period") (ca. 1000 A.D.–1620 A.D.).[5] Known only archaeologically and through the techniques of historical linguistics, these periods encompass remarkable diversity in both time and space, shaped in part by cultural and linguistic developments in the previous terminal Late Archaic period (mean date 1700–700 B.C.).

Proto-Eastern Algonquian in Southern New England in the Terminal Late Archaic

Although earlier interpretations suggested that the people who inhabited southern New England in the Woodland period were relative newcomers, current scholarship indicates that no major population displacement or replacement occurred during the Archaic and Woodland periods (Mullholland 1985). However, glottochronology, the linguistic technique that determines the amount of time which has passed since currently spoken or historically known languages broke away from ancestral or "proto" languages, makes clear that Proto-Algonquian, the parent language from which all historic Algonquian languages descended, separated from an even earlier language stock only about 2500–3000 years ago (Goddard 1978a:586; 1978:70). Even more recent separation has been proposed by Stuart J. Fiedel (1987:3). Not long afterwards, Proto-Eastern Algonquian, ancestor of all eastern Algonquian languages, itself diverged from the central stock, some time around 2500 B.P. (Goddard 1978a:586). Thus, Algonquian languages appear to have been "imported" into the region and adopted by the Native peoples already living there.

Reconstructed Proto-Algonquian includes terms referring to social stratification, earthworks, and authoritarianism (Denny 1989:92–94), as well as to ceramics, the bow and arrow, and possibly to domesticated cucurbits such as squash and gourds (Fiedel 1987:5–7). Such evidence points to knowledge of, and possibly participation in, a complex, technologically sophisticated cultural order prior to the breaking up of the Proto-Algonquian language into its scattered Algonquian language descendants. Semanticist Peter Denny suggests that the mound-building Ohioan cultures that flourished between 3000 and 2000 B.P. were the likely vehicles for the spread of Proto-Algonquian into the Northeast. Denny emphasizes the widespread ideological influence of these complex cultural traditions and suggests that because of their impact, the local populations, speakers of diverse languages now unknown, became bilingual in those languages and in Proto-Algonquian, until the latter completely replaced the original languages (1989:94). Proto-Algonquian may have spread eastward in this manner through the influence of Ohioan mortuary traditions during the Late Archaic. Subsequently, movement of Proto-Iroquoian speakers northwestward into what is now New York and north-central Pennsylvania cut off eastern Proto-Algonquian speakers from the central languages, creating a "Proto-Eastern Algonquian" subfamily, whose languages have been diverging from one another for some two thousand years (Snow 1980:258; Goddard 1978:70).

The breakup of Proto-Eastern Algonquian into the ancestors of the eastern Algonquian languages at the onset of the Early Woodland period may have been associated with the spread of the so-called North Beach phase, itself a descendant of the Ohioan influenced-Mast Forest/Orient cultural system, which was characteristic of north and central Atlantic coastal cultures from 2650 to 1950 B.P. (Denny 1989:99; Snow 1980:278). Comparisons among eastern Algonquian languages suggest that those of southern New England formed a nucleus from which other languages spread, southward probably through language replacement, and northward through the actual migration of the speakers themselves (Denny 1989:98; see also Bourque 1975:43).

Early and Middle Woodland Period Archaeological Patterns

In southern New England, sites dating to the first few centuries A.D. have shown little influence from the otherwise widespread Adena mortuary cult (Snow 1980:279; Mulholland 1985:48), although ties with the later Hopewellian expansion are marked (Ceci 1990:23). Shell mounds with dog burials, some associated with human remains found at several sites in southern New England dating 800–1100 A.D., suggest expanded trade in exotic materials and the increasing influence of Hopewellian mortuary ceremonialism (Kerber et al. 1989). Ceci has found, based on a reanalysis of five well-known sites in Long Island, that "sites of greater complexity and duration" begin to appear during the Middle Woodland (ca. 950 A.D.). She sees evidence for intensified use of anadromous fish, (the hunting of which required group cooperation), increased ceremonialism, and widespread trade in exotic lithics and metals. For example, a six-year-old child was buried at the Tottenville site with nonlocal goods, including hundreds of North Carolina and Florida shell beads (1990:22). There was significant trade in "exotics," such as worked copper from the Great Lakes, mica from Tennessee, and shells and shell beads from the entire east coast. Ceci argues that the coastal Natives were part of the late Hopewellian "world system," an intercontinental network in which Iroquoian people were intermediaries to the coastal Algonquians (22). Bert Salwen too suggests that such influence is marked at some Long Island sites such as Muskeeta Cove at the end of the Middle Woodland (1968:333).

While still relatively unstudied, the Early and Middle Woodland periods in southern New England, as known archaeologically and linguistically, encompassed complex changes associated with the adoption of new languages and social customs, trade in exotic goods, and increasing population aggregation in coastal regions. Evidence from some coastal sites dating to the Middle Woodland period is also consistent with that of other archaeologically known chiefdoms, which are characterized by differential mortuary treatment associated with hierarchy, trade in exotic goods, and the long-term occupation of single sites (e.g., Mulholland 1985:53; Ceci 1990:18; Potter 1993).

The Late Woodland Period in Southern New England: Archaeology and Ecology in the Late Woodland

By A.D. 1000, three distinct ecological regions had emerged in southern New England: maritime/estuarine; riverine; and uplands/

lacustrine. This environmental diversity was related in turn to the increasingly complex patterns visible in the archaeological record, patterns intensified in the fifteenth and sixteenth centuries A.D. by the emergence of maize horticulture, wampum manufacture, and trade. These factors, in addition to the effects of peripheral contact with Europeans, augmented already established trends toward hierarchy and centralization on the coast—trends that were clearly of Native origin. Such trends further contrast with archaeological evidence for riverine and uplands areas, where different socio-political systems were established, and whose different points of intersection with the expanding European presence contributed to the variability of response later characteristic of the region as a whole.

Although coastal sites of the early Late Woodland period show a less marked incidence of elaborate burial treatments than do sites of the Middle Woodland, archaeologists recognize the signs of accelerating population growth and sedentism in riverine and coastal regions (Snow 1980:307; Mulholland 1985:53-60; Barber 1979), signs that have been interpreted variously and as part of a larger debate concerning the nature of settlement pattern, sociopolitical integration, and the effects of European contact in the region.

The "Ethnohistorical" Model: Maize Horticulture and Village Life in Southern New England

From thick warme vallies, where they winter, they remove a little neerer to their Summer fields; when 'tis warme Spring, then they remove to their fields where they plant Corne. (R. Williams 1936:46)

This statement and others like it have become the basis for the "ethnohistorical" model of settlement for the southern New England of the early contact period, a model with profound economic, political, and social implications, and one that has been applied to the period before European colonization as well. The model, based on the comments of seventeenth-century observers such as that quoted above, states that Native settlement was seasonally mobile, with summers spent in scattered homesteads near the coast and winters in concentrated communities further inland. Fall and spring were devoted to fishing and hunting, generally accomplished in small groups from temporary camps (e.g., Marten 1970). Dean Snow, for example, writes that in the early historic period in southern New England, "Main villages were semipermanent sedentary communities built away from the coast. They were most fully occupied during winter seasons and were apparently moved every dozen years or so. . . . during the warm months families dispersed to individual farmsteads of single houses surrounded by horticultural fields" (1980:75–76; a similar argument is made by Salwen [1978:165]).

The importance of Native maize horticulture to the first European explorers and settlers, whose descriptions of native life form the basis of the ethnohistorical model, was profound. Sixteenth- and seventeenth-century European conceptions of land were connected with unvarying regularity to agricultural images and metaphors. Explorers were expressly bidden to evaluate the fertility of soils and agricultural potential of the lands their sponsors hoped to claim (e.g., Champlain 1922). Every apologist for colonization stressed the agricultural productivity of southern New England, usually by describing Native farming practices and products (e.g., Verrazzano 1524, J. Smith 1624). The predominance of descriptions of agricultural practice in these early accounts is thus in large part a reflection of these preoccupations.

One result of this western concern with agriculture is the assumption among modern archaeologists, anthropologists, and historians that farming was the "central" subsistence activity of most of the people of southern New England at contact, and by implication, during much of the preceding Late Woodland period as well. Silver (1981), Snow (1980), and others for example, see maize horticulture and a village-based settlement pattern as important since 1000 A.D.

For much of southern New England, such an assumption is not supported by evidence from a combination of archaeological and historical sources. As Peter Thorbahn has argued, "Except for a few areas in southern New England, such as the middle and lower Connecticut River valley, there is very little archaeological evidence for village-based settlement systems during the Late Woodland period. . . . This is in sharp contrast to most of the rest of Eastern North America" (quoted in Kerber 1988:44). A number of scholars, especially Ceci (1977, 1982, 1990), have been challenged by the discrepancies between the ethnohistorical model posited by Salwen (1978), Snow (1980), and others, and the extant archaeological data. In her earliest examination of the problem, Ceci argued for sparse and infrequent use of the coast in the Late Prehistoric period, followed by the rapid adoption of agriculture and sedentary settlement in response to contact with Europeans (1978, 1982). Her thesis explicitly attempted to reconcile the reporting of "towns" by early explorers such as Verrazzano and Champlain with the lack of Late Woodland village-like sites found archaeologically, as well as with the scarcity of archaeologically recovered maize in southern New England. Ceci concluded that maize horticulture in coastal regions was a response to contact with Europeans and to the related requirements of the developing wampum trade (1990:2–3).

An Alternative Model for Coastal Southern New England

Dismissing the importance of agriculture among the coastal peoples of southern New England in the centuries before contact leaves many questions unanswered. What explains the evidence for population growth and aggregation in coastal regions in the eleventh through the fifteenth centuries? Was the well-ordered seasonal round, intimately linked to the use of coastal resources, as described by early observers, the work of a mere century? What of the evidence for social complexity so often noted by ethnohistorians? A third model, offered by a number of scholars working primarily on fourteenth- and fifteenth-century coastal sites, proposes that year-round or three-season occupation of coastal regions, associated with a broad range of subsistence activities, but not one predicated on agriculture, occured by A.D. 1000. Unlike the model proposed by Snow and Salwen, this alternative does not predict focused "village" settlements, but rather less aggregated communities than are found elsewhere in the eastern Woodlands (but see Custer 1986). Such a model of "conditional" sedentism (Dunford 1992) accounts for the evidence of population aggregation and settlement in coastal areas prior to the sixteenth century A.D., provides a plausible explanation for the depth of cultural practices associated with plant-use, and "decouples" the links previously assumed between sedentism, agriculture, and social complexity (Netting 1990).

Beyond Cultural Ecology: The Social, Political, and Ideological Correlates of Subsistence

The contrasting patterns of coastal, riverine, and uplands economies, and trends toward increasing territoriality and involvement in long-distance and local trade reflected in the archaeology of southern New England also document practice: the daily actions and habitual ways of thought and interaction that were at once most evident to European observers of the Ninnimissinuok and the source of that cultural essence that so eluded those observers. In traditional ethnographies, both those written in the fictitious "ethnographic present" and those that attempt historical situatedness, the "seasonal round" and the parameters of the native material world are always included. They are seldom interpreted, however, in light of the framework of the meaning they help to create. For the Ninnimissinuok, mobility, conditional sedentism, and practices of land tenure thus had specific political correlates, while at the same time reciprocity, and the gendered division of labor, had important social implications. These links are significant in understanding the ways in which daily action shaped, justified, and in some cases altered, the meaning that life seemed to have.

A Review of Studies of Sociopolitical Behavior in Southern New England

Seventeenth-century discussions about variations in settlement pattern and governance and their grounding in a mobile way of life resonated with contemporary concerns about civility, social stability, sovereignty, and property (Jennings 1975; Kupperman 1980; Cronon 1983; Salisbury 1982; Axtell 1985). Modern historians and anthropologists have also debated the relationship between mobility and the evolution of social and political forms from less to more complex (e.g., Upham 1990). Central to contemporary debates is the nature of egalitarianism, the theoretical status of those societies that were neither "bands" nor "states," and the quality of gender relations in such societies. No longer satisfied to argue for a simple equation between "small-scale" societies and egalitarianism, or for that matter, between "tribal" societies and sedentism, ranking, redistribution, and horticulture, scholars now see those societies, "transitional" in evolutionary terms between bands and states, as the very groups that have the most to tell us about the dynamics of culture.

Native North American political organization generally has been characterized by contrasting models: those that focused on evolutionary type, that is the band-tribe-chiefdom-state progression developed by Elman Service (1962), and those that focused on process—that is, the privileging of technology or modes of social production; the examination of the differential effects of environment on different societal institutions; the emphasis on the role of demographic factors; and the placement of explanatory weight on the role of productive specialization, surplus production, and exchange (Upham 1990:2). Southern New England sociopolitical organization has been interpreted both according to evolutionary typologies and those based on technological/processual criteria. The absence of evidence for maize horticulture and sedentary "village" settlement led Ceci to suggest that Long Island Native peoples were organized only into "small bands" prior to European contact (1990:20), an assessment supported by T. J. Brasser for southern New England as a whole (1971:65). Salisbury writes that "the 'chiefdom' and 'tribe' of political anthropology were not to be found in southern New England; the only permanent, supra-familial organization was the band" (1982:48). Other scholars concur with Eleanor Leacock's argument that Native peoples of the Northeast were essentially "egalitarian" in social organization with leadership authority derived from consensus, personal influence, and "acceptance of responsibility for the behavior of kin" (1983:28) (e.g. Salisbury 1982:43; Cronon 1983; Lavin 1988; Carlson et al. 1992:142).

In contrast, scholars such as Anthony F. C. Wallace characterize the political organization of the Northeast as "tribal" or made up of groups possessed of a name, a territory, and a group decision-making mechanism (1957:304; see also Salwen 1978). Thomas further applies the term "segmentary tribe" to polities in southern New England, wherein local, autonomous groups show some higher levels of organization, but he points out that those were of "poor definition and minimum function" (1979:34). Dean Snow, based in part on his understanding of population dynamics associated with increasing dependence on maize as well as on the ethnohistorical model, identifies political entities in the region as "lineal tribes" (following Service 1962:120–39), which, he argued, exhibited "considerable fluidity in political structure above the village or town level" at A.D. 1600" (1980:77).

The arbitrary and inexact character of typological concepts such as "band" and "tribe" is nowhere better demonstrated than in the difficulties of scholars attempting to characterize the nature of political life in southern New England. Bands, the earliest, simplest, and most egalitarian of sociopolitical entities (Fried 1967:67), are known primarily through studies of contemporary foragers, who "map onto" resources by changing residence and adjusting group size, and collectors, who "supply themselves with specific resources through specially organized task groups" (Binford 1980:10). However, most modern foragers and food collectors live in relatively simple ecosystems and on marginal lands and may not resemble any prehistoric people (Yesner 1980:727). "Tribe," a category, merely lumps together those societies that are neither bands nor states.

Much of the data for studies of political organization in southern New England has been drawn from reports of mobile people living in the interior uplands or in the settled villages of the central Connecticut River valley (e.g., D. Gookin 1806). Given the environmental diversity of southern New England, the variety and richness of the archaeological data for the Late Prehistoric period, and the explicit references in the early historic descriptions to hierarchical social organization and hereditary leadership, a characterization of the societies of southern New England as bands does not seem appropriate for any but the Ninnimissinuok of the uplands regions (see chapters 5–7). On the other hand, although important in contemporary formulations of Native identity (Fried 1967:170; Sturtevant 1983:13), the imprecise concept of "tribe" has less utility for interpreting Native cultures of five hundred years ago.

More recent attempts to understand small-scale variable societies such as those found among the Ninnimissinuok have been phrased in terms of process, of region, and of a multidimensional and continuous range of factors including population size, levels of decision-making, control over the means of production, and warfare (Feinman and Neitzel 1984; Earle 1987). Scholars now emphasize the variability encompassed by chiefdoms and stress the continuities between chiefly societies and those of less and greater complexity

(Earle 1987:281). Reports of coastal groups living in southern New England in the early seventeenth century suggest that the people of that subregion were probably best characterized as chiefdoms of marked social hierarchy and centralized leadership, while riverine communities were perhaps more self-sufficient and less hierarchical (Feinman and Neitzel 1984; Upham 1990:3; Earle 1987:279). Sedentism, at least among the coastal peoples of southern New England, was only "conditional" even after the adoption of horticulture; among these people, it was nonetheless associated with hierarchy, inequality, and centralized authority, in part because of the way in which labor was divided and the products of that labor appropriated, and in part because of the way land, central to production, was allocated.

Theories about Land Tenure

Ever since Frank Speck's theory of "hereditary male hunting territories" was deftly refuted by Leacock (1954), scholars have rejected theories of private ownership of land in the precontact Northeast (e.g., Wallace 1957; Brasser 1971; Jennings 1975; Cronon 1983). However, as Irving Hallowell has argued, "Ownership can be defined . . . by the concrete facts and conditions of use" (1943:123). Just as the concepts of "band" and "tribe" do not fully encompass the complexity of southern New England sociopolitical organization, the adjective *communal* does not adequately characterize practices of land tenure there. Instead, the documentary and archaeological data support an argument for a kind of "ownership" linked to notions of personal identity, descent, and intimate use, a constellation of factors distinct from European notions of the same period.

Reciprocity and Its Discontents

The reciprocity considered to be typical of relations among the Ninnimissinuok has been well noted, both in the seventeenth century and by modern students (e.g., Salisbury 1982; Cronon 1983). Such customary sharing is thought to constitute a form of insurance against want for the group as a whole, and is furthermore said to be a form of "redistribution" that levels social inequalities, and ensures positive social relations (Salisbury 1982; Cronon 1983). New scholarship on the nature of reciprocity suggests, however, that it can also lead to asymmetry, and, without an elaborate system of social regulation, often becomes the basis for social inequality. Economic stratification can also exist alongside an ideology of reciprocity. Wealth (in the form of goods or knowledge) can be protected through the exchange of less valued goods or through the establishment of separate spheres of exchange (A. Weiner 1992:7–9). To characterize the Ninnimissinuok as participants in an economic system predicated on reciprocity, is to leave unexamined the intraregional variations suggested by the documentary and archaeological records, and the evidence for the existence of social asymetry present in those same records.

Ranking and Stratification, Private Property, and Regional Integration

Social asymmetry is often conceived in terms of characteristics outlined by Morton Fried, who distinguished between ranked and stratified societies. Ranked societies are those "in which positions of valued status are somehow limited so that not all those of sufficient talent to occupy such statuses actually achieve them" (Fried 1967:109). Stratified societies, on the other hand, limit access to the basic goods, resources, and services that sustain life (110ff). Fried's characterization has been employed to further outline the differences between the evolutionary stages of "tribe" and "chiefdom" (Feinman and Neitzel 1984:42). Traditionally, ranking has been regarded as largely symbolic in nature, and associated with "tribal" levels of organization (Earle 1987:290). Stratification has more generally been linked to chiefdoms and states (290). More recently, however, scholars have come to see that ranking indicates an "incipient" aristocracy, which favors some over others in terms of both wealth and lifestyle and is thus itself a sign of social asymmetry and inequality (291). Such differentiation is often expressed in the dress, comportment, and dwelling places of the highest ranking members of a society, distinctions which were all present at least among coastal people in southern New England.

Discussions of inequality among the Ninnimissinuok and other coastal Algonquians have generally focused on the credibility of seventeenth-century European observers, who were, it is implied, blinded by their own acceptance of the "naturalness" of hierarchy (e.g., Hocart 1970; Salisbury 1982:42–44; Lavin 1988). These interpretations privilege comments concerning the consensus-building style of leadership in southern New England over those describing hierarchy, and the autocracy of the ruling elite. Interpretations that favor egalitarianism and consensus are supported by an indiscriminate use of sources from differing localities within the broader region and fail to recognize the distinctiveness of coastal, riverine, and uplands polities.

Consensus arguments also focus around the issue of property ownership. Seventeenth-century Native statements and European commentary about reciprocity (see chapter 4) have been used most recently to bolster implicitly moralistic contrasts between Native North Americans' "communalism" and English "individualism" and ecological implications of both ways of life (e.g., Thomas 1979; Cronon 1983). Although superior to arguments that lay the blame for the loss of native autonomy on the "fragility" of indigenous culture (e.g., Vaughan 1965), in shifting the onus of failure to ecological conflict, these arguments are nonetheless misleading in their insistence on the simplicity of native social organization, especially in coastal contexts.

Introduction

Leadership in Southern New England

Ranked societies often develop in response to increasing complexities in the decisions that confront groups, where "status differences function to increase the probability of decision implementation" (Fried 1967:101). Therefore, centrality of decision-making is a characteristic of middle-range societies also marked by ranking and/or stratification. The means by which such centralized authority develops has long been debated by scholars. Some favor the notion that a privileged leadership hierarchy arises out of the need to "process" complex information, for example, regarding scheduling, resource distribution, trade, and political relations for large populations (e.g. G. A. Johnson 1978). At the heart of this theory are notions of power and information closure. According to Steadman Upham, "Power relations revolve around the uncertainty, insecurity, and ambiguity associated with access to material and information. The evolution of power relations in small-scale societies occurs when decision-making becomes linked to the use and possession of basic resources . . . relations of power become linked to economy, and profound inequalities result" (1990:11).

Leadership in southern New England was in the hands of sachems—hereditary rulers whom some authors argue were responsible for the redistribution of surplus food and goods acquired through trade. The classic portrait of a chief as the focus of a redistributive network of staple goods in an ecologically diverse region (Service 1962) has recently come under attack. Feinman and Neitzel have demonstrated, for example, that the correlation between redistribution and strong leadership in middle-range societies is only partial, and no more important than several other functions performed by these leaders (1984:56). "Redistributive" chiefs, moreover, do not "manage" the flow of staples, but rather extract agricultural tribute to "finance" their own political activities (Earle 1987). Redistribution, if it existed in coastal southern New England, was of this sort.

Other theorists suggest that chiefs arise through their ability to control surplus or trade in rare or desirable goods, an argument favored by Helen Rountree as an explanation for the rise of the paramount chiefdom of the Powhatan (1989), and Steven Potter, for the neighboring Potomac Valley (1993). Very little is known about the actual production and dissemination of wampum in the late sixteenth and early seventeenth centuries in southern New England, but it seems likely that those groups able to control the distribution of the beads in the early seventeenth century were also those with the most centralized polities, particularly the Narragansetts and neighboring Pequots.

Warfare, and the role played by chiefs in waging war, has also been invoked as an explanation for the development of complex middle-range societies. Robert L. Carneiro's detailed study of chiefdoms suggests that competition over land in environmentally circumscribed regions gives an adaptive advantage to centralized decision-making (1968, 1970), a situation recognized by some scholars studying coastal Algonquian societies (e.g., Dunford 1992; E. S. Johnson 1993; Potter 1993). Alternatively, the importance of warfare as a means of acquiring captive labor might be equally significant in societies where labor, rather than land, was at a premium (Earle 1987:293). The acquisition of captives was frequently noted in seventeenth-century accounts of warfare in New England, and while some were fully incorporated into their captor's communities (Axtell 1985), others were clearly conscripted as servants and slaves (Bradford 1970:397–98). As communities grew, demands by coastal sachems for added labor may have increased.

Chiefdoms are also frequently characterized by the development of a military elite (Earle 1987:297). Warriors trained from youth to lead in battle, such as the *pniese* who served Massasoit of the Pokanoket, often reinforce chiefly control. Indeed, it was these members of a military elite who collected tribute for Massasoit.

Finally, chiefly societies are sometimes understood as the "artifacts" of external pressure, usually from more centralized or powerful states. External threat requires increased centralization of decision-making, organization of defense, and increased involvement in diplomatic and/or trading activities. Both the expansion of the Hopewellian-Ohioan state to the west and the arrival of Europeans in the Northeast have been invoked as causes in the development of complex societies in coastal southern New England (e.g., Thomas 1979:400; Ceci 1990). While the impact of the expansion and collapse of the Hopewell interaction sphere in the Northeast is difficult to evaluate, it is clear that the forces leading to complexity in southern New England were in operation centuries before the European presence was established there.

Recent studies also emphasize the competitive and unstable nature of chiefly power. Chiefs, whose incentives include prestige, a wealthy and comfortable lifestyle, and the "reproductive" advantage of access to multiple sexual and marriage partners, must constantly compete for control of the wealth and the political support that accompanies that wealth (Earle 1987:294). A second problem faced by chiefs and their families is the need to *sustain* such control. According to Fried, regular status inheritance rules may "reduce problems of recruitment, training, and continuity," and a system in which "decision-making positions are effectively inherited would also provide an increased probability of organizational continuity" (1967:101). There is no doubt that rulership in coastal communities was hereditary, and that members of the sachem families or lineages shared in the benefits of high status.

Trigger argues that the implication of some recent studies is that equality is more fragile and short-lived than anthropologists had previously believed. He notes that the Marxist explanation of class conflict as the major cause of social change might be extended to account for change in all societies—that differences of age, gender, and personal prestige found in small-scale societies give rise to conflicts that are similar to those that occur between classes in more complex societies. All social change is thus viewed as being the result of conflict among interest groups (1992:121). Trigger further suggests that both conflicts between groups within a society and the exercise of power by one individual over others are seen in small-scale societies as tendencies that have to be subdued and negated (121). Evidence for conflict and factionalism among the Ninnimissinuok may well reflect these struggles as they do differential access to cultural knowledge.

Scholars concur that the characteristics of chiefdoms outlined above reinforce one another. As Timothy K. Earle argues, "Problems of survival create needs for leadership, and at the same time, opportunities for control" (1987:297). The environmental and social relations that together stimulate the process of centralization are furthermore supported by an accompanying "chiefly" ideology, an ideology that comes to stress the importance of the ruling elite at the expense of the ties of kinship and reciprocity characteristic of egalitarian societies. The ideology of the *sontimoonk* or sachemship, the community/polity most frequently mentioned in Native references to governance in southern New England, functioned in this way. The notion of the sachemship served to articulate and reconcile communities with conflicting interests, to "naturalize" the increasingly unequal interpersonal relationships.

The Unequal Status of Women

The ideology of inequality also affects gender relations and women's status as well. The fact that women, who, in addition to giving birth, are generally responsible for child-rearing, has had important implications for the work they can or are believed able to do (M. Rosaldo 1974:23). Burton, Brudner, and White show that men tend to perform tasks closer to the beginning of "productive sequences" and suggest that control of initial productive stages, or of initial raw materials, enables subsequent control over the entire productive operation, including disposal of products (1977:230–41). That many women cannot, during substantial portions of their lives, perform tasks incompatible with child rearing (i.e., that take place at a distance from home, are physically dangerous, or cannot be interrupted) is frequently thought to be one of the major factors contributing to their confinement to a separate, domestic, or "private" sphere, and to their often rigidly "gendered" work, work often culturally less valued than that of men.

Even where women's work is known to have been of considerable economic value, its significance often has been underplayed. Many analyses of land-use and horticulture in Native North America, for example, proceed without reference to the crucial role of women in the production, transformation, and distribution of plant foods and products. Although women are generally credited with the gathering and processing of wild plants, their role is not acknowledged in the evolution of plant use. Most studies posit a gradual transition from "tolerance" to "encouragement" of such indigenous plants as sumpweed, chenopod, and sunflower, to the active cultivation of maize, without referring to agency (e.g., B. Smith 1989). The anonymity of such a scenario effectively denies women's conscious contributions to plant domestication (Watson and Kennedy 1991:261).[5] The circumstances of the adoption of maize, particularly in coastal southern New England (as described in chapter 2), suggest on the contrary that women played an active role in making the transition to a greater dependence on cultivated crops. The environmentally marginal coastal regions required both a willingness to experiment and extremely intimate knowledge of local conditions on the part of women farmers (Ceci 1977; Demeritt 1991; Watson and Kennedy 1991:266), as well as access to the body of shared knowledge commonly attributed to women, about plants and their habits.

It is not enough, however, simply to acknowledge the contributions of women to the economy. The significance of women's labor lies in how it affected women's experience, their social standing, political influence, and spiritual potency. Women's work among the Ninnimissinuok profoundly shaped the social relations, political structure, and ideology of their societies. However, in coastal communities at least, women were sometimes devalued in spite of their great contributions to economy. Feminist scholars concur that significant contributions to the economy by women are not necessarily correlated with high status or with egalitarian social organization (Mukhopadhyay and Higgins 1988). On the other hand, the low status of women has sometimes blinded researchers to the value of those same contributions.

Both Eleanor Leacock and Karen Sacks suggest that gender asymmetry is due to women's loss of control over the means of production and over their own labor—losses resulting from the expansion of production for exchange and the emergence of hierarchical societies. Sacks focuses on variations within nonstate societies and argues that "it is only when ruling classes replace corporate kin groups as the owners of productive means, thus destroying the economic basis for sisterly relations of production, [that] wifehood gradually becomes the defining attribute of womanhood and the basis for female dependency and subordination" (1974:219). If it is true that hereditary classes were taking the place of kin-groups among the Ninnimissinuok, women's status may have been in decline as a result of reorganization into male-dominated family units.

Finally, as C. Delaney (1986) and D. Gewertz (1984) suggest, ideas about gender are inextricably linked to the larger system of cultural meaning; to cosmology, ideology, and ideas of personhood (Collier and Yanagisako 1987:8). The increasing complexity associated with varied subsistence tasks, growth in the number of outside associations, and in population size among the Ninnimissinuok might have contributed to an increasingly dualistic emphasis on roles and identity. In neighboring Delaware and Iroquois society, for example, sexual dualism was both a strong metaphor and symbolic principle of organization (Fenton 1951:48). Jay Miller suggests that man/woman oppositions are often transformations resulting from an "insistence on differentiation" in which cultural features are reversed, segregated, and redefined on either side of a cultural boundary (1974). This ideology of differentiation, particularly in coastal societies, might well have contributed to the exclusion of women from activities that contributed to the acquisition and maintenance of status.

Kinship and Gendered Ideology

Gender ideology also plays a role in the domain of kin relations. Karla Poewe, for example, suggests that matrilineal and patrilineal descent systems have different implications for interpersonal relations, the former implying unity and equality, the latter, differentiation, separation, and inequality (1981:214). Ortner and Whitehead argue that kinship and marriage are crucial to understanding gender ideology and the sphere of prestige relations that mediates between the organization of kinship and marriage and the organization of gender (1981). They and others also suggest that evidence for women's exploitation implies a developing patrilineal and patrilocal focus. Coontz and Henderson compare patrilocal and matrilocal kin and ask why wives are more exploited in the former—and why patrilocality is so common in kin corporate societies and in the transition to state societies. They find that patrilocal societies have greater potential for expansion and for "internal stratification, both sexual and socio-economic" because of the greater ease with which wealth can be concentrated and the potential for greater fluctuations in lineage wealth in patrilineal societies, both of which hinge on the supply of male-acquired and controlled goods being more variable. This is so because the processes of lineage accumulation and differentiation commonly entail control over the labor and reproductive capacity of wives. Therefore, they conclude, the development of male dominance is inseparable from that of societal inequality (1986:478). If, particularly in the contact period, accumulation of capital in the form of wampum and other scarce goods facilitated a patrilineal organization, women's status (with the exception of that of sachem women) among the Ninnimissinuok may well have been on the decline, particularly in coastal regions.

Cosmology and Ritual

The underlying principles that structured social and political relationships and that accounted for and justified inequalities of class and gender among the Ninnimissinuok were expressed in ritual as well as in cosmology. These principles can be said to have revolved around a number of paired oppositions that encompassed the dualities and contradictions of daily practice. They include: transformation (or impermanence) and fixity; control and powerlessness; dominance and subordination; and autonomy and unity. Such oppositions were manifest in everyday social and economic relations, productive relations that also entailed a classification of beings and forces, of individuals who interceded with them, and of rituals that linked cosmic principles to social experience. Cosmology and ritual, far from representing a sphere removed from the "base" of economic activities, were in reality intimately connected to them.

The Functions and Meanings of Ritual

Ritual, the most elaborated, and ephemeral cultural product of the Ninnimissinuok, was significant both cosmologically and politically. The way in which ritual functions to explain and justify current conditions, and to recreate the sense of *communitas* crucial to the maintenance of such conditions, is most eloquently described in the work of Victor Turner (e.g., 1967, 1969). Clifford Geertz, on the other hand, has emphasized the way in which ritual creates and transforms meaning, weaving the "webs of cultural significance" through which people understand their world (1973). The form that ritual takes also provides clues to the nature of social relations within a community, whether they are rigid and well-defined, or diffuse (Douglas 1970). Ninnimissinuok ritual both justified and transformed.

Ritual was particularly crucial to sustaining political power among those people. Religious sanctions of leadership are said to be common in chiefly societies (Earle 1987:298), and are likely to take the form of rituals marking status, chiefly authority, or the chief's role as an intermediary between the social world and that of the supernatural (Helms 1981). The message of these rituals is reinforced by the support of religious leaders loyal to, or clients of, the rulers themselves. Thus the practice of ritual serves to reinforce the social and cosmological order and, in some cases, to mask or naturalize social inequalities. At the same time, notions of personal and social well-being embodied in ritual reinforced those social bonds of generous sharing and of unity so justly celebrated among the Ninnimissinuok. At the same time, however, rituals that reinforced political power served to transform that power. By the 1640s rituals came to mark the emergence of new social forms and relationships more congruent with the altered circumstances under which the Ninnimissinuok lived.

Recursivity and the Linear Narrative

The linearity imposed by literary convention on an interpretive narrative gives arbitrary prominence to those chapters that occur later in the narrative sequence. However, it is the recursiveness and interplay of various domains of Ninnimissinuok experience that explain much about these people's actions and reactions during the period 1500–1650. Such interplay is documented throughout the following chapters, which draw equally upon the material, ideological and cosmological, in depicting the complex whole that constituted life for the Ninnimissinuok in those centuries of dramatic change.

1.

A Tripartite Settlement Model

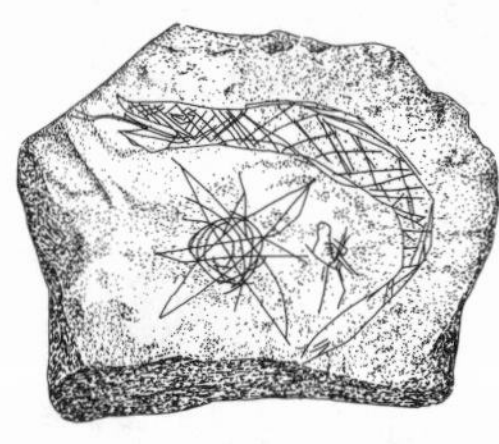

Emerging out of the diversity of the southern New England landscape are three distinctive ecosystems that played a dominant role in the cultural history of southern New England: the estuarine, the riverine, and the uplands. Although fine-grained archaeological analysis of sites in each of these ecoregions is still in its infancy, it is possible to identify general settlement patterns that are characteristic of each one (Map 5).

Estuaries, Coastal Ecology, and Conditional Sedentism[1]

Fragile and bounteous, estuarine ecosystems comprise some of the most unique and significant environments of southern New England. Generally semi-enclosed coastal bodies of water with connections to the open sea, estuaries are characterized by varying mixtures of fresh, brackish, and salt waters (Pritchard 1967; Kerber 1984:14). True

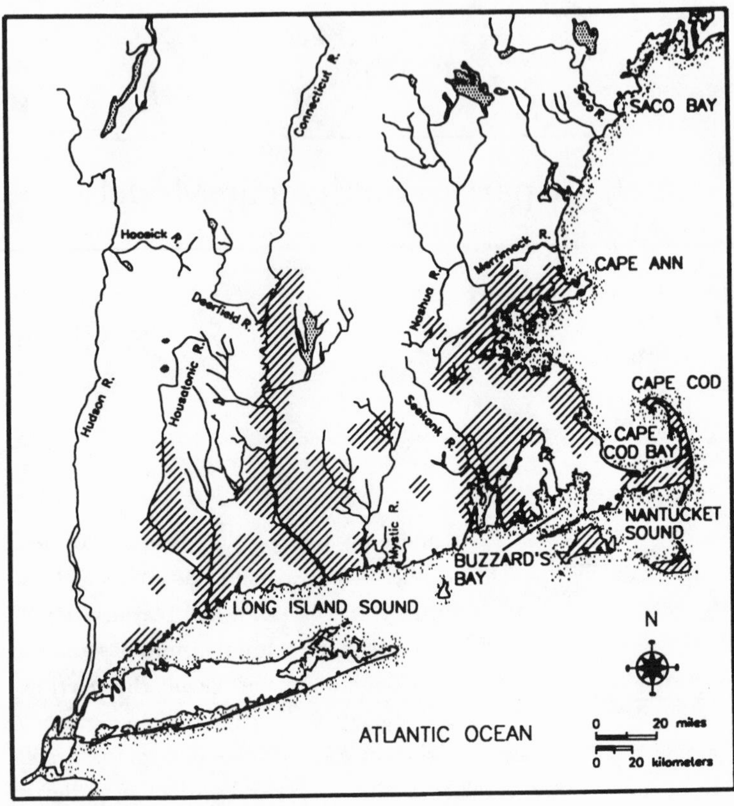

Map 5. Areas of Late Woodland settlement in southern New England. (Artist: Sondra Jarvis.)

estuaries consist of multiple zones, beginning with the water column itself, then extending inland over mudflats exposed only at low tide, which merge with an intertidal zone where marsh grasses flourish, succeeded in turn by a zone of mixed salt and freshwater plant species (Thomson 1958:94–95; Nixon and Oviatt 1973; Niering and Warren 1980).

Once called "ecotones," or "regions of transition between two or more diverse communities" (Odum 1971:157), estuaries are now celebrated for their remarkable biotic diversity. Dincauze (1973, 1974), Barber (1979), and Kerber (1984) argue that estuaries represent uniquely rich habitats for human populations because of the way in which they link diverse ecosystems. Zones ranging from terrestrial to freshwater riverine, freshwater marsh, and salt marsh, are all easily accessible within a relatively narrow strip running from the sea inland. The estuarine ecotone also benefits from what E. P. Odum calls the "edge effect," or "the tendency for increased variety and density at community junctions" (1971:157). Estuaries and other intertidal regions are associated with a number of diverse habitats of great importance to Native subsistence and diet, including the water column itself, the strandflats, tidal rivers, and salt marsh.

Salt marsh "prairies by the sea," so essential to the estuarine profile, encompass more than four thousand acres flung like a fringed shawl along the southern slope of Cape Cod's Sandwich Moraine (Chamberlain 1964:207), reappearing in irregular loops and bands near modern Chatham, Orleans, and Eastham. The chiaroscuro of breeze-ruffled grasses, threaded by tidal creeks characteristic of saltmarsh and tidal estuaries, softens the rocky shores of Martha's Vineyard and Nantucket, and marks much of the coastal region of central Massachusetts, Rhode Island, Connecticut, and Long Island as well.[2]

Salt waters, inundating the intertidal zone at flood tide, permit two varieties of grass to flourish there, the *Spartina patens* and *Spartina alterniflora* (Redfield 1972; Whitlach 1982). These grasses are rich in nutrients important to herbivores, anchor soils in which numerous microbic species thrive and contribute to the creation of a series of linked microenvironments that support uniquely varied plant and animal life (Cronon 1983:31; Yentsch et al. 1966).

The "New England" salt marsh is distinctive both in its history and appearance. Beginning about six thousand years ago salt marshes of the region emerged at the same time the rapid post-glacial rise in sea levels tapered off, but were not fully established until sediment accumulation was able to keep pace with coastal submergence (sealevel rise) some three thousand years ago (Bloom 1963:334). Thereafter, sandbars forming across the mouths of sunken bays enclosed lagoons of still waters, where thin layers of silt and mud were deposited. When soils within these lagoons rose to the level of tidal ebb and flow, the typical grasses of the salt marsh established themselves, and the process of biotic succession could begin (Kerber 1984:17; Thomson 1958:97).

It is abundantly clear that the large variety of animal and plant species present within the estuarine, intertidal, and salt marsh ecosystems, including shellfish, fish, birds, and land mammals, which live or feed in or near the marshes and linked ecosystems, were of great potential use to human populations of the region (Barber 1979:27; Kerber 1984:27–31). Even some of the typical marsh grasses, especially eelgrass, may have been harvested by prehistoric people (Lavin 1988:112). The archaeological record shows a strong correlation between the development of modern estuaries themselves and their use by Native populations throughout coastal southern New England (Dincauze 1973:53;1974:49,50; McBride 1984; Lavin 1988:108). The unique characteristics of the estuarine and estuarine-like environments, especially in those regions where marine mammals and deepwater fish were also regularly available, provided the resources for an equally unique human adaptation (Little 1993a).

This adaptation can be characterized as one of "conditional" sedentism, wherein stable social groupings numbering probably no more than two hundred people occupied more or less bounded estuarine zones for most or all of the year, in some places and at some times establishing largish, dispersed neighborhoods, in others, single or extended family campsites (Dunford 1992). This settlement type has no name in the archaeological or ethnographic literature: It is not "village-based," in that it seems unlikely that villages were ever a common feature of this ecoregional pattern, nor is it the "centrally-based wandering" often attributed to foraging people, for the evidence points to very circumscribed movements within the same rather restricted zones year after year. Such regionally based sedentism had not a single bounded village or series of individual "homesteads" as its focus, but the estuary itself, its human community seemingly (to our partially obscured vision at least) joining and splitting like quicksilver in a fluid pattern within its bounds. A review of archaeological research for the several estuarine regions of southern New England suggests that the pattern was widespread in this region during the Late Woodland period (Map 6).

The Boston Area and Massachusetts Bay

Although much of the prehistoric record of the greater Boston area is obscured by burgeoning urban growth, what remains suggests that by the Late Woodland, there was an increasing concentration of sites of all types, repeated reuse of coastal and estuarine localities, a heavy emphasis on estuarine resources, and a wide range of sites of varying functions within a restricted area of settlement in estuarine environments ranging from the Merrimac to the upper Cape (Dincauze 1974; Luedtke 1980, 1988). Although such concentration has been attributed to the increasing importance of agriculture as a factor in population, the evidence for substantial use of maize in this area is entirely lacking until A.D. 1350.

Cape Cod

On Cape Cod and on the islands of Martha's Vineyard and Nantucket a conditionally sedentary settlement pattern based on estuarine resources was also established by the Late Woodland period, probably without significant contributions from maize agriculture until after 1300 A.D. Frederick J. Dunford (1992, 1993) identifies an "outer Cape" pattern of large multi-component

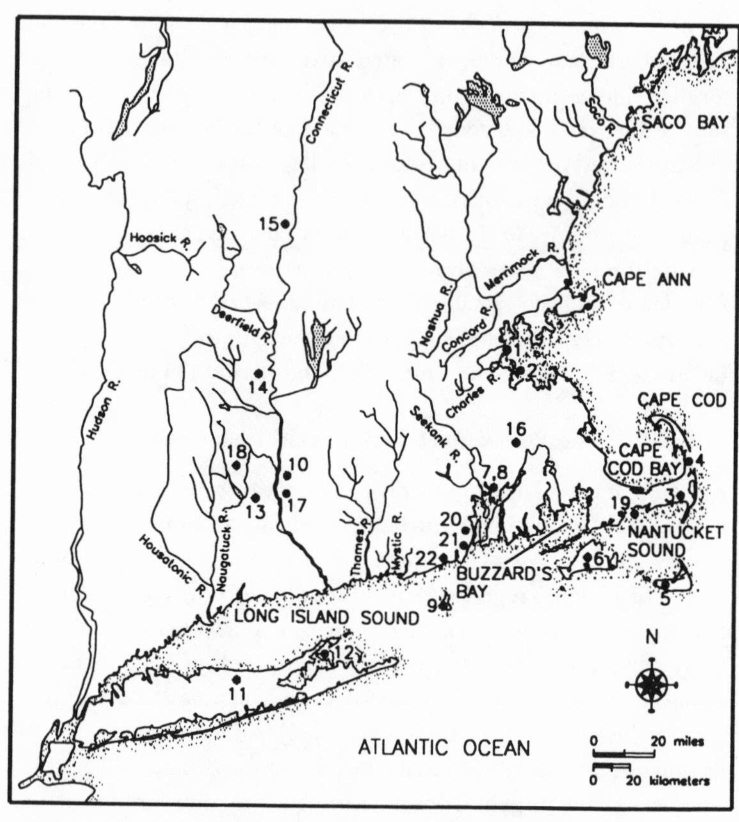

Map 6. Woodland sites discussed in the text. (Artist: Sondra Jarvis.) (1) Charles River Estuary, (2) Boston Harbor Islands, (3) Boland-Brook, (4) Wellfleet, (5) Nantucket, (6) Martha's Vineyard, (7) Providence, (8) Greenwich Cove, (9) Block Island, (10) Morgan, (11) Van der Volk, (12) Shelter Island, (13) Meadow Road, (14) Bark Wigwams, (15) Skitchewaug, (16) Titicut Swamp, (17) Cedar Swamp, (18) Beaver meadow, (19) Sandy's Point, (20) Browning, (21) Campbell, (22) RI 102

shell-midden/residential sites located at estuaries, and small habitation sites located in sheltered areas near freshwater ponds in the early Late Woodland period (1992:3). The latter contain shell and the remains of other marine fauna, implying continued use of coastal resources, especially shellfish (3). Sites of this type include Boland's Pond, in Orleans. This site, which has a radiocarbon date of 915 +/- 120 A.D., although exhibiting evidence for a number of domestic activities, is small, and appears to have been occupied temporarily, by a small number of individuals (1992:5). Based on his analysis of this site, Dunford concludes that "while the historical record clearly suggests that two of the major estuarine communities of the outer Cape, Nauset and Monomoyett, did manifest the demographic, social, political, economic and territorial attributes of sedentary communities, the archaeological record is clearly indicative of periodic residential re-location; a fact not consistent with the traditional definition of sedentism" (1992:9).

Francis P. McManamon finds evidence for moderate-length and long-term occupation of the estuarine region near both Eastham and Wellfleet Harbor in what he calls "nodes of concentrated settlement" and argues that "the overall pattern of prehistoric land-use on the outer Cape shows relatively small areas of intensive settlement and activity with large intervening areas used sparsely, or for activities that have left a sparse archaeological record" (1982:18–19). McManamon and Bradley have also suggested that the people who occupied the Nauset area of the Cape "enjoyed a relatively stable cultural adaptation to an environment rich in subsistence resources." The locations around Nauset Marsh and Wellfleet Harbor "allowed easy access to a variety of micro-environments ranging from tidal flats and salt marsh to freshwater wetland and wooded upland" without movement of "principal residences." They conclude that year-round residence was possible but that "the plans of their villages were more dispersed than those known commonly among the Iroquois and Huron" (1986:40). Such a pattern may well have been due in part to the unique environmental circumscription of the outer Cape in which "the limiting or levelling contingencies of mobility would have been negated," and thus "it did not affect the emergence of those attributes traditionally associated with sedentary communities" (Dunford 1992:9–10).

Nantucket and Martha's Vineyard

Elizabeth A. Little also finds confirmation for a shellfish-based subsistence/settlement model in her work on Nantucket, and suggests that similar patterns obtain on Martha's Vineyard as well (1988). On Nantucket, 56 of 57 inventoried Late Woodland sites are located within 1 kilometer (5–10 minute walk) of a shellfish habitat. Most of these sites also have a southerly exposure, implying November-March usage (1988:76). A smaller sample of sites from Martha's Vineyard also suggests a correlation between shellfish exploitation, southerly aspect, and winter and/or year-round use (Waters and Ritchie, cited in Ritchie 1969).[3]

An analysis of bone collagen taken from human remains found in Late Woodland contexts on Nantucket, in conjunction with that of tissue samples from a variety of flora and fauna known to be represented on Late Woodland sites on Nantucket, further supports the argument that Late Woodland coastal populations relied on a marine-based diet of the sort most likely to have been extracted from estuarine environments (Medaglia et al. 1990).[4] In their study of Nantucket diet in the Late Woodland period, Medaglia, Little, and Schoeninger determined that the Native people apparently subsisted on a diet with a less marked reliance on marine resources than was consumed by a control population of Eskimo, as well as one with less reliance on plant resources than was consumed by a documented group of maize horticulturalists (57) (Fig. 1). Human remains from well-dated Late Woodland burials exhibited no evidence of mal-

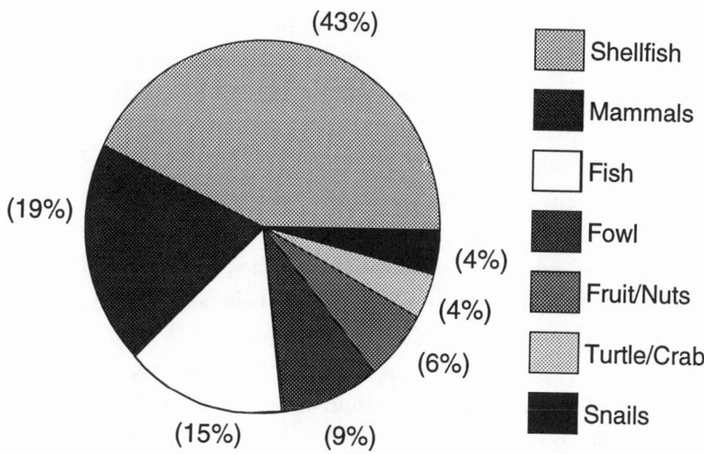

Fig. 1. Late Woodland diet on Nantucket. (After Little 1980. Artist: Shannon Dawdy.)

nutrition, and little or no dental caries, a known associate of maize agriculture in Native American populations. Although small amounts of maize have been recovered from a Late Woodland feature on Nantucket (Luedtke pers. comm. 1994), substantial use of the cultigen has not been established, and since sea mammal remains are also scarce, the authors postulate as a third alternative a diet of intertidal and harbor-dwelling flora and fauna, which would account for a high carbon signature due to indirect consumption of intertidal plants such as Spartina and eelgrass (58; see also Little 1993, 1993a).

Rhode Island

The relationship between settlement, subsistence, and environment is nowhere better demonstrated than in estuarine localities in what is now Rhode Island. The coastal regions of Rhode Island are characterized by two unique but related ecotonal environments: salt-ponds and true estuaries. The southern coast of Rhode Island from present day Westerly to Narragansett comprises a salt-ponds region. Here tidal ponds are sheltered from the ocean by barrier spits, and provide an environment for a wide variety of flora and fauna (Robinson 1987). In addition, the lands adjacent to the ponds are well-drained, relatively fertile, and level. The ponds are fed by fresh groundwater and a few small streams. Springs and glacial kettle holes also provide fresh water (2). Bounded on the north by the morainal ridge, and on the south by Block Island sound, "the region forms a distinct coastal environment that offered specialized resources to indigenous Indian groups" (2).

Estuaries, which likewise constituted a substantial portion of Rhode Island's coastal region, were also heavily used by prehistoric human populations. In the Potowomut River and Greenwich Cove area of southern Rhode Island, for example, intensive exploitation of shellfish coincided with the development of the saltwater estuary, beginning about 2000–3000 years ago (Kerber 1984:150–51). Human settlement was evidently densest adjacent to the estuary itself (155). The focus on settlement near estuaries, which manifests itself with the stabilization of sea-level rise, was accompanied through time by an increasing diversification of resource use, as well as increased cultural modification of the landscape (Bernstein 1990:321).

The relationship between estuarine and estuarine-like environments and a conditionally sedentary life in coastal Rhode Island is further supported by the distribution of sites where evidence of ceramic manufacture and use has been located. Ceramics, frequently associated with sedentism in the archaeological and ethnographic literature, are manifestly unsuited to a mobile way of life, being both fragile and cumbersome, and although traditionally associated with maize horticulture, appear long before maize-use can be documented in southern New England (e.g., Cox 1982:6). The distribution of sites yielding ceramics in Rhode Island is instructive. Anne S. Dowd suggests that sites where ceramics have been found cluster nonrandomly, and reflect a "coastal orientation" (1988:76). Although Dowd suggests an increased dependence on domesticated exotics such as maize as a possible explanation for this clustering, there is no evidence for maize-use in this region corresponding to the increasing appearance of ceramics on coastal and estuarine sites. Instead, David Bernstein argues for an association with native plant use and estuarine exploitation as the basis for sedentary life (1992:9–10; 1993). Peter Pagoulatos also found that Late Woodland sites clustered "toward the coastal margins and near interior river systems" (1990:69). This trend began at least by the first millennium A.D. The environmental zones outlined by Pagoulatos have been further refined through surveys of specific localities, such as the research done for the Route 4 extension near East Greenwich and North Kingstown, Rhode Island. Archaeologists working on that project have found that settlement was focused on an estuarine ecotone, with three-season settlements near the estuary heads, and special use and seasonal camps at special resource locations (Morenon 1986).[5]

Late Woodland sites in coastal Rhode Island have so far failed to yield any maize, despite careful excavation and the use of floatation techniques to recover plant remains. This is the case even when these techniques have recovered evidence for the use of other flora (Bernstein 1992:9–10). The lack of maize itself does not preclude the existence of a marked dependence on predictable plant resources, as evidenced by two sites on the Pettaquamscutt River on the southwestern shore of Narragansett Bay. The Browning site, where a stone spade was found, and the Campbell site, where the remains of carbonized wild rice were recovered in association with a grinding stone in a firepit dating to 850 +/– 145 A.D. (Cox, quoted in Kerber 1988:68), certainly suggest a strong orientation toward such plant-use. Carbonized remains of sunflower seeds were also located at the

RI 102 site in Narragansett, dating at least to 250 A.D. (Morenon 1986). Late Woodland sites on Narragansett Bay have yielded charred remains of nuts such as hickory, acorn, and hazelnut, with an emphasis on hazelnut and hickory, fruits including cherry, raspberry, and grape, and leafy plants such as chenopods (Bernstein 1992:4–5).

The Providence Cove Lands site in present-day Providence, Rhode Island, dating to the Late Woodland period, also contained large numbers of carbonized plant remains. These included at least five edible native species and a large variety of terrestrial and aquatic fauna (Bernstein 1992:8). Another Late Woodland site of some significance is the Lambert Farm site, which, although 1.5 kilometers inland from Narragansett Bay, yielded both marine resources and carbonized floral remains, especially hickory (Kerber et al. 1989).[6]

Recent archaeological investigations in the Narragansett Bay region thus demonstrate that a wide variety of plant resources were gathered and "encouraged" by the peoples who occupied the region. According to Bernstein, "Increase in subsistence output was seemingly achieved through an intensification of the collection of a few key resources and an overall diversification of the subsistence base" (1992:1).

Strong evidence for a long tradition of conditional sedentism also comes from an Early Woodland period village excavated by Kevin McBride on Block Island, located within the estuarine boundaries of the Great Salt Pond. This large, 3-acre site provides evidence for year-round settlement of a group of 200 people, living in long-houses 10–20 meters long, and subsisting on wild plants, game, fish, and shellfish nearly 1000 years before maize horticulture became important in the region (Jaworski 1990).

Archaeological data from Rhode Island indicate that conditionally sedentary occupation of coastal regions has been the norm in that region since the early Woodland period. While coastal occupations are generally not "village-like," they are clustered and diverse, and demonstrate multiseasonal occupation, often based on estuarine resources, and a heavy reliance on predictable, wild plant resources,

(Bernstein 1993). Rather, the data presently available point to a conditionally sedentary occupation of coastal regions with several centuries of time-depth, and a broad-range subsistence base in which maize horticulture played a late and minor part.

Connecticut

This interpretation is also confirmed by McBride's work in coastal Connecticut (1984:308) (Map 7).[7] According to him, this region was characterized during the early Late Woodland period by "a number of seasonal camps located in riverine areas, with temporary and task-specific sites situated in terrace and upland zones. Temporary camps are all located within the riverine ecozone, and nearly half within the developing tidal marshes within the riverine ecozone, a pattern similar to one recognized by Dincauze on Charles River Estuary" (1973:74). McBride finds that there is no evidence for year-round settlement during this period but some evidence for increasing sedentism (1984:312).

The patterns noted by McBride are also supported by other scholars working in Connecticut. Lucianne Lavin's analysis of settlement pattern for southern New England is based on environmental reconstructions (1988:101). She too notes the richness of estuarine environments and their association with increasing site density and estuarine development (108) In addition, Lavin points out the association between increased ceramic sherd frequencies on sites of the Middle and Late Woodland and increased use of marsh vegetation (112; Braun 1980:7–8). This increase in coastal populations corresponds with a decline in interior sites (Dincauze 1974), a decline possibly due to nucleation (Lavin 1988:110).

Long Island

A survey of Long Island sites finds that although large coastal shell middens, mortuary sites, and manufacturing locations are most

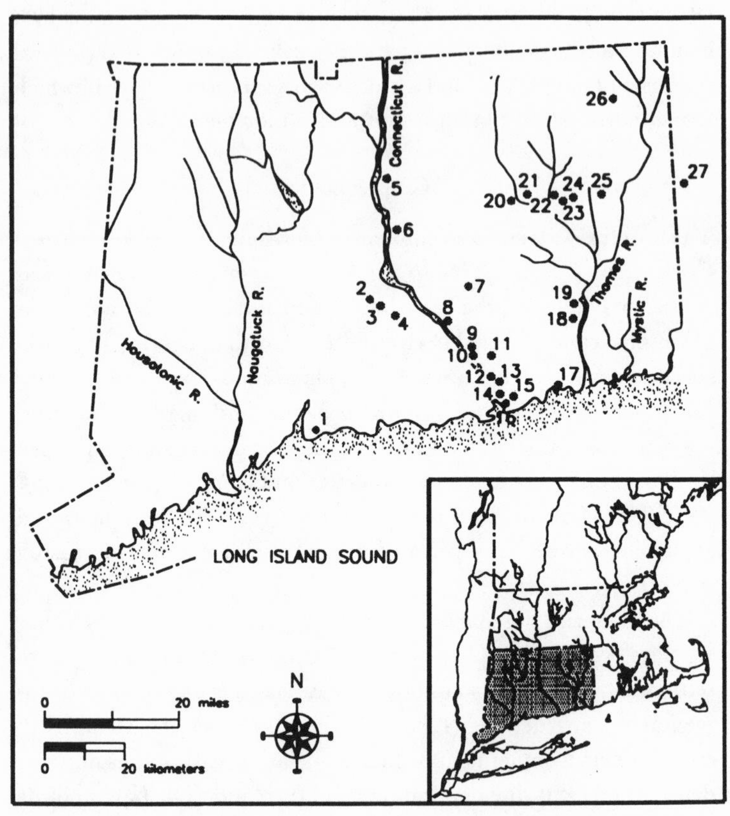

Map 7. Woodland site distribution in coastal Connecticut. (After McBride 1984. Artist: Sondra Jarvis.)

(1) Waldo-Hennessy, (2) Nick's Niche, (3) Fielding, (4) Hackney Pond, (5) 6-HT-116, (6) Hollister, (7) Roaring Brook, (8) Pollard Point, (9) Selden Point, (10) Selden Island, (11) Coudert Ledge, (12) Hamburg Cove, (13) Cooper, (14) Kaiser I, (15) 105-30, (16) Broeden, (17) Mago Point, (18) Fort Shantok, (19) Shantok Cove, (20) Ballymahack, (21) Beaver Brook, (22) Pete's Dive, (23) 1480, (24) Pearl Harbor, (25) Paradise Lake

frequently reported and excavated, Long Island coastal regions actually show great diversity of site type (Lightfoot et al. 1985). While confirming the Late Woodland coastal and estuarine focus of settlement, a recent survey of Shelter Island designed to test this pattern found that a great variety of sites were often clustered in a small area (5.9 hectares) including small shell middens, lithic workshops, quarry sites, and lithic scatters (72–75). The Van der Volk site, a Late Woodland shell midden on Mount Sinai Harbor, excavated by David Bernstein, also documents year-round occupation without reliance on cultigens (Bernstein pers. comm. 1994). This and other surveys further support a settlement model of limited mobility and site diversity within a restricted estuarine/coastal region, a "conditional sedentism" similar to that found in other coastal regions of southern New England.

Ossuaries and Conditional Sedentism

Additional evidence for a conditional sedentism with strong links to local territories comes from ossuaries located in coastal southern New England, all of which date to the beginning of the Late Woodland period (McManamon and Bradley 1986:18; Bradley 1989) (Map 8). Although Luedtke (pers. comm. 1994) suggests that these ossuaries may be "holdovers" of Middle Woodland burial practices, they have also been linked to the development of conditional sedentism in the early Late Woodland period. McManamon and Bradley suggest that ossuaries in other areas of the Northeast are "linked closely with sedentary villages," and "that the burial ceremonies that generated ossuaries seem to have been designed to reassert social ties among villagers who resided in neighboring villages." The authors also believe that the presence of an ossuary supports a model of "year-round" occupation (1986:24–25). Bradley argues that the presence of such ossuaries indicates that "group

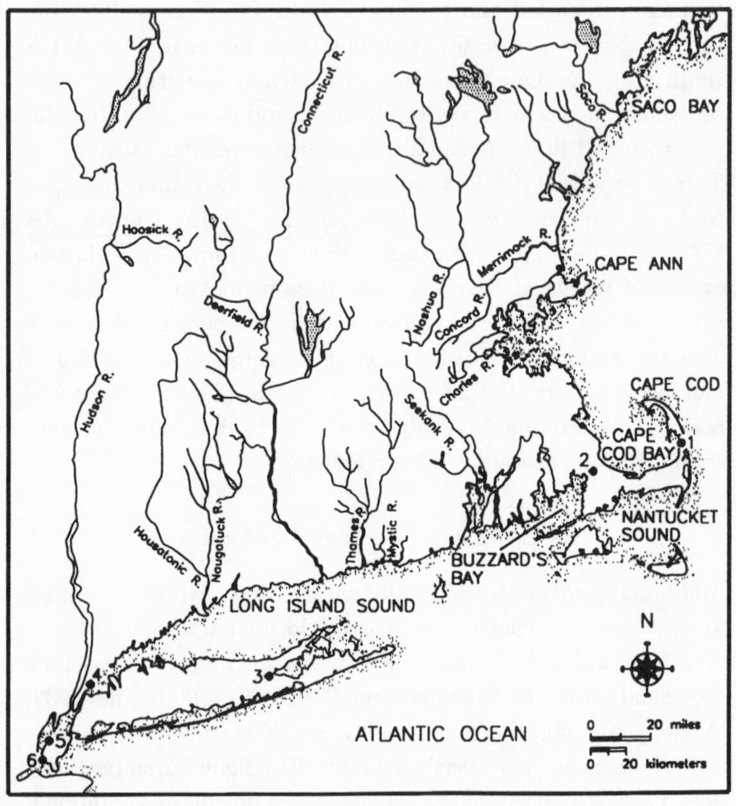

Map 8. Ossuaries in southern New England. (After Bradley 1989. Artist: Sondra Jarvis.)

(1) Indian Rock, (2) Grove Field, (3) Conklin, (4) Archery Range, (5) Bowman's Brook, (6) Tottenville

identity was stronger and was more locally defined than has been suggested traditionally," and that "it may have been expressed more clearly in mortuary terms than in either settlement or material culture patterning" (1989:21).

A Tripartite Settlement Model

The estuarine focus of settlement in coastal regions of southern New England in the Late Woodland period encouraged a lifestyle of regulated and habitual activity, with complexities associated with seasonality, scheduling, and increasing territoriality. This pattern, intensified after the adoption of maize horticulture in the coastal regions, was still present during the period of European contact and settlement. It contrasted with settlement adaptations that emerged in the second important ecoregion of southern New England: the riverine bottomlands of the Connecticut River Valley.

Riverine Adaptations

While the tidal marshes, snaking creeks, and gently sloping eelgrass meadows of southern New England have their abrupt boundaries, none rival in variety and contrast those of New England's large river valleys, especially that of the Connecticut River itself. Rough falls and rapids in the northern reaches near the Canadian border flatten to broad bottomlands in what is now central Massachusetts and northern Connecticut. Estuarine at its mouth, the tidal marshes of the Connecticut extend northwards fifteen to twenty miles, as far as Whalebone Cove, near Hadlyme (McBride 1984:26, 42), and then beyond to the loamy floodplains suitable for agriculture. These plains, lined by rows of ancient, stranded shorelines, sometimes meet abruptly with lofty terrace walls.

As their setting contrasts with that of the coastal estuaries, so the prehistoric inland river valley settlement and subsistence patterns contrast as well. McBride has found an increase by the beginning of the Late Woodland in the use of upland areas, an increase in site size and frequency, and increased aggregation in riverine areas. Sites include with increasing frequency storage pits and the remains of cultigens such as maize (1984). He and others argue that the major contrast between inland and coastal Connecticut River settlement/subsistence patterns is the presence of large, sedentary, agricultural villages.

The Morgan site, located on the floodplains of the Connecticut River at Rocky Hill, south of Hartford, is an example of such an agriculturally based Woodland village site (Lavin 1988a, pers. comm. 1993). The site has been radio-carbon dated to A.D. 1170 +/- 90, A.D. 1320 +/- 70, and A.D. 1360 +/- 70. A deep, single-component site, it covers several acres, and appears to have been occupied continuously during the late twelfth through the fourteenth centuries (Lavin 1988a:7). The site exhibits evidence for multiseason domestic occupation, and for the presence of craft activities such as ceramic pot and pipe manufacture. It is significantly located near a clay source (Lavin 1988a:13). The many ceramic pots recovered from the site show evidence of connections with coastal people, as well as "increased contacts with Native American societies north and northwest of the Morgan site," especially the groups presumably ancestral to the Mahican and Iroquois of the Mid-Hudson and Mohawk vallies (13). Pipe bowls are similarly decorated, showing influences of the indigenous Windsor tradition to the south and the Hudson/Mohawk styles to the west.

Reddened earth pit features found at the Morgan site were possible roasting, steaming, and smoking pits, reused as trash pits. Remains of shellfish such as quahog and soft-shell clam suggest either trade or trips downriver to shellfish beds (13). Some pits contained upright pots, suggesting storage (one had a maize kernel in it) and reuse of the site on a seasonal basis. Another feature contained a "cache" of deer antler with the stone "shovel" used to dig it found near the top (digging tools were found near the tops of other pits as well). Postholes appear to have encircled pit features. Others formed lunar-shaped patterns, perhaps for windshelters or smoking racks (Lavin pers. comm. 1993). Archaeologists have recovered nearly one hundred maize kernels from the site, along with the remains of at least eighteen other edible species, particularly chenopods, hickory, chestnut, and butternut. Windsor hoes have also been found at the site (Lavin 1988a:17).

Floral and faunal remains suggest late spring to early autumn occupation at the Morgan site. The site was not used in winter, probably because of flooding in late winter and spring (18). Lavin concludes that "the early and relatively numerous presence of maize kernels at Morgan illustrates economic differences between the Late Woodland societies in interior Connecticut and those on the coast." She suggests that maize was an important staple of the inland Natives: "Lacking the year-round wild resources provided by coastal marshes and marine environments, they needed a productive, reliable, and storable food to support their growing communities during the starvation period of winter and early spring. Maize horticulture was the answer" (1988a:18–19; see also 1988:113).

The large riverine sites noted by both Lavin and McBride are also identified by Kenneth L. Feder for other parts of north-central Connecticut. For example, the Meadow Road site at the confluence of the Farmington and Pequabuck rivers near New Britian, which dates to 1120 +/– 70 A.D. to 1230 +/– 20 A.D., is a large site covering nearly five acres (Feder 1990:62).

By the Late Woodland period several villages have also been identified on the central Connecticut floodplains. One of these, known as the Bark Wigwams site, comprises an area of several acres, and contains evidence of essentially year-round residency based on maize horticulture (see also Garman 1991). Ceramic styles, lithics, and other material items indicate strong ties with peoples of the Hudson drainage, whose villages theirs closely resemble (Johnson and Bradley 1987). The central Connecticut Valley was also rich in migratory fowl, anadromous fish, and many species of animals, trapped for meat and fur (Thomas 1979:103). Sites in this region reflect this variety and document the continued importance of many native plants, such as berries, nuts, and sumac. Nuts and cultigens were dried and stored in large underground pits, sometimes lined with grasses (Bendremer et al. 1991) or bark.

Other sites located on the upper Connecticut River also support interpretations by Johnson and Bradley (1987) and Lavin (1988a).

The recently excavated Skitchewaug site, near Springfield, Vermont, shows evidence of maize horticulture since early Late Woodland times. Here, the remains of two semisubterranean housepits with as many as fourteen layers of occupation, central hearths, and internal, grass-lined storage pits (Heckenberger et al. 1992:131–32), imply nearly year-round settlement, with emphasis on warm months, and on possible abandonment during spring floods. Storage pits show reliance on small-to-medium mammals, fish, and a large variety of plants, including cultigens (135–36, 140). The authors argue that "maize agriculture was significantly different from earlier patterns of presumed plant management" and that while coastal people derived the majority of their diet from estuarine resources, riverine groups often found their most dependable resources in the river floodplains. However, since the best agricultural lands were also located in the floodplains, maize agriculture, even at riverine sites, may not have adversely affected the scheduling of pre-existing activities (141–42).

It is this riverine "model," predicated on three-season or year-round occupancy of a large village, based on dependence on agriculture, with ancillary use of uplands locations for hunting, fishing, and collection of other resources, that has dominated the archaeological literature of the Northeast. Identified in the early twentieth century by scholars working in New York, it has been the standard by which all other New England sites have been judged, and found wanting (Dincauze 1993:33). Although this pattern is manifestly evident in the riverine sites of the upper Connecticut Valley, it does not apply to the equally complex coastal adaptation discussed above, or to the uplands interior sites of southern New England that are just beginning to receive scholarly attention.

Uplands Interior Adaptations

While the river falls and bottomlands cut a swath through southern New England combining drama and placidity, the meandering uplands, dotted with lakes and marked by rolling oak-hickory forest, are in some ways the most mysterious of landscapes. At the beginning of the second millennium A.D., mile after mile of wooded terrain merged with deceptive subtlety into vast inland swamps, encompassing some of the rich biotic diversity of the estuary, albeit more seasonally. Small, medium, and large lakes, the products of the uneven retreat of glacial ice, were set like jewels in the green expanse of trees. The uplands were threaded with streams and rivers, large and small, some so meager as to even today go unnamed, moving toward the sea or mingling with the waters of those inland bogs that became the focus of much human activity in the Prehistoric period.

The prehistory of the Northeast is complicated by the relatively rapid postglacial evolution of the landscape and the changing nature of these interior wetlands. Brona Simon has found, for example, that the prehistoric use of the Titicut swamp wetlands area of Bridgewater and Raynham, Massachusetts, changed as the swamp itself evolved. In the Late Woodland period, when Titicut was primarily a red maple/cedar swamp, characterized by high biomass and high seasonal productivity, Native use focused primarily on "specific, seasonally available resources" (1991:72). At the same time, its inaccessibility to major rivers may always have made it less desirable as a year-round settlement base than the nearby estuarine, riverine, and wetlands ecoregions of the Taunton River and Assawompsett Pond (72).

Curtiss Hoffman argues that neither nucleated settlements nor maize horticulture were present on nonriverine upland sites in central Massachusetts. He suggests that "the village sites which have occupied so much of the attention of researchers will be seen against a background of pervasive cultural conservatism, in which large population concentrations and dependence upon horticulture were absent" (1989:24). The small Cedar Swamp 3 site (980 +/– 70 A.D.), for example, was in the middle of a swamp, with no evidence of agriculture or storage features although it was possibly a year-round site. Hoffman argues that "the economy of the occupants appears to be oriented exclusively toward swamp resources," and that "the overwhelming character of the adaptation at the Cedar Swamp sites appears to have been local, non-horticultural, multi-seasonal, and self-sufficient, involved very little in regional exchange." Hoffman and others see this uplands pattern as part of a "lacustrine adaptive pattern [dating] from at least the 6th millennium B.P. continuously through to the Late Woodland" (26).

Here the vexed question of the relationship between the interior people and those of the coasts or river valleys, becomes significant. The ethnohistorical model of seasonal transhumance, which has been employed in much of the archaeological literature, implies that uplands sites were simply "outliers" for centrally based foragers or horticulturalists. Late Woodland sites in the Robbins Swamp in northwestern Connecticut, for example, which was extensively occupied in earlier periods, appear to have been only seasonal and/or temporary camps. The swamp seems to have been culturally "empty" space in the Late Woodland, with settlement focused to the north and west in the Housatonic drainage (Nicholas 1991:92).

Others argue that the differing patterns of upland lacustrine and lowland and coastal sites indicate entirely different cultural orientations. Cox et al., for example, have argued that coastal sites are larger, have a wider range of tool types, have more local lithic materials, and less intricate features than interior sites (1985; see also Leveille and Van Coughyen 1990:52). The "Beaver Meadow Complex," associated by Kenneth Feder with the western uplands of the Farmington Valley, is characterized by the presence of sites dated to both Archaic and Woodland times. Feder argues that their location in virtually identical micro-environmental settings, their great similarity in functional artifact assemblages, the presence of similar ecofactual material, and their indistinguishable raw material assemblages, together indicate indisputable continuity in the form of prehistoric upland usage in the Farmington Valley. He notes that this supports a hypothesis of "prehistoric differentiation" between the Farmington Valley uplands and the lower Connecticut Valley, and, perhaps, between the uplands and the Farmington Valley floodplain sites on the eastern margin of Farmington Valley (1990:67).

Finally, McBride argues for the possibility of both an uplands-oriented lacustrine adaptation and one based on seasonal transhumance in central and eastern Connecticut. He hypothesizes that the Willamantic River was a boundary between "two distinct settlement systems" in the Middle and Late Woodland (1992:16) and suggests that the western corridor was exploited seasonally or for specific resources by peoples oriented toward the Connecticut Valley. The highlands east of the Willimantic River, on the other hand, were occupied year-round by a presumably distinct group during the Late Woodland (16).

A Tripartite Settlement Pattern

In summary, archaeological evidence for the Late Woodland period suggests three distinct settlement types, associated with specific eco-regions: estuarine "conditional sedentism" based on reliance upon a wide variety of marine and estuarine resources; riverine village-based sedentism, with a heavier dependence on corn-beans and squash horticulture; and a culturally conservative uplands lacustrine adaptation. Whether some or all uplands peoples were connected in some way to coastal or riverine groups is unclear; it is possible that at least in some areas their adaptation resembled most closely the mobile patterns described by French Jesuits for Natives of the lower Champlain Valley in the early seventeenth century (Day 1978:150).

The environmental contrasts of southern New England and the distinctive settlement patterns associated with them were related to the developing social modalities of the Late Woodland period in that region. On the coast, limited access to environmentally restricted resources and increasing localized populations may well have created the necessary conditions for emerging centralization, hierarchy, and managerial control known cross-culturally to be most commonly associated with "middle-range" societies or chiefdoms (Carneiro 1968, 1970; Earle 1987:294), conditions reifying linguistic categories and historical knowledge already present among the Ninnimissinuok of that area.

Riverine sites, on the other hand, showed a village-like organization with dependence on horticulture, from at least 1000 A.D. The archaeologists who work on such sites find that they most closely resemble the agricultural villages of the ancestral Mahican and Mohawks, both of which were, in historic times, clan-based, matrilineal, and essentially egalitarian people (e.g., Brasser 1978), with strong village autonomy. This raises the possibility that an entirely different social dynamic was at work on these riverine sites. Such an admittedly speculative hypothesis is consistent with cross-cultural links between committed horticulturalists and matrilineality (e.g., Douglas 1971; Goody 1976), and with the evidence for shared ceramic styles between the two areas (Lavin 1988a; Johnson and Bradley 1987).

Uplands interior sites are less well studied but potentially represent a third organizational type, one best characterized as a "collecting" pattern (Binford 1980) typical of logistically organized hunter/gatherers. It is tempting to suggest that such people were organized patrilineally or bilaterally, as were many of their northern neighbors (Day 1978; Snow 1978). Their relations to riverine and coastal groups seem especially enigmatic, and it may be that what appears to be a separate adaptation was in fact only evidence of seasonal or occasional use by larger communities living on the coast or on river floodplains. The complexities of the interrelations between the separate ecozones in southern New England are clear, however, and make the region as a whole one of remarkable "eco-social" variability. Such variability was intensified in the fourteenth and fifteenth centuries A.D. by the growth of long-distance trade and the addition of maize horticulture to coastal subsistence patterns. These developments form the subject of the following chapter.

2.

Maize, Trade, Territoriality, and Wampum: The Archaeological and Linguistic Evidence

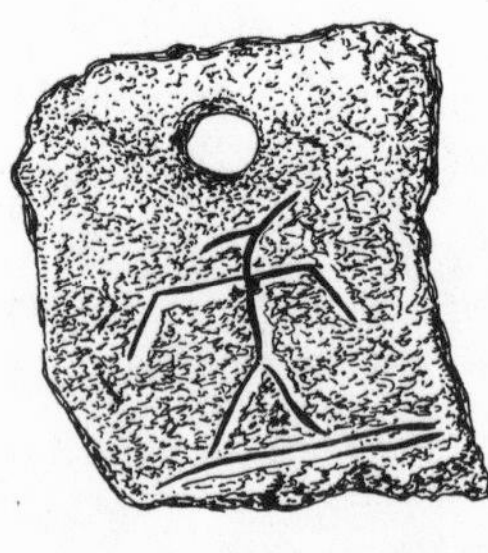

The contrasting "eco-social" patterns emerging from the archaeological record of the southern New England region in the period 1000–1300 A.D. continue into the fourteenth and fifteenth centuries, but their outlines are harder to identify. An overall increase in complexity of sites, and an increase in their number, add to the difficulty of their categorization and study. Furthermore, sites of the terminal Late Woodland are most often components of stratified sites, and in the absence of datable artifacts or organic remains, are often difficult to distinguish from components deposited in earlier centuries.

However, four linked trends can be identified in the archaeological record, trends of great social and historical significance in southern New England. These include: the adoption of maize by coastal people; participation in local and long-distance cultural interaction and trade; the development of local identities (territorial and ethnic); and the emergence of wampum as a sacred substance in the Northeast.

Maize, Trade, Territoriality, and Wampum

The Arrival of Maize in Coastal Southern New England

Maize and at least one of its usual companion plants, squash, may have been known to Algonquian speaking peoples before the segregation of the eastern Algonquian language subgroup near the beginning of the first millennium A.D. Patrick Munson reports a near-universal term for maize for Central and Eastern Languages, suggesting that speakers knew of it before the split (1973:118).[1] Yet in spite of its "availability," corn and most other domesticates apparently entered the diet of southern New England coastal peoples relatively late. Snow's 1980 model for southern New England argues for the establishment of maize horticulture there by 1000 A.D. as an explanation for increasingly dense coastal settlement (1980: 331–32). Ceci has argued persuasively against this model. She points out that most maize samples from coastal sites date later than those of the New York interior and that maize seems to have been little more than an occasional supplement to Native diet depending on the quantity and size of kernels. She suggests further that the "little Ice age" of 1550–1880 A.D. and poor soils also contributed to the problematic nature of agriculture on the coast even during the historic period (1990:18–19).

Since the publication of Ceci's reappraisal of coastal New York archaeology, maize has been reported on more than forty sites in southern New England (Bendremer and Dewar 1994; Cassedy et al. 1993) (Map 9). Jeffrey C. Bendremer and Robert E. Dewar find that maize appears to have diffused from the upper Susquehanna River Valley and the Delaware River Valley, to the Connecticut River Valley, Cape Cod, and Martha's Vineyard. Based on this distribution, they argue for movement via water transportation. They further suggest that the appearance of maize before 1300 A.D. was associated with areas characterized by warmer temperatures and inland, riverine locations (1994:387). A similar argument is

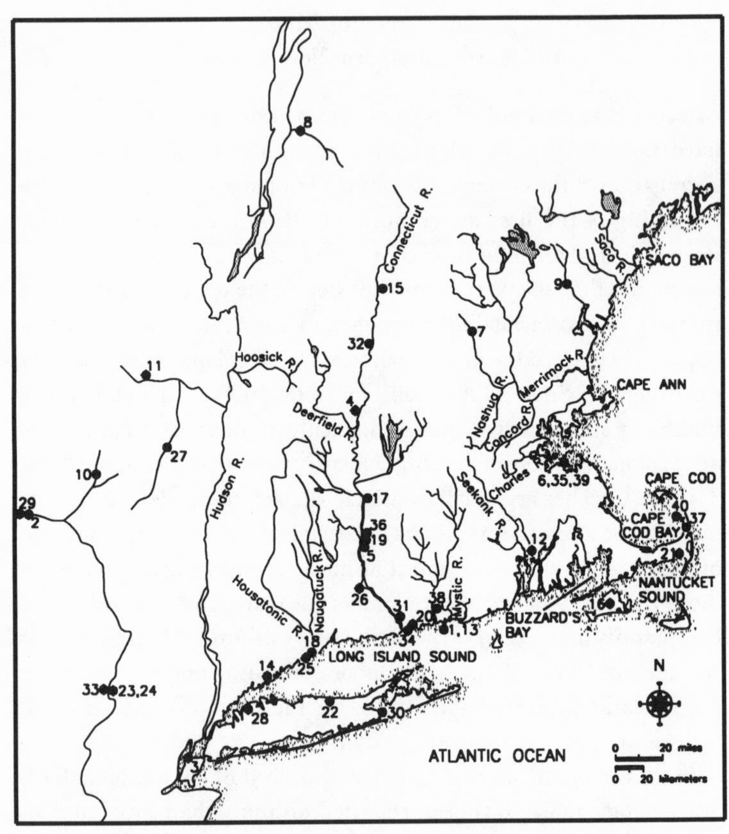

Map 9. Sites containing evidence of maize. (Artist: Sondra Jarvis.) (1) Barlow Pond, (2) Boland, (3) Bowman's Brook, (4) Bridge Street, (5) Burnham Sehpard, (6) Calf Island, (7) Campbell, (8) Donahue, (9) Early Fall, (10) Fortin, (11) Getman, (12) Gardner's Neck, (13) Hawk's Nest, (14) Highland, (15) Hunter, (16) Hornblower II, (17) Indian Crossing, (18) Indian River, (19) Kasheta, (20) Mago Point, (21) Malluzo, (22) Matinecock Point, (23) Medwin Knoll II, (24) Medwin North, (25) Muskrat Hill, (26) Morgan, (27) Nahrwold I, (28) Pleasant Hill, (29) Roundtop, (30) Sebonac, (31) Selden Island, (32) Skitchewaug, (33) Smithfield Beach, (34) Tubbs, (35) World's End, (36) 6-HT-116, (37) 19-BN-288, (38) 72-31, (39) HL-6, (40) Krusen/Rainey

posited by David Demeritt, who contends that agriculture would most likely be established in those areas where soils were well-drained and workable with native stone, shell, and wooden tools, where temperatures were warmest during the critical growing season, and where sites combining southerly exposure, drainage, and frost protection could be most easily located (1991:195). These criteria are most readily met in the lower Connecticut Valley, and to a lesser extent in the Massachusetts Bay region, precisely those areas where the earliest dated maize kernels have been recovered (Bendremer and Dewar 1994:387) (Map 10). Demeritt suggests that outside of these temperate areas, people would have been less likely to commit to a heavy dependence on agriculture (1991:196). Support for this argument come from Bendremer and Dewar's survey of fourteenth-century sites, fewer of which contain maize than is found in sites of previous centuries, presumably because of the effects of the documented decline of temperatures at the northern limits of maize cultivation after 1300 A.D. (1994:390).

The arrival of maize in coastal southern New England has been called a "non-event" in the sense that it had little immediate effect on settlement patterns or on previously established subsistence practices. In Connecticut, coastal populations with access to a wide variety of resources probably also stored foods and "encouraged" indigenous plants like chenopods, nut trees, and berries from an early period. Horticulture itself merely reinforced this long-established subsistence routine (McBride and Dewar 1981).

Similarly, in the Massachusetts Bay region, agriculture became increasingly important by about 1300 A.D., especially on and near Boston Harbor (Luedtke 1988:60), and led to changes in use of the larger islands close to shore, which appear to have been incorporated into "defended" territory as agricultural lands (Luedtke 1980:73). But in spite of the increased emphasis on horticulture, Barbara E. Luedtke sees little change in settlement pattern following the appearance of maize (1988:61).

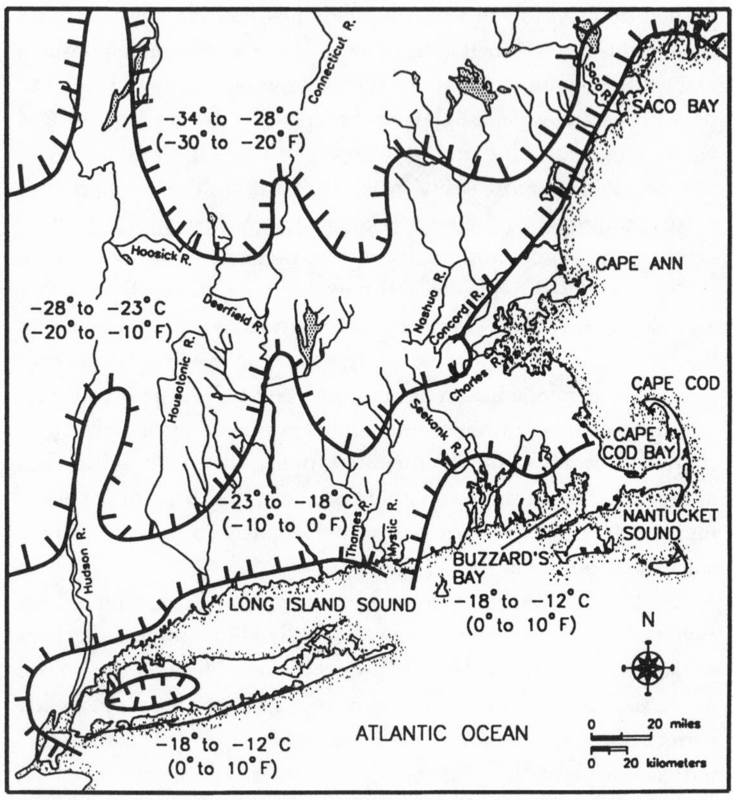

Map 10. Average temperature ranges in southern New England. (Artist: Sondra Jarvis.)

Elsewhere the same patterns emerge. Sites on Cape Cod show continual reuse, with evidence for limited dependence on agriculture in the highest strata. The Krusen/Rainey site (1220 +/- 70 A.D.), a multi-component site located on the north shore of a small pond in Orleans, on Cape Cod, which yielded Late Woodland ceramics and projectile points in association with a "diversity of faunal and floral remains, including several kernels of charred corn (Maiz de Ocho)," shows such evidence of reuse over an extended period of time (Dunford 1992:7–8).

Theories Concerning the Adoption of Horticulture in Southern New England

The causes of a change in orientation toward maize horticulture by coastal people is the subject of some debate. On Cape Cod, sometime between 1000 and 1300 A.D., shellfish use began to decline, perhaps as a result of overuse. It was at this time that a "fundamental shift" is said to have taken place in subsistence activities, in which agriculture began to intensify (Dunford, cited in Little 1988:73; see also Shaw 1992). Other explanations refer to the increasingly evident, although still poorly understood, presence of nonlocal lithics and ceramic styles in southern New England, the former of which may indicate the arrival or influence of newcomers (McBride 1984:140–44; Lavin 1988:110). Snow argues, for example, for the movement of some Munsee-speaking populations north and east into the lower Hudson drainage in the Late Woodland period, movement which would have put additional pressure on local populations (1980:333). These varied explanations are difficult to evaluate with the evidence now in hand, but it appears that a number of factors encouraged an already burgeoning coastal population, and led to the appearance of local diversity as well.

A Modified Boserupian Model

To date, the archaeological evidence seems to support a modified version of Esther Boserup's model of agricultural development.[2] In Boserup's view, agriculture, and its resultant social and economic changes, often follows a population increase that has been triggered by other factors (1965). In southern New England, compelling archaeological evidence for population aggregation in coastal regions occuring well before any indication of dependence on horticulture, suggests that farming, at best a risky proposition in most areas of coastal southern New England, was adopted late, and as part of an increasingly complex interaction between ecological and internal and external social conditions. It appears that the richness and diversity of coastal estuaries both permitted and encouraged large, conditionally sedentary populations, but that the carrying capacity of these estuarine regions was ultimately surpassed, putting stress on natural resources and necessitating the adoption of alternative food-producing strategies. Population growth in coastal regions may also have been one of the effects of the expansion of centralized polities to the west and south.

That conditions in coastal regions of the sort outlined above existed in the period dating after 1300 A.D. is suggested by archaeological evidence for household dispersal. By 1300 A.D. individual "farmsteads" begin to appear on Cape Cod, made up of single households and surrounded by fields, storage pits, and shell middens. These farmsteads, dispersed around the perimeters of estuaries, were year-round habitations (Dunford cited in Little 1988:73–74). Household dispersal of this type may also have been linked to the limited availability of arable land, found in small "patches" in the coastal zone, a soil distribution pattern favoring dispersed settlement pattern (Luedtke pers. comm. 1994). A pattern of household dispersal emerged in the period coinciding with the widespread adoption of maize agriculture by people living on Connecticut's coastal plain as well. There, in contrast to Cape Cod, small, variable seasonal occupations began to appear in the uplands, occupations that appear to have been associated with the activities of nuclear or extended families (McBride 1984:360; McBride and Bellantoni 1982:63). Champlain's maps and other early descriptions also document the dispersal into family homesteads in coastal southern New England (Map 11).

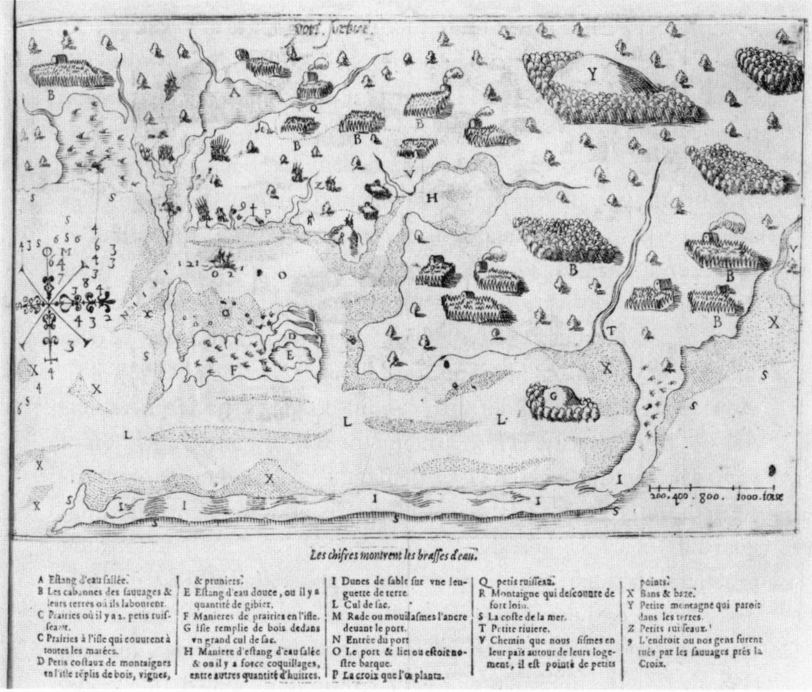

Map 11. Champlain's map of Port Fortune, Chatham, Massachusetts, circa 1605. (Courtesy of the John Carter Brown Library, Brown University.)

Links between a Boserupian model of agricultural development and the archaeologically documented break-up into households in coastal regions can be found in cross-cultural studies of horticultural people undergoing population stress. Historically, such intensification in areas of growing population density has been accompanied by a breakdown of sectorial fallowing and nucleated communities in favor of dispersed compounds of permanently tilled fields. Under these conditions, the kind, amount, and especially quality of labor that intensive cultivation demands are provided most effectively by the independent family household, which derives most of its own subsistence from its agricultural efforts (Netting 1990:39–43). Household dispersal under such conditions, and especially in situations of land scarcity, is also accompanied by the intensification of techniques and increased labor demands, such as the use of multistoried, interplanted gardens, intensive and frequent weeding, guarding of fields, and the use of fertilizer (26–29). The farming practices in such areas show remarkable similarities to those described in early seventeenth-century sources for coastal southern New England, including the maintenance of multistoried gardens (Winthrop, Jr., 1889), the use of children to guard the fields, intensive weeding and worming (R. Williams 1936:170), and most interestingly, the use of fish fertilizer.

Fish Fertilizer: Native or Not?

In 1975, Ceci argued dramatically and convincingly that the technique of fertilizing corn hills with fish, a technique introduced to the Pilgrims by the Patuxet Native Tisquantum (Squanto) (Bradford 1970:85), was in fact of European origin. Ceci saw no evidence for such a practice in similar horticultural groups, argued that the labor involved in such efforts was too great, and, finally, suggested that Tisquantum was familiar with European fertilizing practices as a result of his sojourns among the English prior to the

Pilgrims' arrival (1975). This argument did not go unchallenged. Several scholars have since suggested that while fish fertilizer might have been impractical in inland locations, it was perfectly feasible on the upper Cape, where annual herring runs brought tons of fish literally to the doorsteps of Native farmers (Russell 1980, Salisbury 1982; Nanepashemet 1993).

Fish remains in planting hills have been recovered from the Sandy's Point site on Cape Cod, where what appears to be a single-family dwelling is associated with an early seventeenth-century planting field, a field that shows evidence of intensive effort to supplement and maintain soil fertility (Mrozowski 1992, Mrozowski and Bragdon 1993). Regardless of whether fish fertilizer was "aboriginal," it was, as Netting reminds us, and as the site at Sandy's Point suggests, most frequently associated with intensive agriculture in areas of restricted arable land, and with growing populations, dispersed into nuclear families for the purpose of producing and consuming food (Netting 1980:29, 39–43; Mrozowski and Bragdon 1993; Mrozowski 1992).

Horticulture As a Supplement to the Estuarine Adaptation

At the same time, physical evidence of joint disease in adults buried at the RI 1000 site near Kingston, Rhode Island, where the remains of adults who would have been born between 1600 and 1640 are buried, suggests that horticulture was still only one subsistence strategy among many employed by coastal people. Much of the joint degeneration detected in the skeletal remains was comparable to that found in hunting-gathering populations, although wear at wrist joints in the majority of females was consistent with wear found in horticultural populations. However, there was no evidence of the iron deficiencies commonly associated with newly established horticultural systems, suggesting that the population represented at

RI 1000 was well nourished from a variety of resources (Kelley, Sledzik, and Murphy 1987:13). This admittedly ambiguous evidence seems to support an argument in favor of only a moderate commitment by the early seventeenth century to horticulture, and for horticulture practiced primarily by women, at least in coastal Rhode Island.

Contrasts with Riverine Horticultural Adaptations

The people of the middle and upper Connecticut Valley were, of course, fully committed to horticulture by A.D. 1300. Only on upper river floodplains do large, village-like sites appear (McBride 1984: 228–29; Heckenberger et al. 1992:126; Johnson and Bradley 1987; Lavin 1988a). Furthermore, it is only in interior riverine locations that maize has been found with the remains of other cultigens such as beans, squash, and sunflower, and with the large, grass-lined storage pits thought by archaeologists to indicate a committed horticultural lifestyle (Bendremer et al. 1991; Bendremer and Dewar 1994; Heckenberger et al. 1992:134). Locations where such remains have been found include Late Woodland period villages such as those at the Morgan site, Late Woodland/early historic settlements at Guida Farm/Palmer, and the Bark Wigwams site (Lavin 1988a; Johnson and Bradley 1987:21–22); and historic-period villages at Agawam, Norwottuck, Pocumtuck, Squakheag, Quabaug, and Woronoco (Day 1965:246, Thomas 1979:6, 96).

Thomas suggests that the crucial factor in determining community size and settlement distribution in the central Connecticut Valley was the availability and fertility of lands suitable for horticulture. He proposes a figure of ½–2½ acres per household (1979:109). This figure is consistent with one given by Daniel Gookin for the Nipmuck, who were said to raise 40 bushels of corn per acre (1806:170). Although the needs of an individual family might not exceed 1–2 acres, a high ratio of fallow to cultivated land was required by the techniques employed by the Native people,[3] such that communities rarely exceeded 400 people, and were generally spaced approximately 25 miles apart (110–14).

The varieties of planted corn included the eight-rowed flint, and a northern adapted variety with a shorter growing season, and a smaller yield (Thomas 1979:100). John Winthrop, Jr., Governor of Connecticut, noted that a companion crop of multicolored beans was planted when the cornstalks reached a height of six to eight inches; the beans used the cornstalks as support and kept the soils surrounding the mounds free from weeds (Winthrop, Jr., 1889:1066, cited in Thomas 1979:101).

Archaeological investigations at Fort Hill, near Hinsdale, New Hampshire, a Squakheag settlement dating from 1663 to 1664, have recovered the remains of at least one species of *cucurbitae*, which included squashes and pumpkins (Thomas 1979:Appendix V). Other late prehistoric and early historic sites from the region have yielded evidence for the use of maize, beans, and sunflower (Bendremer et al. 1991:336).

These and other sites on the middle and upper Connecticut River demonstrate a commitment to maize horticulture with its accompanying sedentism, nucleated settlement pattern, and dense population, exhibiting many similarities with sites of the central Hudson and Mohawk valleys to the west. It is thus probably no accident that these middle Connecticut Valley sites also reflect other cultural linkages with their western neighbors, particularly the presence of similar items of trade.

Long-distance Trade and Cultural Interaction

Evidence for participation in local and long-distance cultural interaction and trade is particularly strong at riverine, agricultural villages, and is reflected both in trade items and in more ambiguous ceramic patterns. The strength of trade networks can be traced in part through the appearance of exotic goods on these terminal Late Woodland sites. Copper from Nova Scotia and the Great Lakes, shell from the south and mid-Atlantic coasts, and lithics from the Susquehanna region all have been recovered. McBride has found nonlocal lithics on sites of this period on the Connecticut River as well in coastal Connecticut (1984:329–30). In surprisingly early contexts, some dating to the twelfth and thirteenth centuries, exotic goods from Europe, which evidently were traded south from Greenland and the Labrador coast, made their way onto what are called "protohistoric" sites on the Saint Lawrence drainage, the Champlain valley, and what is now eastern New York (Fitzhugh 1985). Dating from a later period, such sites contain objects of smelted copper or copper alloy (Johnson and Bradley 1987:10), often refashioned into projectile points, cutting tools, or ornaments and glass beads (Bradley 1983). Although prehistoric trade routes may not have continued in use throughout the terminal Late Woodland (Bradley 1987:41; McBride and Dewar 1987:316), they were clearly serving by the early seventeenth century as conduits for the distribution of European goods. Glass beads found at the Bark Wigwams site on the middle Connecticut, for example, are of early seventeenth-century Dutch origin, and presumably arrived from the southeast, while Jesuit rings and other objects of French origin were traded south from the Saint Lawrence (Johnson and Bradley 1987:13).

Ceramics as Evidence for Culture Contact

Ceramics also speak to the topic of cultural contact and trade. Studies of ceramic style and distribution in southern New England have been plagued by disagreement over terms and methods, and a tendency to link local ceramics to the better-established New York sequences, sequences not applicable to the majority of ceramics found on southern New England sites (Snow 1980:319–20). Scholars such as D. S. Byers and Irving Rouse identify three ceramic traditions for central Connecticut, the East River, Owasco, and Windsor (1960:25). The Windsor pots, generally conical and uncollared, contrasted with the collared, shell, or grit-tempered pots of the East River and Owasco traditions. These latter traditions were thought to be New York-based, while the Windsor tradition was thought to be of local origin (26–27). Byers and Rouse interpret the evidence from the Guida Farm, where all these types have been identified, as a reflection of migration of New York-based East River people into Connecticut in the Late Woodland period (28). Salwen has suggested that the ceramics from Muskeeta Cove on Long Island represent a "blending" of styles typical of coastal Connecticut, the Hudson River Valley, and regions as far south as central New Jersey, indicating some sort of cultural interaction from ca. 900 A.D. (1968:339). More generally, the constricted-neck, castellated pots found typically on sites in central and eastern New York, the Housatonic river, in the Connecticut River Valley, and in other parts of southern New England (e.g., Moffett 1957:8), have been interpreted by many authors as reflecting "Iroquoian" influence in southern New England, particularly during the period 1300–1600 A.D. (Petersen 1990:33–34).

Lavin has argued, however, based on ceramics from the Morgan site, near Rocky Hill, Connecticut, that the collared pots previously considered "late" and "Iroquoian" in most areas of southern New England can be dated for this region to 1170 A.D., contemporaneous with the adoption of wild grain and maize horticulture in the Connecticut River Valley. She also notes that such pots are well adapted to the preparation of vegetables and grains, and may reflect an increased use of such foods in southern New England (Braun 1980). Lavin's data suggest that a regional "horizon" style or ceramic tradition was shared by agricultural Iroquoian and Algonquian speaking peoples of the middle and upper Connecticut in the Late Woodland period (Brumbach 1975; Petersen 1990:36).

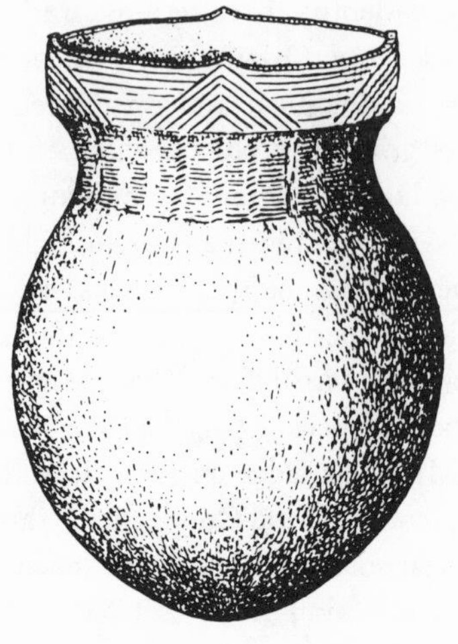

Fig. 2. Ceramic vessel from a Late Woodland context in southern Connecticut. (After Willoughby 1935.)

Such a shared tradition was combined, however, with ongoing trade relations between the Connecticut River people and the Iroquoian cultures of what is now central and eastern New York. Later ceramics from the Morgan site, for example, show marked similarities with those of central New York, and connections with the Hudson valley appear to grow stronger through time (Lavin et al. n.d.:11-14). Lavin et al. argue that "the similarity in ceramic assemblages between Morgan and the Markham Pond site of west-central New York suggests that such a great array of pottery types and attributes traditionally considered diagnostic of discrete cultural phases reflects the confrontation of two distinct societies and as such may be used to identify this kind of social interaction" (21). The vast majority of the ceramics from the Bark Wigwams site, near Northampton, Massachusetts, a Late Woodland/early historic period village, "share many similarities with ceramic traditions associated with the Five Nations and St. Lawrence Iroquois" (Johnson and Bradley 1987:7). Most archaeologists also agree that ceramics on many sites in Vermont, Maine, and northern Massachusetts reflect both trade and migration of western and northern populations into New England in late Woodland times (Peterson 1990:37).

These influences are probably best understood in light of interregional socio/political relations. Snow suggests, for example, that pressures were being exerted in the Late Woodland on coastal people in western Connecticut territorial groups by expanding Munsee populations from the south (1980:330, 333).

Territoriality

Such "foreign" influence was undoubtedly one factor leading to the development of territoriality, which some scholars see emerging in the archaeological record in the terminal Late Woodland. Dyson-Hudson and Smith (1978:23) argue that "territorial behavior is expected when the costs of exclusive use and defense of an area are outweighed by the benefits gained from this pattern of resource utilization." The defense of territory, in their view, will become cost-beneficial when resources are both predictable in time and space, and abundant (24). Archaeologists are beginning to recognize the signs of territoriality in southern New England in the Late Woodland period, when agriculture in riverine locations, and a mixed estuarine-farming adaptation on the coast, provided such conditions.

Traditionally, territorial groups have been distinguished through analysis of ceramic style and differential distribution, although the evidence is ambiguous in the Late Woodland period. According to McBride, by 1500 A.D. "there appears to be a trend toward increasing variability in ceramic assemblages between the various village sites located throughout the lower Connecticut" (1984:141–44), variability that implies an increasing differentiation into locally defined polities (see also Snow 1980:331). Lavin also sees evidence for clustering of ceramic styles in coastal Connecticut (pers. comm. 1993). On the other hand, Luedtke argues in favor of stability of ceramic styles throughout the Woodland period in the Massachusetts Bay region (1986), and Goodby has found no evidence for the marking of "tribal" differences in ceramic style in the Narragansett Bay region (1992:14). If territoriality was on the increase, it appears to have been most intense on the Connecticut coast.

Arguments supporting both internally motivated territoriality, and that generated through trade or pressure of expanding polities to the west, have been advanced by archaeologists. In the early historic period, agricultural produce, lithics, and even pottery were traded throughout the New England region (R. Williams 1936:159–60). If territorial groups did exist, then restricted resources must have been exchanged with those without territorial access to such resources, further accelerating trends toward local boundary maintenance. For example, Dunford suggests that on Cape Cod, "environmental circumscription" led to increasing territoriality (1993:12). This territoriality, reflective of estuarine adaptations established during the Woodland period, was exacerbated by the introduction of agriculture after 1300 A.D. (24).

Territoriality can also be marked by the presence of fortified sites. Early historic period references suggest that sites on the middle Connecticut and the upper Merrimac may have been palisaded (Snow 1980:333). Snow attributes this to a defensive response to the expansion of Munsee and Massachusett speakers northward into the lower Hudson and upper Merrimac regions respectively (333; see also Byers and Rouse 1960:27–28).

However, to date, no fortified settlements dating prior to the period of European exploration have been identified archaeologically in southern New England, in contrast to the Mohawk and Hudson valleys, where such sites were common in the Late Woodland period (E. S. Johnson 1993:249). If territoriality was a factor in southern New England prior to the arrival of Europeans, it was not visible in the archaeological record except possibly in coastal Connecticut, where the shellfish used to manufacture wampum were most readily available.

Wampum as a Sacred Substance and As a Commodity

The first beads that can truly be called wampum beads, tubular beads made from the columellas of the *busycon canaliculatum* and *busycon carica* whelks, and from the purple of quahog shell, averaging 5.5 mm in length and 4 mm in diameter, appear on Middle and Late Woodland sites of Hopewellian association, as well as on sites of inland and coastal New York (ca. 200–1510 A.D.) (Ceci 1990a). Ceci regards this as evidence for "the existence of an inland-coastal exchange network for marine shell in the northeast before European contact" (49). Wampum was being woven into narrow belts or bracelets during the Late Woodland period, and in that form is found in increasing numbers in interior New York sites in the sixteenth century A.D. (50).

Evidence for wampum in the archaeological record comes primarily from contexts that suggest its important ritual significance, particularly in Iroquoia (e.g., Snow 1980:85; Bradley 1987:67, 178–80). Its origins are also associated with mythology and with shamanistic practices (Ceci 1990a). Although it was only after the introduction of steel drills by Europeans in the seventeenth century that wampum use became truly widespread, it was becoming increasingly important from 1000 A.D. on. (Ceci 1990:22–23; 1990a; Slotkin and Schmidt 1949). The role of southern New England societies in the acquisition and distribution of shell, wampum blanks, and wampum beads before the coming of Europeans is poorly known, but it is likely that its trade was controlled locally. In the earliest period of widespread use, it also is possible that it formed part of a "separate sphere" of exchange involving only wampum and other symbolically charged goods, a sphere in which only sachems could participate. A later example of this restriction of the use and distribution of wampum is suggested in Bradford's comment that

> all the Indians of these parts and the Massachusetts had none or very little of it, but the sachems and some special persons that wore a little of it for ornament. Only it was made and kept among the Narragansetts and Pequots, which grew rich and potent by it. (1970:203)

The developing wampum trade was thus likely to have been a factor in the emerging centralization of leadership among the Ninnimissinuok of the coast since the control of valuable commodities and their associated ritual knowledge are often found among chiefly societies (Earle 1987:296), serving as an impetus to competition among "peer-polities" (297).

While the desire for wampum was presumably most intense among peoples to the north and west of the predecessors of the seventeenth-century Ninnimissinuok, it was the coastal people who supplied the raw materials and possibly the bead blanks that fueled the trade. As Paul Robinson has pointed out, these shells were most abundant and accessible in tidal locations in what is now Rhode Island and coastal Connecticut, and this abundance may have contributed to the territoriality that was becoming increasingly evident in the archaeological record in the two centuries preceding contact with Europeans (1990).

Intraregional Contrasts

While the southern New England region as a whole participated in the trends outlined above, there were contrasts between the peoples of the riverine, coastal, and uplands interior zones, the broad outlines of which can be seen in the archaeological record.

Although some families may have lived in outlying "hamlets," located in the middle Connecticut Valley, Thomas suggests that the primary settlement in this region was nucleated, (Thomas 1979:397). It is only at these middle Connecticut Valley sites that evidence for a committed horticulture is found, including remains of a variety of cultigens and large underground storage pits. Sites on the middle and upper Connecticut River have mixed ceramic assemblages, indicating much stronger evidence of relationships with Iroquoian groups to the west and of an earlier involvement in long-distance trade.

Coastal sites, on the other hand, show increasing dispersal into household units, less commitment to agriculture, and a concomitant reliance on estuarine-oriented resources. Some sites show clusterings of local ceramic styles indicative of territoriality and increasing ethnicity as well. Although the evidence for the involvement in long-distance trade is more ambiguous on coastal sites than on those of the middle and upper Connecticut River, it is clear that the role of wampum in the configuration of coastal sites is significant.

Uplands sites, on the other hand, show little evidence of an emphasis on either farming or estuarine resources. Few trade goods or wampum beads are found on these sites (e.g., Hoffman 1989; Feder 1990). Data is lacking to determine whether the conservation exhibited at uplands sites is due to their ancillary function or to the survival of an older hunting/collecting pattern in these regions.

Other contrasts, most apparent between Iroquoian sites and those of the coastal Algonquian-speakers, may also be applicable to the contrast between coastal and riverine sites within the region. According to Bradley, although trade goods appear in very early contexts on several sites in Iroquoian territories of the fourteenth and fifteenth centuries, few if any such goods appear in Algonquian sites. Two questions concern Bradley: Why are protohistoric sites of people like the Pokanoket not visible, and why are European trade goods more common on Iroquoian sites five hundred kilometers further inland? He suggests that the Algonquian and Iroquoian groups were distinguished by different structures—that people such as the Onondaga were egalitarian, whereas the Pokanoket were stratified, and so goods were more evenly distributed among the Onondaga while they were concentrated among Pokanoket, a concentration that would lower their archaeological visibility (1987:38). Thus the absence of trade goods in graves in coastal southern New England before A.D. 1550 may reflect not lack of hierarchy and complexity, but its established presence, a hierarchy reinforced by the increasing intensity of trade in the fourteenth-seventeenth centuries A.D.

In sum, archaeological evidence suggests that in spite of a well-established emphasis on agriculture in central and upper Connecticut River Valley sites, maize horticulture in coastal areas was part of a different settlement dynamic. Although there is some disagreement among archaeologists, recent evidence suggests that the estuarine adaptation did not require any supplement from maize horticulture until approximately two centuries before contact with Europeans, and that factors of population density, territoriality, and resource distribution created conditions in which experimentation with agriculture became worthwhile. In these circumstances, the dissolution into household units during the terminal Late Woodland period in coastal regions may have signified not a decline of social complexity, but an acceleration of the processes leading to social asymmetry, wherein (among other things) women's labor as farmers came to benefit the nuclear or extended family. In addition, the managerial skills required to make efficient use of limited agricultural land (including the use of fish fertilizer) may well have motivated increasingly powerful chiefs, who, according to cross-cultural studies, often seek new and more productive agricultural techniques to maximize their competitive positions (Earle 1987:295). This process coincided with an increased competition for land in coastal regions, a condition known cross-culturally to initiate or encourage the development of chiefdoms (Carneiro 1968, 1970; Thomas 1979:116; see also Dunford 1992). Control over the whelk columella supply and wampum production in coastal regions in the Late Woodland period was also a condition likely to foster more centralized leadership (Ceci 1990:23). Both the process leading to household autonomy and the one leading to growth of chiefly power owed only a small part of their intensity, I would argue, to the effects of contact with Europeans.

Although it appears that maize was ultimately adopted by most of the Native people encountered by Europeans in southern New England, its importance to the local economy varied widely and was the result of dramatically different local trajectories. The differing social forms and leadership structures emergent from these varying trajectories were largely consistent with environmental conditions and adjustments of established antiquity in southern New England. The archaeological data suggest that the tripartite model of settlement was overlain, or interconnected by, intraregional networks of trade, and that territorial boundaries were established in order to control that trade and protect vital resources within constricted environmental settings. Both trade and the desire to protect restricted resources may have served to encourage the coalescence of territorially based "ethnic" groupings and the rise of chiefly families and hereditary leadership, processes often associated with European presence (e.g., Comaroff and Comaroff 1992). However, to argue that such groupings and leadership patterns were solely the result of such presence conflicts both with the archaeological record and with cross-cultural studies of societies traditionally intermediate between bands and states. Furthermore, the complexity visible in the coastal archaeological record by A.D. 1000 (Dincauze 1974:53; Snow 1980:320; Ceci 1990:19) owed little to maize horticulture, except in the Connecticut River Valley. Elsewhere, sedentism, hierarchy, involvement in long-distance trade, and territoriality, once thought to be closely linked to the development of agriculture, now appear to have emerged without its impetus yet to have characterized societies in coastal New England during the Late Woodland.

3.

The Quotidian World: Work, Gender, Time, and Space

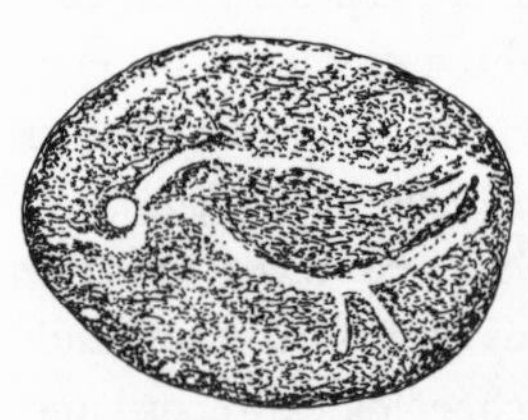

A traveler in Ninnimissinuok country, when approaching the cleared circumference of the busy coastal homestead, was met by people who were eager to hear news, share food and lodging, and conduct business. Seated in the comforting smokiness of the wigwam, the newcomer was received with generous, undemanding courtesy. For the visitor with leisure to observe, the comings and goings of women and children, whose work it was to nurture crops and gather wild plants as they ripened, and of men, who returned with game or fish, or with sharp stone tools fashioned nearby, took on the look of order. It was here, at the homestead, that the majority of family business was conducted, where children were raised and instructed, where food was prepared and stored, and the daily interactions that served to maintain and define social relations were played out.

Food, offered to visitors regardless of the hour of their arrival, although simple in appearance, often called for long hours of advanced preparation. *Aupúminea-naw-saùmp* (R. Williams 1936:11), or cornmeal boiled in water, required the harvesting, drying, shelling, parching, and grinding of corn, grown, as we have seen, at some cost by the coastal Narragansett, Pokanoket, and Massachusett. Other cultigens and wild plants had to be peeled, cored, and/or dried. Nuts and berries, although eaten fresh, were also laboriously dried and later pounded into meal, or boiled or crushed for their oil (95–96). Water, their only drink before the coming of Europeans, had to be hauled and kept cool and clean.

Perhaps cuisine varied in different regions. William Wood, in contrast to others, discusses the importance of seasonal availability of foods:

> In wintertime they have all manner of fowls of the water and of the land, and beasts of the land and water, pond-fish, with catharres and others roots, Indian beans, and clams. In the summer they have all manner of seafish, with all sorts of berries. (1977:86)

Unlike the Narragansetts, the "Aberginians" "seldom or never make bread of their Indian corn, but seeth it whole like beans, eating three or four corns with a mouthful of fish or flesh" (86). Hospitality in their area included "unoatmealed broth made thick with fishes, fowls and beasts boiled all together, some remaining raw, the rest converted by over-much seething to a loathed mash" (88).

Squash and pumpkins were available both earlier and later than maize. Although English observers say less about them, they do remark on their "wholesome" quality, whether these foods were cooked, mashed, steamed, or added to stews (e.g., R. Williams 1936:101). Likewise beans, of many colors and textures, could be baked or boiled fresh or dried and soaked and added to whatever was in the pot. Gookin mentions "bean cakes" as well. Gookin, who lived with the Massachusett and Nipmuck people of regions west of Massachusetts Bay beginning in the 1650s, noted also that:

Fig. 3. Southern New England mortars and pestles. (After Willoughby 1935.)

Their food is generaly boiled maize, or Indian corn, mixed with kidney-beans, or sometimes without. Also they frequently boil in this pottage fish and flesh of all sorts, either new taken or dried, as shads, eels, alewives or a kind of herring, or any other sort of fish, but they dry mostly those sorts before mentioned. (1674:150)

Special or ceremonial foods among the Narragansett included boiled chestnuts and a pudding made of "beaten corne" mixed with "a great store of blackberryes somewhat like currants" (Johnson 1910:162).

The sounds of daily activity were punctuated by the constant thump and grind of the mortar and pestle called either *tackunck* or *weskhunck*. (Fig. 3) The heavy pestles, of both stone and wood, crushed the parched corn into a fine meal, *nokake*, a traveling food of universal use, and the basis for stews, cakes, and other baked or fried breads sounding remarkably like tamales and tortillas. Lounging before the central fire, or one of the two or three fires that might have burned simultaneously in a larger house, the visitor would see the results of hard and constant labor all around him. The *wétu* or dwelling itself was formed from arched poles lashed together to form a dome-shaped frame, over which mats were stretched in winter and finely dressed chestnut bark in summer. The interiors of the *wetuomash* were lined with *mannotaúbana*, which Roger Williams likened to "hangings," or with embroidered mats made by the women (R. Williams 1936:32).

Storage bags and baskets of all sizes were hung from the rafters and stacked on the floors of the wetuwash. The bags, woven of hemp, could hold as many as six bushels. (Fig. 4) Folded bark "boxes" of several sizes held stored food, clothing, and even water. Some of these were decorated with incised or painted designs, and were reputedly both sturdy and long-lasting. Delicately carved wooden bowls and spoons made by the men were used for serving and eating.

Other tools included chipped-stone, bone, or copper-tipped arrows, spears, and harpoons, stone and (later) imported iron axes, clamshell hoes, skillfully woven cording and nets, bone needles, stone awls, and traps of wood and cord.

Wood, providing one of the most complete early accounts of Native "manufactures," tells

> Of their several arts and employments, as first in dressing all manner of skins, which they do by scraping and rubbing, afterwards painting them with antic embroiderings in unchangeble colors. . . . Their bows they make of a handsome shape, strung commonly with the sinews of mooses; their arrows are made of young eldern, feathered with feathers of eagles' wings and tails, headed with brass in shape of a heart or triangle, fastened in a slender piece of wood six or eight inches long which is framed to put loose in the pithy eldern that is bound fast for riving. . . (1977:108)

Water transport was provided by two sorts of canoes,

> either of pine trees, which before they were acquainted with English tools they burned hollow, scraping them smooth with clam shells

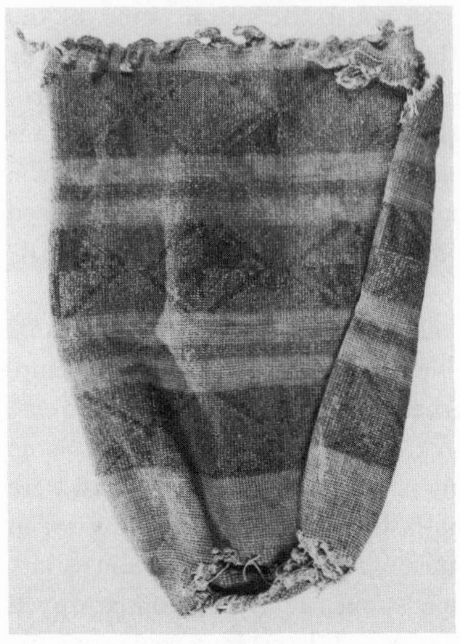

Fig. 4. Woven Bag, Mohegan. (Courtesy of the Connecticut Historical Society, Hartford, Connecticut.)

or oyster shells, cutting their outsides with stone hatchets. These boats be not above a foot and a half or two feet wide and twenty foot long. Their other canoes be made of thin birch rinds, close ribbed on the inside with broad, thin hoops like the hoops of a tub. These are made very light. (109)

The tired traveler was invited to sleep, sharing skin- or mat-padded platforms with the host, his wives, children, and other household members. The platforms, raised two feet off the ground, encircled the perimeter of each house and were wide enough so that each sleeper might be as close to or far away from the central fire as desired. Few blankets were needed, for "their fire is instead of our bedcloaths" (R. Williams 1936:19). The undivided interiors of the wigwams imparted a sense of sociability, even as they lay sleepy in the darkness; one, then another, would sing to themselves, much to the consternation of English visitors, whose rest was disturbed by that "barbarous" sound. The peace of the night was sometimes broken by an unfamiliar noise, such as an alarm. (Heath 1963:67). An approaching Dutch or Englishman would cause *wauwháutowaw* or shouting. Any who had an evil dream would "fall to prayer at all times of the night, especially early before day." (R. Williams 1936:19). Others might *mâuo*, "cry and bewaile," a lost husband, wife, or child (43). Perhaps because their sleep was not uninterrupted at night, any who slept by day were left undisturbed, with a dish of food kept warm for them, for when they awakened (43).

At rest, or upon the arrival of a newcomer, men might share tobacco, the only crop they grew themselves, in pipes they kept suspended around their necks and down their backs, or in massive pipes of wood or stone, often traded from the Mohawks to the west (45). The talk on such occasions was measured, each man speaking deliberately, without interruption. If the occasion was of moment, "many of them will deliver themselves either in a relation of news, or in a consultation with very emphaticall speech and great action, commonly an houre, and sometimes two houres together" (55). More intimate conversations undoubtedly took place in the *pésuponck*, or sweatlodge, and in the *wetuomemese*, or women's menstrual hut, into which no man might set foot (31, 197).

Women's Work

Maize, the variety commonly known as northern flint or *Maiz de Ocho*, with eight-rowed, multicolored ears, was planted in successive crops and harvested in late September or early October. Called *weachimineash* in Massachusett, its related terms included *meechu*, 'eat,' and terms for 'raw grain' and 'fruit.' Although there is little archaeological evidence for companion crops, many historic descriptions name beans (called by the English "French" beans) of many colors, a variety of squashes (Massachusett *ask∞tasquash*), and pumpkins, which were planted within a single field. Corn was planted in mounded hills, and when it was sprouted and sturdy, bean seeds were added to the same hills, so that the runners might cling to the cornstalks as they grew. Squash vines trailed alongside and over the mounds, protecting the roots of the corn plants and preventing weeds from establishing themselves. The elegant simplicity of this arrangement was noted in the seventeenth century and has been praised by modern agronomists for its nitrogen-fixing and weed-discouraging character. Nutritionally, the combination of corn and beans provided nearly complete protein, while the squashes added flavor, vitamins, and textures.

Fields were cleared by burning the trees and chopping down and removing the charred remains, although it is not likely that stumps were removed until they had rotted. Parties of related men and women cleared and prepared the fields, but women alone were responsible for all horticultural tasks (with the exception of the planting of tobacco). Depending on the soil and location of the field, no amendment other than ash was required in the first years of planting. Women scraped the soil with hoes into hills a meter wide and separated them from other hills by about one meter. (Fig. 5) After the corn sprouted, the mounds were hilled again to protect the roots of the corn until the squash was established.

In coastal areas vigilant attention was paid to weeds and insects in the fields. Each mound was examined daily for pests and choking plant competitors, and small huts, where children kept a lookout for birds who threatened both the young seedlings and the mature grains and fruits, were erected in each field. The Narragansett kept tame hawks to frighten bird thieves from the fields as well. Josselyn wrote that a farmer would collect the worms that attacked the roots of the growing corn, place them in a bark dish, and "set it swimming," thereby ridding the field of the pests (1988:83).

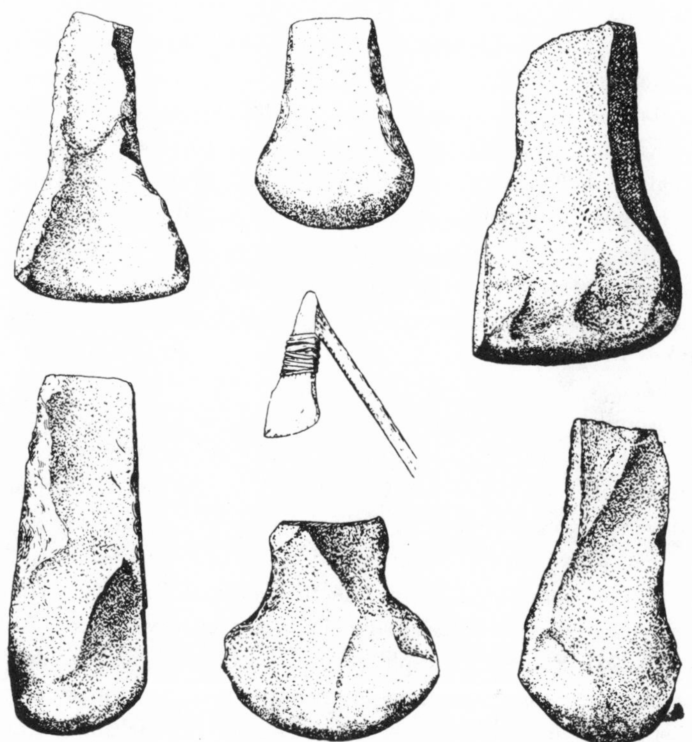

Fig. 5. Hoe blades, Connecticut River Valley. (After Willoughby 1935.)

In less productive or older fields, among the Pokanoket, fish fertilizer was commonly used (see chapter 2). Evidence of early seventeenth-century use of fish fertilizer, as well as of intensive weeding, multi-storied cropping, and short-term fallow, regardless of the origin of these practices, is another indicator of horticulture practiced under duress. Fertilizing and short-term fallowing practices, also associated with marginal agriculture, were also noted among the Narragansett and Niantic (Winthrop, Jr., 1889:1066) and among the coastal people of Cape Cod and Massachusetts Bay (Champlain 1968:87–88).

Harvesting of green corn began in late July, accompanied possibly by festivals, although none are clearly recorded in southern New England. Fully ripe corn was harvested in late September and dried in heaps before shelling. Shelled corn was stored in underground "barnes" lined with mats or grass, often doubly protected in baskets or clay pots, and later, in brass, copper, or iron pots acquired through trade. The storage pits were covered with sand or earth, and sometimes with boards or rocks, which protected them from thieving animals.

Women's contributions to diet by way of their shellfish-collecting have received less attention from archaeologists and ethnographers than is merited. Cheryl P. Claassen points out that women are universally acknowledged as shellfish gatherers, arguing that "it is at least in part the unacknowledged but widely recognized identification of women with shellfishing that is responsible for the common reputation of shellfish and molluscs as a low priority foodstuff" (1991:277). Both ethnographic and archaeological evidence from southern New England argue for the importance of shellfish in the diet of the Ninnimissinuok—hence the significance of women's contributions to that diet, particularly in estuarine environments, but also among inland people, who either traveled to the coast to procure shellfish or traded for it with coastal groups.

Sickìssuog, one of the several varieties of clams (or other bivalves) available in the estuarine regions, were dug at low tide. According to Roger Williams, "this fish, and the naturall liquor of it, they boile, and it makes their broth and their *nasaũmp* (which is a kind of thickened broth) and their bread seasonable and savory, instead of Salt" (1936:114). The quohog, called *séqunnock* or *poquaûhock*, "the Indians wade deepe and dive for" (115). Women collected lobsters for their husbands to use as bait, diving for them in calm and rough weather. "The tide being spent, they trudge home two or three miles with a hundredweight of lobsters at their backs" (Wood 1977:113). Clams were winter food for the Aberginians, and again, it was the woman's job to carry them from the clam banks (114).

Shellfishing required a detailed knowledge of animal habitats and seasonal availability. Quahog generally lie just under the sand and mud from high tide level to a depth of fifteen meters (Little 1986:50). They can be collected by digging and are available all year. Scallops live in deep water, protected by eel grass. In the late fall, after the grass dies back, storms will wash a multitude of scallops onto the beach. They might also have been collected with hand nets from a boat during the summer.

The channeled whelk live in deep water in winter, but come inshore near low tide level in early summer, and some remain there until October (51). The American oyster is available and edible at all seasons (52) and is easily harvested from sandy surfaces from mid-tide level to twelve meters. The softshell clam is also easily available all year, at mid-tide to one meter below water surface. All these species, and some less common as well, are sometimes cast up on shore, particularly during winter storms. These shellfish can be gathered by men, women, adolescents, and children with little or no equipment. Such collecting is a sociable task, one regarded in many cultures as an opportunity for social converse, rather than as "work" (Claassen 1991:285).

Processing fish and shellfish was probably an important and time-consuming task. Black and Whitehead remind us that shellfish preservation and storage "were a firmly established part of the cultural repertoire of the Northeast coast at the time of European contact," and that there is no necessary relationship between preservation and horticulture (1988:26). While they maintain that limited evidence for storage and processing of shellfish has been recovered (24–25), Russell J. Barber (1982:101) identified storage pits for shellfish at the Wheeler's Site, a Middle-Woodland, fall-occupied site on the lower Merrimack estuary; such pits were common throughout southern New England during the Woodland period. Narragansetts preserved the abundant bream by drying it in the sun or smoking it (R. Williams 1936:113). Aberginian women were obliged to fetch their husband's catch from the boats, "which done they must dress it and cook it, dish it, and present it" (Wood 1977:114). In the summer, lobsters were laid on scaffolds in the sun, with smoky fires underneath, "till the substance remain hard and dry," (114). Other fish were also cured in this way, cut in thin strips, and moved inside at night and during wet weather (114).

Shell itself was a significant material in the manufacture of symbolically significant objects throughout the Northeast from archaic times to the historic period (Hammell 1987; Claassen 1991) (see also chapter 2). Wampum, strings of beads made of whelk and quahog shell, had become by the early historic period a powerful "engine" in the developing fur trade, although its significance to Native people in terms of symbolism and ideology is still only poorly understood (Ceci 1990a; Hammell 1987). Information from European observors about wampum manufacture suggests that both men and women made wampum beads (e.g., Peña 1990; Ceci 1990a). However, it appears that the beads had their greatest significance when woven into belts, which was apparently the work of women (Rowlandson 1913; Pena 1990:27).

The collection and use of wild plants among southern New England people were activities rich in folk knowledge and tradition. Wood notes that Indian women gathered flags and rushes, and dye plants "of which they make curious baskets with intermixed colors and protractures of antic imagery" (1977:114). He also includes a list of numerous herbs and medicinal plants although he does not mention their use by Native people (e.g., 1977:36). Josselyn, himself a trained naturalist, recorded dozens of plants used as remedies by Native people (1988:43–59). Most early explorers listed the fruits and nuts available in the region, especially the grape, strawberry, currants, plum, acorn, and hickory nut. In the early twentieth century both anthropologist Gladys Tantaquidgeon (1930) and naturalist Edward Burgess (1970) recorded extensive information about plant use among the Natives of Martha's Vineyard. Howard S. Russell's exhaustive discussion of such plants reveals an elaborated knowledge of their nutritional and curative properties among Native people of the region. Forced by the silence of the earliest observers to seek data from eighteenth- and nineteenth-century discussions of herbal lore, Russell demonstrates conclusively the constant importance of these wild resources and hints at the time-consuming nature of their collection, preparation, and use (1980:56; 130–32).

Among the most important of wild plants was the bullrush, employed in the manufacture of the mats that covered both the interior and exterior of the wétu. Historians at the Plimoth Plantation museum estimate that it took seven to ten mats to cover the exterior of a single-family dwelling, each of which required a week's worth of work to complete. Such mats, moreover, would have required replacing every two to three years. (Fig. 6) Interior mats would last longer, but because of their finer and more decorative design, would have taken longer to create (Nanepashemet pers. comm. 1993). Although the weaving and use of mats by Native women of the Northeast have received little attention, it is probable that mats were of great significance to Native society. Annette Weiner points out that cloth, in which category she includes woven mats, has long been ignored as a significant cultural product associated with women. As perishable products, cloth and woven mats cannot be conserved as effectively as stone, metal, and shell, and thus rarely serve as "inalienable" possessions, but the production of woven materials is laden with symbolic import, and the quality and amount of labor involved in such production contributes to the value of all woven materials (1992).

Among the Ninnimissinuok, mats served a variety of significant functions. They covered the wetuomash, protected drying corn

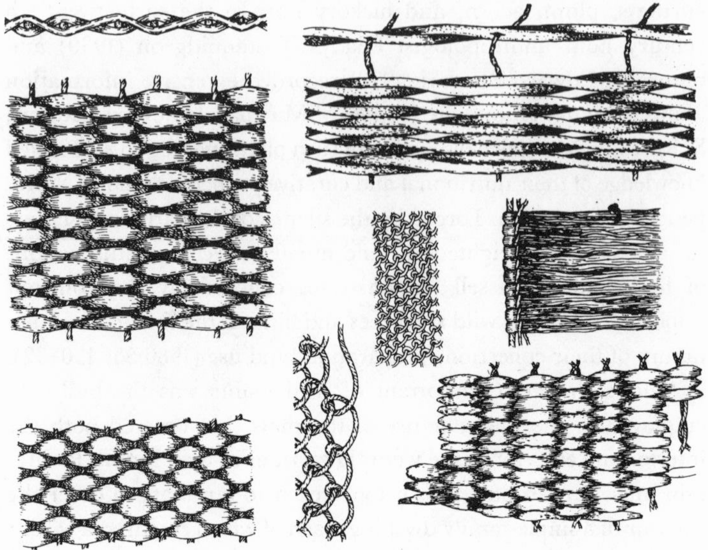

Fig. 6. Weaving techniques, southern New England. (After Willoughby 1935).

after harvest, and lined the pits where corn was stored. Especially fine mats adorned the interiors of sachem's houses. Finally, mats wrapped the bodies of the deceased, including the bodies of important people, which were sewn into markedly "curious" or ornate mats (R. Williams 1936; Winslow 1910, Sewall 1973). Inversely, mats were removed from the houses of any who had died. It appears that in southern New England, as elsewhere, mats emphasized social differences and marked ritual occasions.

Women were responsible for moving their homes and establishing new domestic space, an often onerous task. The women, said Wood, were "poor tectonists," whose duty it was to construct the smaller summer houses, as well as the large winter (long?) houses that could shelter fifty men (1977:113), and to move such structures "on their backs, sometime to fishing places, other times to hunting places, after that to a planting place where it abides the longest" (113).

If Roger Williams is to be believed, it was women (at least among the Narragansett) who made pots as well (1936:160). Pots were fired from local clay, tempered with finely ground shell in the Late Woodland period, and shaped into rounded, thin-walled containers, sometimes with collared rims. Such construction reflected the increasing importance of plants in Native diet, prepared in a form well suited to slow-cooking of vegetable-based stews and potages (Braun 1980). Increasing evidence of interactions with Hudson and Mohawk valley peoples in the Late Woodland period in the form of competing ceramic traditions suggests that women themselves brought new ideas into communities, or played an active role in adapting their potting skills to new conditions, both social and economic. Classic ethnographies have associated earliest prehistoric pottery with women as potters whose work was confined to domestic consumption and to practicing a technology that required only rudimentary techniques, while portraying early commercial pottery technology as "labor intensive and time-consuming." As with agriculture itself, the assumption is that "labor extensive activities with low economic yields are engaged in by (all) women, whereas labor intensive activities are innovative and lead to commercialization, the (exclusive) domain of men (Wright 1991:195). Among the Narragansett, however, Roger Williams implies some craft specialization involving women: "They have some who follow onely making of Bowes, some Arrowes, some Dishes, and (the Women make all their earthen Vessells) . . . " (1936:159–60). Archaeological evidence for increased trade in ceramics in the Late Woodland period also suggests that women, transformers of clay into pots, were active producers of goods that were used to forge connections beyond their own communities.

Men's Work

Wood, speaking of the Natives of the Naumkeag, said that at fishing the Ninnimissinuok were "very expert," they "being experienced in the knowledge of all baits, fitting sundry baits for several fishes, knowing when to fish rivers and when at rocks, when in bays, and when at seas" (1977:107; see also R. Williams 1936:116). With strong nets of woven hemp of their own manufacture, men caught sturgeon up to eighteen feet long by day, while at night they speared the huge fish by attracting them to torches held above their swift, but fragile canoes (Wood 1977:107). Sleepy seals were taken from the rocks where they basked so that they could ice fish for pikes, perch, bream, and other fish (108). Ocean fishing was also possible from the larger, sturdier dug-out canoes (R. Williams 1936:107; Plane 1991). Nets strung across narrow rivers or coves imprisoned bass, which were then dispatched with harpoons, spears, or arrows (R. Williams 1936:112–13).

The available species of fish and shellfish, and the methods for taking them, affect seasonal scheduling and social organization as well. Fish could be taken from shore, in shallow waters, and from boats. In the protected bays, summer flounder, skate, and dogfish could be, and still are, caught at night with torch and spears (Andrews 1986:42; Wood 1977:108). In shallow waters, weirs would be effective for schooling fish such as herring (alewife) and mackerel. Fish such as striped bass and sturgeon, which run into saltmarsh creeks and ponds at high tide, and return to deeper water with ebb tide, could be caught with a combination of barrier and net, or speared at the crossing places (Andrews 1986:43–44). White perch and other small fish may have been caught with nets or with baited lines and hooks. Many fish swarm at barrier beaches or in brackish ponds, including eels, white perch, winter flounders, yellow perch, and pickerel. These are easily caught with minimal equipment. Eels can be caught through the ice in winter and as they sluggishly migrate back to sea in the spring (45).

Deep-sea fishing was more dangerous and required heavier equipment, very little of which has survived archaeologically. Cod, pollack, hake, scup, tautog, sea bass, and bluefish all require large hooks and heavy lines or spears, and some are not easily caught. The presence of these fish in shell middens and other archaeological contexts implies that much well-crafted fishing equipment did exist, although perhaps it was too valuable ever to have found its way into discard heaps. Men were responsible for the fashioning of such equipment, and some of it was buried with its owners.

Several species of fish require the manufacture and maintenance of equipment such as weirs, channel barriers, nets, and traps. Stranded fish or schooling fish corralled in salt ponds were probably best harvested by a cooperative group. The weaving and maintenance of nets was a serious investment of labor, and required safe and permanent storage, suggesting possibly a family activity (Andrews 1986:46).

A second male activity was hunting and trapping birds. Seemingly endless numbers of migrating birds passed over southern New England in spring and fall (Josselyn 1988:68–74). Keen observers of avian behavior, men of the Ninnimissinuok hunted each species according to its habits. Ducks, geese, and swans were taken with bows and arrows; cormorants at night while sleeping; and geese, turkies, and cranes, with nets (R. Williams 1936:90–91). Pigeons by the thousands were caught and eaten as well, especially during the spring and "at Michaelmas" (Wood 1977:50).

Men's hunting of these and other animals involved movement away from domesticated space, and was conducted among the Ninnimissinuok in several ways, each with its specific social correlates. The group deer drive, a vigorous but relatively short-lived activity, in which as many as three hundred people beat the woods for deer (R. Williams 1936:171), required coordination and leadership, as well as a sense of community and shared goals. Trapping, on the other hand, was both a more lengthy and more intimate activity, for trapping parties were generally smaller, made up of groups of men, and if the trapping grounds were not too distant from the permanent settlement, the parties included their wives and children as well. Crude bush shelters of bark and rush housed the hunters as they tended their traps, which sometimes numbered as many as fifty within the care of a single hunter (171–72). Hunters from the Saco River region went out in small parties in deep snow, hunting with dogs and snowshoes, running sometimes half a day after a snow-hampered moose (Josselyn 1988:98). Ingenious spring traps set at the mouth of large, V-shaped deer hedges secured game at night when the men themselves could not lie in wait. Traps for moose, bear, wolves, and foxes were common, as were weighted traps for beaver and otter, animals "too cunning" for the English to catch (Wood 1977:107).

Hunting wild animals was of necessity carried out beyond the confines of the homestead or hamlet, in the culturally "empty space" identified archaeologically by the sparseness and ephemeral nature of sites. Fishing too took men away from shore, closer to the deep and mysterious places where only other-than-humans dwelt (see chapter 7). Their focus as producers, then, was on those objects and denizens of the forests and waters that required travel, time, and danger to procure. Prestige associated with these activities presumably accrued to men as a result (Ember and Ember 1990:140ff.).

Men were also engaged in the transformation of at least some of what they acquired through trade and the hunt. From lithics, both exotic and local, they created the bulk of (surviving) tools, including those such as pestles, used by women. Men were carvers as well, famed for delicate bowls and spoons made of burled wood, often (at least in the early historic period) adorned with naturalistic carvings of animals. Large stone pipes, if not imported from the Mohawks to the west, were carved from soft steatite into marvelous animal figures, made to be passed around amongst men sitting in conversation or in ritual meeting (Fig. 7). Sculptures of unknown

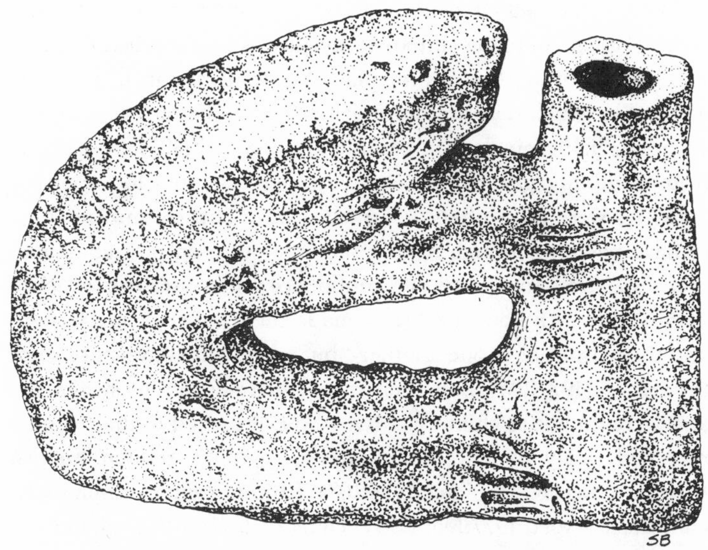

Fig. 7. Bear effigy pipe. (Courtesy of the Haffenreffer Museum of Anthropology, Brown University. Artist: Seth Ballou.)

significance have also been recovered from Late Woodland archaeological contexts in southern New England; depicting animals and people, they were often carved in an abstract, if ultimately naturalistic style, probably by men (Willoughby 1935, Trent 1982:82–83). Cross-cultural research in art and stylistic design suggests that geometric designs, like those on Native bags, are common in societies where communalism and group solidarity is privileged over individualism. Naturalistic forms of idiosyncratic design are more typically found among those groups that favor independence and individuality (Ember and Ember 1990:307). Perhaps the differing styles of men's and women's art in southern New England reflect contrasting qualities of male and female life in that region.

The habitual actions associated with "making a living," especially those of men, were accompanied by just as many scheduled and unscheduled opportunities for play. As Wood saw it, it was their games "in which they are more delighted and better experienced, spending half their days in gaming and lazing" (1977:103). Aside from gambling games (to be discussed in chapter 10), sporting activities were most often described. Many of these appear to us to have been functional, in that they served to encourage marksmanship, strength, agility, and confidence under pressure. Practice from youth with bow and arrow made them superior marksmen, and they also shot at one another "but with swift conveyance shun the arrow" (1977:105). Both men and women were strong swimmers, and were taught as children. Men who overturned in their canoes returned safely to land, sometimes dragging a sodden English traveler along (R. Williams 1936:109). Running games emphasized endurance (Wood 1977:105; R. Williams 1936:71). Although football was sometimes played in large teams, for rich prizes donated by spectators, (also discussed in chapter 10), Wood concluded that "It is most delight to see them play in smaller companies, when men may view their swift footmanship, their curious tossings of their ball, their flouncing into the water, their lubberlike wrestling, having no cunning at all in that kind, one English being able to beat ten Indians at football" (1977:105).

The hardiness encouraged by games, sports, and lifelong practice served the Ninnimissinuok well in one of the most important, but most poorly understood, of mens' pursuits—what Roger Williams called "businesse." According to Williams, "among themselves they trade their corne, skins, coates, venison, fish &c" (1936:159). Echoing the comments of earlier explorers, he claimed that "who ever deale or trade with them had need of wisedome, patience, and faithfulnesse in dealing: for they frequently say *cuppànnauem*, you lye, *cuttassokakómme*, you deceive me" (162). Furthermore, "they are marvailous subtle in their bargaines to save a penny. . . . they will beate all markets and try all places, and runne twenty thirty, yea forty mile, and more, and lodge in the Woods, to save six pence" (163). From the English, they sought heavy, dark-colored cloth, iron tools, needles, ceramics, metal kettles, bottles, and looking glasses, and later, wampum itself (160–65).

Native men also plied the coasts for trade, in vessels which, by the mid-seventeenth century, incorporated European features. In 1638, John Josselyn observed an "Indian pinnace . . . made of birch-bark, sewed together with the roots of spruse and white cedar . . . with a deck, and trimmed with sails" (Josselyn 1988:23).

Paths criss-crossed most "stony and rockie" places, and many men were capable of running eighty to one hundred miles in a single day, returning in two days (R. Williams 1936:71). Their knowledge of the forests and topography of their homelands astonished English settlers, who were often guided by them through miles of seemingly trackless woods, safely to their destinations (Williams 1936:71; Wood 1977:90–91). Lavin et al. have argued that a great deal of western trade was conducted via inland rivers, which formed a network stretching thousands of miles, linking the Ninnimissinuok with large urban centers in what is now Ohio, as well as with coastal peoples from present-day Florida to Nova Scotia, extending to the Caribbean and south America as well (Lavin et al. n.d.:16–17; see also Tanner 1989). Shell, copper, and lithics from many locations found their way to the Ninnimissinuok, and no doubt other perishable goods as well. The growing importance of wampum in the fifteenth and sixteenth centuries A.D. (see chapter 2) provided the Ninnimissinuok with a desirable local commodity, which was not only portable and nonperishable, but became a medium of exchange and a symbol of trade and diplomatic linkages.

The division of labor between men and women, labor that appears to have been of greatest benefit to the household unit itself, was cross-cut by another dimension, that of labor performed in larger groups, such as the clearing of planting fields. Roger Williams recalled that:

With friendly joyning they breake up their fields, build their Forts, hunt the Woods, stop and kill fish in the Rivers, it being true with them as in all the World in the Affaires of Earth or Heaven: By concord little things grow great, by discord the greatest come to nothing. (1936:99)

Cooperation was required to fertilize large fields in those areas where fish fertilizer was used (Ceci 1975). Organized labor parties (probably mostly of men) burned the undergrowth to encourage edible plants and game, participated in the massed hunting of rabbits and deer, and netted sturgeon and other large fish. Another source of animal protein probably harvested in groups was stranded whales, particularly the long-finned pilot whale (Bradley, Spiess, and McFee 1991). These mammals are subject to mass strandings on the Cape and nearby islands, in part because of their gregarious habits, and in part because of the unique characteristics of the ocean currents and coastal configurations of the region. Strandings, both natural and induced, have been recorded from as early as 1620 in the Cape Cod Bay, particularly at Wellfleet and Eastham, and have "substantial time depth" archaeologically as well. Bradley, Spiess, and McFee find that most strandings occurred late summer to early winter. Documented strandings by year from 1800 to 1990 occurred on average at least once per decade (1991:1–2), with an overall frequency of 39 percent of the time. Pods of blackfish ranged in size from 2 to 500, with an average of 70 animals. Although intermittent, the caloric impact of a stranding event was significant, as each whale represented the equivalent of 36 deer. Thus, a pod of 70 whales would represent the food value of 2,420 deer!

Even the Narragansetts occasionally encountered a stranded whale or blackfish, which they cut out "in severall parcells, and give and send farre and neere for an acceptable present, or dish" (R. Williams 1936:113). Bradley, Speiss, and McFee argue that:

mass strandings may have encouraged the formation of local groups as the most efficient way to organize the labor required for effective utilization of this opportunity. At the same time, the variability in strandings may have served both as a limiting factor on local group size, and as inducement for the establishment of intergroup collectives. This form of social organization would have (i) maximized the opportunity to exploit a stranding when and where it occurred, and (ii) minimized the risk of shortage by spreading it through a reciprocal network. (1991:2)

Men's habitual work generally was not done by women, and although men occasionally assisted at women's tasks, it was always especially noted (e.g., R. Williams 1936:99). The division of labor separated men and women both experientially and spatially. Men were concerned primarily with activities that took place away from the homestead: deep-sea fishing, hunting, the manufacture of tools, trade and warfare. Women's work centered around domesticated, familiar, social spaces: clearings, tidal pools, clam banks, and shallow ponds. Women's work required little supervision, or coordination with that of other women, although they often worked in groups, fostering an "organic" solidarity, in contrast to the "mechanical" order experienced by men, who worked by necessity as part of a team in hunting, fishing, and trading.

The duality of men's and women's work and the imprint of habitual action on social life were linked to other rhythms that were in part ecological and in part social. These included seasonal shifts in the kind of work being done and relocations of some or all family members according to yearly cycles of temperature and availability of resources within a given ecoregion.

The Seasonal Cycle

The calendar of the Native peoples of the interior river valleys was framed according to a predominantly agricultural cycle. Notes in John Pynchon's journal include references to month names, which generally highlighted farming tasks:

They recken but 12 months to ye yeare as we doe and they make ye yeare to begine in Squannikesos (as far as I yet can understand ym) & so call ye first month Squannikesos—part of Aprill & pt. of May, when they set Indian corne

2. msonesque nimock kesos—pt. of May & pt. of June, when ym women weed their corne
3. tow wa kesos—pt. of June & part of July, when they hill Ind corne
4. matterl la naw kesos—when squashes are ripe & Ind beans begin to be eatable
5. mi cheen mee keso—when Ind corne is eatable
6. pa/s/ qui taqunk kesos—ye midle between harvest & eating Ind Corne
7. pe pe narr—bec: of white frost on ye grass and g/round/
8. qunnikesos
9. pap sap quoho, or about the 6th of January. Lonatanassick: so caled bec: they account it ye midle of winter
10. Squo chee kesos—bec ye sun hath [not] strength to thaw
11. Wapicummilcom—pt. of february and part of march, bec ye ice in ye river is all gone
12. Namossack kesos—pt. of march and pt. of Aprill, bec of catching fish. (quoted in Thomas 1979:96)

No such calendar has been recorded for coastal people among the Ninnimissinuok, and it is probable that it would not reflect the same emphasis on horticulture as that of the river dwellers known to the Pynchons. However, for both coastal and interior people, the passage of time was marked by the seasonal quality of work, as well as by the movement of sun, moon, and stars:

They are punctuall in measuring their Day by the Sunne, and their night by the Moon and the Starres, and their lying much abroad in the ayre; and so living in the open fields, occasioneth even the youngest amongst them to be very observant of those heavenly lights. (R. Williams 1936:62)

The constellations they knew were *Mosk* or *Paukúnawaw*, the great bear, *shwishcuttowwáuog*, the "Golden Metewand," *mishánnock*, the morning star (80), and *chippápuock*, the "brood hen," known to us as the Pleiades. Verrazzano's first description of the Natives of Narragansett Bay reads in part: "when sowing, they observe the influence of the moon, the rising of the Pleiades, and many other customs derived from the ancients" (1970:139).

Ceci notes that in southern New England, planting was timed with the disappearance of the Pleiades from the western horizon and harvesting with its reappearance in the east, a period marking the length of the frost-free season in the Northeast (1978:305). These signs, as well as the onset of spring anadromous fish runs indicated that it was safe to set the precious seed corn. Natives had other means of determining the beginning of the frost-free period, including the size of buds on trees, the warmth of the soil, and the appearance of certain animals and birds. Ceci suggests that such knowledge was crucial to peoples farming in marginal zones. Such yearly recurrences and lunar, terrestrial, and solar cycles marked the wheeling seasons as regular and predictable, orderly to those with eyes to observe.

Space, Time, Mobility, and the Cultural Landscape

The cyclicity and repetitiveness of subsistence activities not only contributed to the definition of time, but also defined meaningful space. Action that takes place in the world has a spatial dimension, directly related to habitus as well. As mentioned earlier, Giddens labels this multidimensional quality of the lived world as *locale*, arguing that "virtually all collectives have a *locale* of operation, spatially distinct from that associated with others and carrying the connotation of space used as a setting for interaction (1990: 205–207). For the Ninnimissinuok, locale included a seasonal, interactive, and cosmological dimension as well (see also chapter 8). Their daily and seasonal activities served "to build into a geographical setting a behavioral one" (Merleau-Ponty 1962:112), such that the "scene itself [became] a force in the motivation of the action" (Burke 1962). Space took on social and political meaning, and sites for socially important events were carefully selected for their symbolic contributions to action (Kuper 1972:423). Locales also include a temporal dimension: like Erving Goffman's "regions," they are defined in terms of time/space criteria (e.g. night/bedroom) (1959). For the Ninnimissinuok, time was linked to place as they moved through the seasonal subsistence round.

Although settlement remained anchored within restricted territories, seasonal removals to hunting and fishing camps were common. In winter some peoples abandoned wind-beaten coastal localities for sheltered south-facing locations. Houses themselves might have been moved when fleas or dust threatened to overwhelm the inhabitants, while agriculture fields were shifted every dozen years. Among the Narragansett the principal shift was only "a little neerer" their summer planting fields from the "thick warme vallies, where they winter" (R. Williams 1936:46).

Royalist Thomas Morton found much to admire in these seasonal removals, which he compared favorably to those of the English upper class:

> After the manner of the gentry of civilized nations, [they] remoove for their pleasure, some times to their hunting places where they remaine keeping good hospitality, for that season; and sometimes to their fishing places, where they abide for that season likewise: and at the spring, when fish comes in plentifully, they have meetinges from severall places, where they exercise themselves in gaminge, and playing of juglinge trickes, and all manner of Revelles, which they are delighted in, that it is admirable to behould, what pastime they use, of severall kindes, every one striving to surpasse each other, after this manner they spend their time. (1947:20)

Other English observers, however, were disturbed by the rapidity of these moves, the seeming impermanence of a life wherein "in halfe a day, yea, sometimes at a few houres warning," a house and home, indeed, an entire community, could be transferred in a new location (R. Williams 1936:47). Although Josselyn pointed out that the people of the Saco River region spent the majority of the year "at the Sea-Side," he also remarked that, "I have seen half a hundred of their wigwams together in a piece of ground and they shew prettily, within a day or two, or a week they have all been dispersed" (1988:296). To those used to marking the landscape with permanent structures, it was disconcerting to lodge one night in a wigwam and return again the next night to find it "gone in the interim" (Williams 1936:47).

For the Ninnimissinuok, in contrast, mobility imposed a cosmological, moral, temporal, and social "grid" on a familiar landscape. Maps drawn by Native people of New England and elsewhere reveal this sense of socially defined space, with proximity associated with familiarity and power (Smith 1979:25–26; Allen 1987). Delaware and Powhatan maps, for example, depict communities as residing within concentric circles or domains, with Powhatans or Delawares occupying the center (Waselkov 1989:300ff.).

Winslow, a frequent traveler with the Ninnimissinuok, also remarked,

> Where any remarkable act is done, in memory of it, either in the place, or by some pathway near adjoining, they make a round hole in the ground, about a foot deep, and as much over; which when others passing by behold, they inquire the cause and occasion of the same, which being once known, they are careful to acquaint all men, as occasion serveth, therewith; and lest such holes should be filled or grown up by any accident, as men pass by, they will oft renew the same; by which means many things of great antiquity are fresh in memory. So that as a man travelleth, if he can understand his guide, his journey will be the less tedious, by reason of the many historical discourses [which] will be related unto him. (Winslow 1910:352)

Movement through the landscape thereby linked living populations with the past.

The landscape created and used by the Ninnimissinuok in the sixteenth and seventeenth centuries was also one showing visible signs of social and cultural "management." Native people exercised control over plant and animal species through land clearing, especially in the yearly "burning off" of the undergrowth. Burning increased the food supply for heath hen, passenger pigeon, wild turkey, and deer (Day 1953:339). The association between certain species of nut trees such as chestnut at village sites was probably attributable to burning as well (339–40).

The practice of burning off the forests created a "parklike" landscape, where game animals could move freely and fruit-bearing bushes could thrive. These burning practices also discouraged secondary growth and scrub trees (Day 1953:335; Cronon 1983). In the riverine interior and the Boston Bay region, forest clearing for agricultural lands created substantial open space, and fallow fields provided additional habitats for productive fruit-bearing plants. Swidden techniques improved the estuarine ecotones as well (Thomas 1976). Land clearing was deliberate and also the inevitable effect of the prodigious use of wood for heat and cooking. The Natives were said to use extensive fires, all day, all seasons of the year (Cronon 1983:49). Day estimates that much land around camps and villages was cleared when trees were felled for firewood (1953:330).[1]

These observations are quite consistent with the reports of early English observers who noted the extraordinarily open character of the southern New England coastline. Verrazzano wrote of what was probably Narragansett Bay in 1524, "there the fields extend for xxv–xxx leagues (75–90 miles); they are open and free of any obstacles or trees, and so fertile that any kind of seed would produce excellent crops. Then we entered the forests, which could be penetrated even by a large army" (1970:139).

Farming, burning, clearing, and encouraging Native flora and fauna created a landscape managed by human hands—a primarily social landscape, which also varied regionally, seasonally, and according to the habits of the local inhabitants. The broad farmlands of the river valleys may have looked quite different from the more "naturalized" coastal estuarine communities, which in turn starkly contrasted with the heavily forested, "lightly" inhabited uplands.

Summary

The separation of men's and women's work was intimately tied to the Ninnimissinuok sense of time and space, and to a culturally determined image of the world. Women's work generally was domestic, and confined to the environs of the homestead. Men, on the other hand, were hunters, deep-sea fishers, and warriors. Their horizons were wider than those of women, encompassing that part of the landscape untamed by fire or cultivation and that part of the ocean far from the strandflats where shellfish were gathered. Both men and women sometimes did each other's work, and sometimes shared work together. This and other complexities and contradictions in the lives of individuals notwithstanding, the separate patterns of work made for a gendered world. At the same time, changes in work and in locale according to season and need endowed the landscape with social significance and made visible the passage of time. The complex interplay between ecological and social factors that shaped patterns of work and play among the Ninnimissinuok was accompanied by an equally compelling ideology. Like all ideologies, those expressed and acted upon by the Ninnimissinuok made sense of the quotidian world and of the social relations that structured daily activities, while they served both to maintain and to reproduce those relations. The metaphors and models that defined this ideology form the basis of the following chapter.

4.

Metaphors and Models of Livelihood

It goes without saying that the Ninnimissinuok had explanations and understandings about the ways in which work was to be conducted, and by whom, and how such work was connected to the orderly processes of social life. Interested Europeans often remarked on this work code, made explicit in Native talk and action. Clearly linked to the Natives' economic needs and long-established patterns of livelihood, such a code was also embedded in the Native languages themselves.

Themes or "key" symbols characteristic of the Ninnimissinuok are apparent in the verbal expressions recorded by Europeans, which shed light on their economy and explain their ideas about reciprocity, land tenure, and the relations between humans and the supernatural world. The "emic" explanations of Native people, and of their seventeenth-century European observers, form part of a complex commentary on these issues, which now occupy the interest of modern historians and ethnographers as well.

Reciprocity

A central theme in seventeenth-century commentary on Native life, and one much discussed by students of southern New England, is sharing or reciprocity.[1] For many peoples whose economies involve "primary exchange," that is, direct exchange of one sort of goods for another, sharing is a social event, which demonstrates affectivity and the desire to establish and maintain sustaining relationships (Bird-David 1992:30). As Nurit Bird-David points out, the economic value of sharing also lies in its occurrence—in that it secures recurrence—rather than in the value of the resources involved in the particular transaction (30).

Reciprocity, a nearly universal social phenomenon (Mauss 1967), was indeed a powerful "engine" of social action among the Ninnimissinuok, and the sharing of goods and services a truly "social activity" (Gudeman 1986:40). Generosity and sharing were obligatory in Native social relationships. Roger Williams wrote, for example, "It is a strange truth, that a man shall generally finde more free entertainment and refreshing amongst these Barbarians, then amongst thousands that call themselves Christians" (1936:16). Travelers both Native and English were entertained without stinting, regardless of the time of their arrival, and feasted until all food was consumed. Their hosts gave up their beds for them, made available their tools and other possessions, and cheerfully provided their services as guides. These socially sanctioned expectations ensured that resources would be distributed fairly, that the helpless would be provided for, and that community interdependency would be continuously reinforced.

As a result, no one in a Native community was allowed to go hungry or unclothed, no request for goods or service was to be denied, and ungenerous actions were counted among the most heinous of antisocial acts.

However, people often complained bitterly about their miserable condition, and boldly requested the goods of others. Roger Williams said of the Narragansett:

> They adde *Nanoüe*, give me this or that, a disease which they are generally infected with: some more ingenuous, scorne it; but I have often seene an Indian with great quanties [*sic*] of money about him, beg a Knife of an English man, who happily hath had never a peny of money. (1936:164)

These requests were based on what was visible, and desirable, in the possession of others (Bird-David 1992). In contrast to Marshall Sahlins, whose classic *Stone Age Economy* (1972) linked reciprocity and prodigality to a "zen" disregard for possessions, Bird-David argues that although food collectors are not interested in possessions in the abstract, "it is equally apparent that they delight in abundance when circumstances afford it and that they consume ostentatiously what they have" (1992:31). "Demand sharing" and the ethos of generosity ensured some measure of economic leveling, but only by placing some individuals, at least temporarily, at a social disadvantage, where their status was marked linguistically by the use of stock phrases of humility, such as *Cowaúnckamish*, 'I pray your favour' (R. Williams 1936:2). Petitioners became enmeshed in ties of obligation, which were strongly backed by social mores. Wood remarked that "As they are love-linked thus in common courtesy, so are they no way sooner disjointed by ingratitude, accounting an ungrateful person a double robber of a man" (1977:88).

As Nicolas Peterson has pointed out, "demanding and deference go hand in hand" (1993:869). The culturally defined role of giver is to provide aid and sustenance, which leads to a situation where "hierarchy and authority thus come to be presented in the guise of concern and nurturing, and in consequence, generosity becomes the complement of authority" (Meyers quoted in Peterson 1993:869). Petitions written in Massachusett in the late seventeenth century reflected this set of linked premises, being prefaced by expressions such as "we are pitiful" and "we beeseech you" (Goddard and Bragdon 1988:173, 179). The alternating roles of petitioner and donor, social links forged through reciprocity, seemed especially threatening to the English, whose shirking of their obligations was a major source of misunderstanding between Natives and newcomers (Salisbury 1982).

In the never-ending cycle of giving and receiving, people would also engage the help of intercedants, preferably those with more power than themselves. To become someone's advocate was a mark of superiority, as superiors, both human and other-than-human, were begged, *kenootamwanshinnan*, to "speak on our behalf" (Goddard and Bragdon 1988:373, 635).

For both men and women, the socially determined practices of livelihood were sources for "primal, focal, or axiomatic metaphors." Such metaphors become the dominant idiom for constituting and expressing events, and had an organizing force for a broad range of behavior (Gudeman 1986).[2] They also served as models for relations with the supernatural. According to Steven Gudeman, "In many exotic models human qualities and relationships provide the imagery; material objects and processes are seen as having the qualities of the supernatural, dead or live humans. Securing a livelihood, consequently, is an exchange between this socially close other and the self" (1986:44).

Hunting rituals among the Ninnimissinuok (e.g., Josselyn 1977:97–99) (see also chapter 10) suggest that the natural world was seen as a sharing partner and was thus "morally bound to share food and other material resources" (Sahlins 1972:31). For the Ninnimissinuok, as for many other Algonquian-speaking people, "nature" was a set of agencies, animate rather than inanimate, and the relations of human beings to such agencies were conceived in terms of social relations and conducted according to the same proprieties (Bird-David 1992:2; Gudeman 1986:43–44). As the universe was socially constituted, relations with the other-than-human were conducted along the same lines as were those with human beings. People demanded a share of the bounty that was available, and were confidant that, in exchange for deferential behavior, or by virtue of their status as "petitioners," their requests would be granted.

Reciprocity among the Ninnimissinuok was thus not simply about generosity, or egalitarianism, nor did its presence adequately delineate the difference between "middle-range" societies, such as those of the Ninnimissinuok, and nascent capitalist societies, such as those of the English settlers. Instead, reciprocity was linked to a different set of expectations about human relationships, about the supernatural, and about nature and its products.

Prodigality

Many European observers of Native cultures in the Northeast commented on the "prodigality" of the people they encountered. Wood noted of the Aberginians with some distaste:

> At home they will eat till their bellies stand forth, ready to split with fullness, it being their fashion to eat all at some times and sometimes nothing at all in two or three days, wise providence being a stranger to their wilder ways." (Wood 1977:87)

Wood's remarks mirrored similar sentiments expressed by Jesuit observers of Algonquian-speaking hunters living to the north of the Ninnimissinuok. The "prodigal" tendency to consume most or all of what was available was counter to European notions of prudent management (Le Clercq 1919:110; Biard 1897:107).

Such prodigality is, however, according to Sahlins, characteristic of hunting/foraging people, for whom "beginning in subsistence and spreading from there to every sector, an initial success seems only to develop the probability that further efforts will yield smaller benefits" (1972:30–31, 33). Prodigality, like generosity, is best understood, as Sahlins has argued, not as lack of foresight, but as evidence of a different attitude about the future, one that is "predicated on abundance" (33). Abundance was in fact seasonal, but its existence, like scarcity in western culture, was the underlying assumption that motivated perception and action (Bird-David 1992). Although prodigal patterns of consumption may have been more marked among the northern or inland collector/hunters, the accompanying expectations about nature were evidently widespread throughout southern New England and were reflected not only in the positive value placed on generosity and hospitality, but also in the language of intimate possession.

Language and Intimate Possession

Algonquian words, Edward Sapir once said, are like "tiny imagist poems." Like all Algonquian languages, the best-known languages of southern New England—Massachusett, Narragansett and Mohegan-Pequot—are largely made up of constructions that combine verbal notions with nominals in an infinite variety of possibilities, each one exquisitely tailored to the context in which it is created. Because of their context-dependent nature, Algonquian words often are, like the imagist poems they resemble, uncompromisingly concrete, pointing directly to the heart of each referent's being. In addition, Algonquian languages seem to confirm Benjamin Lee Whorf's insights about the ways in which grammatical structure influences the unconscious patterning of thought (1956). Research suggests that these languages influence thought and experience in their form and structure, in the deictic functions of naming and reference, and through iconic patterning (e.g., Hallowell 1955; Goddard and Bragdon 1988:594). Links between people and their surroundings were marked in language use, which in turn reinforced expectations and understandings about the "naturalness" of experience.

The Massachusett term for house, *wetu*, is an instructive instance. It is one of a class of dependent nouns common to Algonquian languages, nouns that generally cannot be employed without reference to intimate ownership, and that are expressed in differing pronomial prefixes: *n-* (first person); *k-* (second person); and *w-* (third person). Other nouns in this category include kin terms and body parts (Eliot 1896:11–12). One would say *neek*, 'my house,' but *keek*, 'your house,' and *week*, 'his or her house.'[3] The intimate quality of associations between owner and house are mirrored in other related terms. The terms *wetahtu*, 'sister,' and *weetomp*, 'kinsman/friend,' for example, are semantically related to *wétu*, and express the intimacy of the shared dwelling place experienced by siblings (Trumbull 1903:279). The intimate quality of the relationship between house, self, and close kin is well-expressed in these related terms and was presumably invoked each time such words were spoken.

The subtleties of notions of intimate possession in southern New England were also marked in metaphorical expressions. Seventeenth-century Massachusett-speaking people sometimes used the term *meechu*, 'eat,' as a metaphor for possession and use of land and its products. One such surviving expression regarding a tract of land translates, "We have eaten it all, I and my children . . . we have used it all my children and I" (Goddard and Bragdon 1988:81). The term *meechu* in turn is related to words for fruit, and possibly to *weatchimin*, the word for corn (Trumbull 1903:237). In English, the common metaphor "to have is to eat" is reflected in such expressions as "I'll have dinner." In Massachusett, a comparable metaphor "to eat is to have" was employed.[4] To eat of the fruits of the land was to own it, to use it was to establish propriatory links extending to one's children (Bragdon 1991).

For the Ninnimissinuok, what James Weiner has called the "existential space" was structured not by Euclidean geometry, or as mediated through a Cartesian sense of bounded self, or even in light of the anthropologically revered contrast between nature and culture. For these people, lived space was constituted through life activity (J. Weiner 1991:32), through the intimacy of shared lodging and consumed food. These perceptions also have relevance to the question of "land ownership," an often debated issue in writings about the Ninnimissinuok.

The Phenomenology of Usufruct

Early descriptions of land tenure among the Massachusett are contradictory. Edward Winslow of Plymouth implies that the sachem, as leader and symbolic representative of the community, had sole authority to distribute land:

> Every sachim knoweth how fare the bounds and limits of his owne country extendeth; and that is his owne proper inheritance, out of that, if any of his desire land to set their corne, he giveth them as much as they can use, and sets them their bounds . . . (1910:347)

At the same time, Roger Williams claimed that among the closely related Narragansetts, land could be exchanged or sold by ordinary individuals:

> I have knowne them to make bargaine and sale amongst themselves for a small piece, or quantity of ground. (1936:95)

Other early descriptions document the customary power of the sachem to distribute parcels of land, but suggest that land tenure was a complex matter. Sachems could allot land in a variety of ways, for several purposes, and receive a variety of payments. Land could be set aside for an individual's lifetime only or might be granted to a man and his heirs forever. The sachem granted land to kinsmen or loyal followers, often in return for a series of small payments or gifts, and in later years, for a single, larger payment. Failure to pay could sometimes lead to the loss of lands allotted by the sachem, who might then assign them elsewhere (Bragdon 1981:106).

Among the sachem's prerogatives was the right to grant use-rights to land or to its products. The sachems of the islands were entitled to grant shares in drift whales and other "wreck goods" within their domains as well. They also could retain certain rights, particularly hunting and fishing privileges, after granting access to the lands to another (R. Williams 1936:95; E. Winslow 1910:347). Many scholars have suggested that while Native notions of land ownership were superficially similar to those of the English, the power of decision-making with respect to land alienation rested with the community as a whole (e.g., Wallace 1957:305), and that the sachem's power to alienate land was unnaturally emphasized, perhaps created, by Europeans in their desire to negotiate land transactions with single representatives of the Natives (Wallace 1957; Brasser 1971; Jennings 1975).

Seventeenth-century court records from Martha's Vineyard and Natick mention disputes between sachems and their subjects over wrongful alienation of land, but the majority of such disputes are over the legitimacy of a sachems's claims to leadership and hence the right to allot or alienate land, not over the alienation itself (Bragdon 1981:109). At the same time, observations such as that by Roger Williams quoted above indicate that although the sachem was able to exercise prerogatives of land allotment and even to alienate land, his or her rights were effectively limited by the equally powerful claims of Native families to lands they farmed and hunted on, rights that could only be abrogated in exceptional circumstances. As Sahlins points out,

> the household in tribal societies is usually not the exclusive owner of its resources . . . But across the ownership of greater groups or higher authorities, even by means of such ownership, the household retains the primary relation to productive resources. The family enjoys the *usufruct*, it is said, the use-right, but all the privileges entailed are not obvious from the term. The producers determine on a day-to-day basis *how* the land shall be used. And to them falls the priority of appropriation and disposition of the product. (1972:93; all emphases his)

In a sense, "land ownership" was about identity for the Ninnimissinuok. Technically "controlled" by the sachem and the corporate groups, access to land was in fact predicated on need and active engagement with it (J. Weiner 1991:40), usually within the context of the household. To make use of land was to be a member of the corporate community, to eat its products was to "own" the land from which they were gathered. To lack these privileges was to be only a "non-member" or servant, one without name (R. Williams 1936:5).

The movement from place to place, along accustomed paths, from dwelling to dwelling, past each named spot, through a landscape visibly altered by human actions, accentuated the impression of the seamlessness of daily experience. The cycles of sun, moon, and stars, of seasons and seasonal work, continually reinforced the sense of repetition, of growth, death, and regeneration. The division of labor, the materials worked with, and the tasks carried out, further enhanced these ideas. Finally, the language used in daily experience complemented these connections, marking the iconic relations between people and things, actions and words. The quotidian world "made sense" of social relations, and as we shall see, those with the supernatural. Through metaphor and extension, these relations in turn colored the decisions and actions that allowed social life to be reproduced.

Habitual action, the customary work, talk, and thought of women and men, thus can be seen not only as a means of "making a living" but as a source for basic understandings of time and space, of sociopolitical relations, kinship, and gender identity. It is these latter issues that are the subject of the following chapters.

5.

The Sachemship and Its Defenders

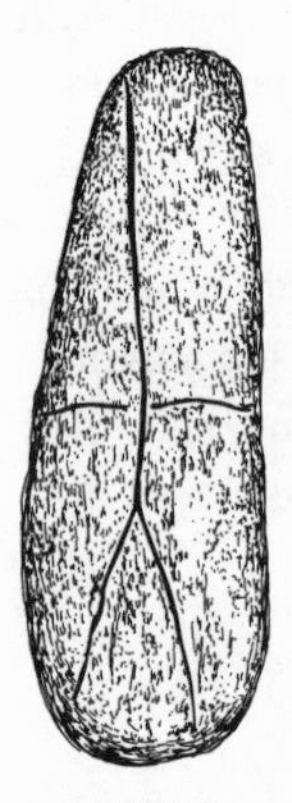

The local polity, the face-to-face community in which social relationships were forged, was known to the Ninnimissinuok as the *sontimooonk*, or sachemship. Each had a hereditary leader, usually male, known as a *sontim*, or sachem. Early descriptions of the Narragansett refer to a dual sachemship, wherein a community was led by two men, related by blood or marriage (R. Williams 1936:202; Lechford 1833:105). "The old Sachim will not be offended at what the young Sachim doth; and the young sachim will not doe what hee conceives will displease his Uncle" (R. Williams 1936:140). The sachemships survived longest on the islands of Martha's Vineyard and Nantucket, and the best descriptions of them come from early reports by English settlers there and from public records such as deeds, which provide valuable detail about the workings of the sachemships in the seventeenth and early eighteenth centuries (Bragdon 1981; Little 1980, 1990). Membership within the sachemship was either inherited, along with concomitant land rights, or achieved through marriage or consent of the sachem and his or her council (Bragdon 1981:128). The sachemship was made up of those who "defended" it (*kannootammanshittogik*), whether kin or followers of the sachem. Loyalty went beyond that given to the present sachem, and rested with the sachemship as an ongoing social grouping, to whom one's ancestors had belonged and to which one's own posterity would be loyal.

According to Wood there were some sachems, elsewhere called *ketasontimoog*, or "great sachems," whose authority went beyond the bounds of a single community:

> A king of large dominions hath his viceroys, or inferior kings, under him to agitate his state affairs and keep his subjects in good decorum. (1977:98)

Edward Winslow also noted a hierarchical political organization among coastal societies:

> Their sachims cannot be all called kings, but only some few of them, to whom the rest resort for protection and pay homage unto them; neither may they war without their knowledge and approbation; yet to be commanded by the greater, as occasion serveth. Of this sort is Massassowat, our friend, and Conanacus, of Nanohigganset, our supposed enemy. (1910:346)

The sachemships, at least in coastal areas, were associated with specific territories. The earliest known European visitor to Martha's Vineyard claimed that the island was divided into four major sachemships, Chappaquiddick, Gay Head, Nunnepog, and Takemmeh. Each of these were also divided up into sub-sachemships under the rule of "petty" sachems (Banks 1911:39). Edward Johnson observed similar divisions on the mainland (1910:41). Roger Williams notes that rivers sometimes served as boundaries for sachemships (1936:167), and other writers observed that the bounds of these territories were widely recognized.

A well-known description of the sachemship reads:

> Their government was purely monarchical and as for such whose dominions extended further than would well admit the Princes personal guidance it was committed into the hands of Lieutenants, who governed with no less absoluteness, than the Prince himself: notwithstanding in matters of difficulty, the Prince consulted with his nobles, and such as whome he esteemed for wisdom; nobles were either such who descended from the Blood Royal, or such on whom the Prince bestowed part of his dominions with the Royalties, or such whose descent was from Ancestors, who had time out of mind been esteemed such. Their yeomen were such who having no stamp of Gentility, were yet esteemed as having a natural right of living within their Princes dominion, and a Common use of the Land, and were distinguised by two names or titles, the one signifying subjection and the other Tiller of the Land. (M. Mayhew 1940:7–9)

The *ahtaskoaog*, or "principal men," of each community, often called "nobles" by contemporary Englishmen, had a number of rights and responsibilities. The ahtaskoaog advised the sachem, and early descriptions imply that the sachem's wishes were not binding without the consent of his advisors (M. Mayhew 1694:7; R. Williams 1936:202). It is probable that the principal men were also responsible for affirming the succession of a new sachem. When Peuskenin, son of the sachem Josiah, became sachem in 1701, the chief men of Takemmeh petitioned the Massachusetts Bay government to recognize the legitimacy of the sachem chosen at a "a proper or lawful meeting" (Goddard and Bragdon 1988:133). One or more chief men were almost always witnesses at any land exchange performed by their sachems, suggesting that their consent was necessary.

The so-called *missinnuok* or "common people" also participated in decision-making. On Martha's Vineyard and Nantucket, people who do not appear to have been highly ranked were listed as witnesses on documents regarding land and in other disputes over dominions and relations with outsiders (Bragdon 1981:124). However, Little argues that in general in the seventeenth century only sachems and their families played a significant role in land transactions, and the common people appeared only in birth, death, and marriage records (1990).

There were other categories of community members whose rights and responsibilities are more obscure. The *pniesesok* described by Edward Winslow collected tribute for the sachem, led warriors in battle, and claimed a special relationship with Abbomocho. Winslow devotes significant commentary to these individuals, but they are not mentioned elsewhere, and the origin of the title is unclear as well (Winslow 1910:344–45). Perhaps they were similar to the military leaders or "valiant men" called *múckquompaûog* or *keénompaûog* by the Narragansett (R. Williams 1936:184). It is significant that both the Pokanoket and the Narragansett sachems had a specially trained military elite in their service, a common characteristic of chiefly government (Earle 1987:297). Finally, there appears to have been a class of people who inherited the status of servant or slave. According to Matthew Mayhew of Martha's Vineyard:

> there lived among them many families who although the time of their Fore fathers first inhabiting among them was beyond the Memory of man, yet were known [to be] strangers or Foreigners, who were not privileged with common right, but in some measure subject to the yeomanry, nor were not dignified in attending the Prince, in hunting or like exercise; unless called by particular favor (1940:9).

The hierarchical nature of Native society, commented on by many observers, was marked in clearly differentiated status attributed to different classes and in the presence of a permanent class of servants or slaves.

The Role and Function of the Sachem

From the English point of view, the sachem's most important prerogative was the right to allocate land. Winslow also wrote,

Fig. 8. Portrait of Ninigret, Eastern Niantic sachem. Painted in 1681. (Courtesy of the Museum of Art, Rhode Island School of Design. Gift of Mr. Robert Winthrop.)

Every sachim knoweth how far the bounds and limits of his own territory extendeth; and that is his own proper inheritance. Out of that, if any of his men desire land to set their corn, he giveth them as much as they can use, and sets them their bounds. (1910:347)

If deer or other game were slain within the sachem's territories, part was offered to him as well. Most scholars and contemporary sources agree that a payment was given in return for the use of such lands or for rights to resources located within the sachemship's bounds. Testimony about such practices in the 1640s was given by Joel, an Indian "aged about 70 years," in 1718:

> when I was young many years agoe, I saw several Indians in the fall of the year carry corn to Simon Wekits mother then I asked my father why so many Indians carried corn to that old squaw Every fall. he told me that Island called Oister Island was hers and that corn they carried to her was to pay her for their planting on her land. (MHS, misc. bound MS, April 30, 1718)

In addition to distributing land and land rights, the sachem was responsible for conducting diplomatic activities, receiving visitors, and dispensing justice (Wood 1977:97). As an upholder of the law, the sachem had the grave responsibility of judging and punishing thieves, murderers, and other wrongdoers. In keeping with his or her status as representative of the social polity, the sachem was in some areas required to kill, with his (or her?) own hands, any judged guilty of crime. That sachems took such responsibilities seriously is suggested by several incidents where they sought council within their territories, and even from outsiders, before making decisions of such weight (e.g., E. Winslow 1910:290–91).

Another of the sachem's prerogatives, which attracted much attention among the English, was the right of the local ruler to all "wreck goods," especially to beached whales, to the skins of all deer killed in water within the sachem's domains, or to the skins of all rare or valuable animals such as black wolves. Wunnatukquannumou, queen sachem of Martha's Vineyard, deeded to Matthew Mayhew and Thomas Dagget a portion of land within her "dominion or sachemship," but reserved for herself:

of every whale so stranded one flook or part of the tayle, and one finne to be severed at the . . . bone, and a yard square in the blubber to be the said Natuquanum and her heirs . . . forever. (DCHS, unbound MS, 1696)

Although a great deal of attention has been paid to the sachem's role in land distribution and diplomacy, very little has been paid to his or her role as a group trade representative and organizer of long-distance trade. This equally salient feature of the sachem's responsibilities was crucial to the spiritual health of the group (see chapter 8) and also provided a means to strengthen his or her own position. Early descriptions of encounters with Natives almost invariably describe the presence of the sachem or leader at trading sessions (e.g., Champlain 1968:82; Brereton 1968:43-44). Bourque and Whitehead have made a convincing case for the personal control of coastal trade by Micmac and Abenaki sachems (1985). Presumably it was the sachem's responsibility to ensure the safety of such transactions by establishing reciprocal relations with other groups, and to represent the group in encounters with unknown peoples. Thomas also suggests that trade was a method by which sachems maintained alliances, preserved local autonomy, and avoided hostilities (1979:405).

The Nature of the Sachem's Authority

There is considerable historical and theoretical debate about the extent of the sachem's authority. Roger Williams was careful to point out, as were most observers, that

the sachims, although they have an absolute monarchie over the people, yet they will not conclude of aught that concernes all, either Lawes, or Subsidies, or warres, unto which the people are averse, and by gentle perswasion cannot be brought. (1936:142)

Daniel Gookin, who was most familiar with the Nipmuck, also found that

> Their sachems have not their men in such subjection, but that very frequently their men will leave them upon distaste or harsh dealing, and go and live under other sachems that can protect them; so that their princes endeavour to carry it obligingly and lovingly unto their people, lest they should desert them, and thereby their strength, power, and tribute would be diminished. (1806:154)

These remarks have led some historians and anthropologists to conclude that the power and status of the sachem was more ceremonial than real.

On the other hand, Wood remarked that although the sachem:

> hath no kingly robes to make him glorious in the view of his subjects, nor daily guards to secure his person, or court-like attendance, nor sumptuous palaces, yet do they yield all submissive subjection to him, accounting him their sovereign, going at his command and coming at his beck, not so much as expostulating the cause though it be in matters thwarting their wills, he being accounted a disloyal subject that will not effect what his prince commands. (1977:98).

The sachem's subjects paid a kind of tax, or tribute: "Once a year the pnieses use to provoke the people to bestow much corn on the sachim. To that end, they appoint a certain time and place, near the sachim's dwelling, where the people bring many baskets of corn, and make a great stack thereof" (E. Winslow 1910:347). Tribute payments also took the form of labor, usually preparing planting fields for the sachem's use, but by the late seventeenth century, they took the form of payments in money as well (Little 1980).

Although some scholars interpret these payments as a form of redistribution (Salisbury 1982:47; Eric S. Johnson 1993:226–27), it seems more likely that the tribute collected by the sachems was not redistributed except through the medium of diplomatic gifts or great feasts, feasts that served primarily to reinforce the power of the sachem. Consider what "a few" of the people to whom John Eliot preached had done for their sachem in "two years past":

> At one time they gave him twenty bushels of corne, at another time more than sixe bushels; two hunting dayes they killed him fifteen deeres; they brake up for him two acres of land, they made for him a great house or wigwam, they made twenty rod of fence for him, with a ditch and two railes about it, they paid a debt for him of 3.li. 10.s, only some others were contributors in this money; one of them gave him a skin of beaver of two pound, at his returne from building, besides many dayes workes in planting corne altogether and some severally. (Whitfield 1834:141)

The sachem was distinguised by his or her wealth, derived through trade, tribute, and, if male, the work of multiple wives. The fact that the sachem did not (or could not) always hoard the goods acquired through tribute payments or trade did not negate his or her power and influence, except in English eyes. Among the Ninnimissinuok, as among the Trobriand kula traders, power and prestige accrued to those who *channeled* wealth as well. Moreover, the tribute paid by subject groups was not simply "ritualized exchange" (Salisbury 1982:47), but was specifically linked to military protection.

Warfare and the Sachemship

Sachems had determinative power in decisions concerning war (R. Williams 1936:186–87), and apparently participated in combat as well. In spite of the voluminous writings about Native warfare in southern New England, its conduct and motivation, as well as its principal protagonists, are poorly understood. The dual sachemship noted among the Narragansett is suggestive of the separation of "war" and "peace" chiefs in other Algonquian-speaking groups, but is never so described by contemporary observers. Many scholars have suggested that Native warfare was distinct from that of Europeans in several respects. In the late precontact period, raids were evidently conducted for three reasons: "valor," "revenge," and to acquire captives. Roger Williams's discussion of Narragansett warfare suggests all these motives (1936:182–91). Raids were also a common strategy of "recruitment" for groups who had need of personnel, usually women and children (Axtell 1985:304–306). Individual needs for wives and children became, because of Native notions of obligation, group needs. So too, individual desires for revenge, and for insult, "a great kindling of warres amongst them" (R. Williams 1936:186), were taken up by the group. Sachems sometimes challenged one another to single combat as well (Hirsch 1988:1192).

The development of the martial character of the sachemships may be reflected in the increasing incidence of fortified settlements in southern New England. Palisaded settlements dating to the early decades of the seventeenth century have been identified on the Connecticut River (Thomas 1979; Pretola 1986), the Mystic River (McBride 1990), at Fort Shantok (L. Williams 1972), the Taunton River (Taylor 1976), the Thames (McBride 1993, 1993a), and six locations on Long Island (Salwen and Mayer 1977; Solecki 1950:9, 19).

Warfare was sometimes employed as a means of exerting authority over a tributary group or of extending the dominion of a particular sachemship (E. S. Johnson 1991, 1993). As Hirsch points out, "Native hostilities generally aimed at symbolic ascendancy, a status conveyed by small payments of tribute to the victors, rather than the dominion normally associated with European style conquest" (1988:1190). Such warfare increased throughout the seventeenth century and induced shifting alliances, such as the Quabaug alliance with the Mahicans and Mohawks, and later with Cutshamokin of the Massachusett (Thomas 1979:64, 75). Structurally, tributary groups took on the role of petitioner to the most powerful of the local sachems, who became their "advocate" and defender. This pattern was consistent with alliances some sachems contracted with the English in later decades (57).

The tendency toward regional centralization associated with warfare may have arisen relatively late in the development of chiefly societies in southern New England. Champlain wrote of the Indians of New England in 1605 that "they have chiefs, whom they obey in matters of war, but not otherwise, and who engage in labor and hold no higher rank than their companions" (1922). As Salwen points out, later accounts, postdating settlement, changes in trade, and newly introduced diseases indicate fewer aggregations with more powerful chiefs (1978:168). What James Axtell calls "voting with their feet" (1985:143), the tendency among the "common people" of the Ninnimissinuok to abandon one sachem for another, frequently described in the early seventeenth century, may well have only occurred within the context of the wider local jurisdictions presided over by the *ketasontimoog*, or great sachems.

Conflict and Cultural Knowledge

The terrible disruption caused by epidemic diseases had a significant impact on sociopolitical relations in southern New England in the seventeenth century. If there were established ways in which specific individuals achieved status within a community, as was true for many similarly situated peoples, some of these paths were no doubt disrupted by the massive loss of legitimate "candidates." The only descriptions of Native political behavior come from the years after the epidemics, when asocial and antisocial behavior must have been at its nadir. These conditions were ripe for the emergence of "big men," strong leaders whose claims to office were based on personal charisma and the establishment of wide networks of obligation and support, rather than on heredity (Thomas 1979).

Certainly competition and intrigue marked the relationships between some sachemships in the decades following English settlement in New England. Indeed, Thomas has argued that "from a period prior to initial European exploration until the 1680's, the political scene in New England was one of an ever-changing collage of personalities, alliances, plots, raids, and encounters which involved every Indian and colonial village" (1979:30). Several men, including Tisquantum of the Patuxet, and most dramatically, Uncas of the Mohegan, have been evaluated in light of their attempts to attract followers, to undermine the power of "legitimate" sachems, and to overthrow the power of one sachemship in favor of another (Humins 1987; Burton and Lowenthal 1974; Metcalf 1974, E. S. Johnson 1993).

Tisquantum, or Squanto, the only surviving member of the Patuxet community (once located at Plymouth) and the Pilgrims' "special instrument sent by God," was "assigned" to them by Massasoit of the Pokanoket. Tisquantum had been in Spain and England, and had also spent some months at the English fishing posts in Newfoundland (Salisbury 1981; Humins 1987:58–59). Although appointed by Massasoit, he appeared, from the English perspective, to act frequently as if to enhance his own power and prestige. For example, he spread rumors among the neighboring Massachusett that the Pilgrims stored "the plague" in a secret hiding place, and that only he, Tisquantum, could protect them from it. He urged the English to regard the arrows wrapped in snakeskin and sent by the Narragansett as a threat. He attempted to direct the Pilgrims' trade northward to the Massachusett, and for this and other reasons, was ordered to be executed in traditional manner by Massasoit, who sent his own knife to the Pilgrims to carry out the deed. Tisquantum's death, "of an Indian fever" in October, 1622 was sudden, and accompanied by a severe nosebleed, considered by the Pokanoket a sign of witchcraft intervention (Humins 1987:67). Tisquantum has been interpreted as establishing himself as a chief in the eyes of the English, but is also considered responsible for actions that undermined truly peaceful efforts on the part of Massasoit, the legitimate sachem (Salisbury 1981).

Uncas, who was born around 1588, was the son of a "subordinate Pequot sachem." In 1626 Uncas married the sister of Sassacus, grandson of the powerful Pequot sachem Woipequand, his own cross-cousin. In 1634 Uncas challenged Sassacus's right to rule, basing his claim both on his mother's and his wife's lineages. Sassacus prevailed, but Uncas's ambitions coalesced with those of the English in their desire to control the wampum trade and settlement in Connecticut (Jennings 1975; Ceci 1990a; E. S. Johnson 1993). After the massacre of four hundred Pequots at Mystic fort in May of 1637, and the subsequent deportation, enslavement, and dispersal of the remainder of their population, Uncas emerged as sachem of the Mohegan, presiding over these newly "created" people as well as over the surviving Pequots. Uncas went on to engineer the murder of Miantonimi, the Narragansett sachem, in 1643 (Metcalf 1974:654–57). Uncas also sought to strengthen his position through marriage, the skillful use of disinformation, and the establishment of political alliances (E. S. Johnson 1993:69–70), strategies common among rulers in chiefly societies (Earle 1987:294).

Both Peter Thomas and Eric S. Johnson argue that Uncas's behavior was consistent with the patterns of authority that characterized Native polities in seventeenth-century southern New England, wherein strong individuals, hereditary "petty chieftains," or "big men" drew together "unstable political alliances" with the support of "a broad kin base, a number of warriors, and a superior access to economic resources" (Thomas 1979:32; E. S. Johnson 1993; see also Burton and Lowenthal 1974; Metcalf 1974:652–53). Historian Richard Metcalf has concluded that "Indian societies were . . . as conflict-ridden as white societies," and that individual Native leaders such as Uncas should be understood as masters of "seventeenth-century *realpolitik*" (1974:665, 657).

I suggest, however, that leaders like Uncas emerged not merely in response to English presence, but because chiefdoms already existed in coastal regions, whose organizational structures were capable of exploitation. In contrast, historic communities of the middle Connecticut valley such as Norwotock show no overarching political organization, each village acting as an autonomous group, under the rule of a sachem, whose successful leadership depended in large part on skill and personal influence. Deeds from the 1640s also indicate that women in these Connecticut communities had a larger say in political decision-making and in the allocation and sale of land than did women in coastal regions (Thomas 1979:135–36). It is probably not coincidental that these people were not only politically allied with the matrilineal Mahican to the west (as well as by the 1640s to the Narragansett [Salisbury 1987]) but were also, like their western neighbors, committed horticulturalists of long standing.

The Sachem as Advocate and Mediator

However urgent a given sachem's quest for legitimacy within their Native communities, his or her position was also of a symbolic importance that, although interconnected with political machinations, in the long run superceded them. The sachem was a representative of the community with a pivotal or transformative role. He or she faced inward, to the community, regulating interpersonal relations, land allocations, and disputes, and saw to the redistribution of surplus resources. The sachem was intimately connected to others through ties of affection and kinship, and to the continuity of the sachemship through descent and marriage. At the same time, the sachem mediated contacts between the world outside of the community, just as the powwaw and priest (to be discussed in chapter 9) mediated the group's contacts with the supernatural. The sachem entertained visitors, coordinated a cadre of messengers and information gatherers, and personally visited all communities within his or her territories. He or she also served as a delegate to councils of more influential sachems.

As the embodiment of the sachemship, the sachem was continually subject to special scrutiny with regard to home, dress, and behavior. Always visible, the sachem traveled yearly throughout his or her territories accompanied by a large group of advisors, kinsmen, and guards (Wood 1977:98). The comings and goings of the sachem were usually accompanied by great ceremony (E. Johnson 1910:161; M. Mayhew 1940:7; Bragdon 1987, 1987a). The sachems' dress and ornament were more elaborate than those of their subjects, and their houses were larger and more richly decorated (Mayhew 1727:167). Polygyny was most common among sachems, whose first wives, and often subsequent wives, were of high status as well. The sachem's public demeanor was also prescribed. Dignity of office was maintained through strict protocol involving elaborated discourse strategies (Bragdon 1987). Special structures were sometimes erected to conduct diplomatic business, such as the mat-covered "state-house" constructed for the parley between the English and the two Narragansett leaders Conanacus and Miantonimi (E. Johnson 1910:162). Several noted sachems presided over ritual as well.

The importance of spiritual well-being is also closely tied to the political, symbolic, and ritual importance of the sachem in southern New England. A. M. Hocart argues that sachems, like kings, are "part . . . of an organization to promote life, fertility, prosperity by transferring life from objects abounding in it to objects deficient in it" (1970:3). According to Hocart, the king's duty is not to be the governor, but "the life of the group" (1970:99). Because the king is the microcosm, and the macrocosm must be bountiful, the king must himself be rich. He must also be generous, and have nothing of his own (Hocart 1970:202).

Consistent with, or perhaps because of, his or her importance in warfare, the sachem was also assigned the role of "protector," a role made more necessary during the perilous decades of the early seventeenth century when raids necessitated the construction of fortified settlements and the abandonment of vulnerable settlement locations (Ceci 1990; Wood 1977:76–78, 102):

Sachems were personal advocates and champions: Beside their generall subjection to the highest sachims, to whom they carry presents: they have also particular protectors, under sachims, to whom they also carry presents, and upon any injury received, and complaint made, these protectors will revenge it.'' (R. Williams 1936:141).

In return for tribute and humble respect, the subjects could expect their sachem's advocacy in matters personal as well as spiritual. *Cowaúnckamish*, 'my service to you,' and *cuckquénamish*, 'I pray your favor,' were phrases addressed to sachems by their followers as "the party reverently doe obeysance, by stroking the Prince upon both his shoulders, and using this word" (R. Williams 1936:2).

In sum, at least in the coastal groups, the sachem was the symbolic embodiment of the group, made all the more significant as households became the primary unit of production. From a functional point of view, the sachem was responsible for maintaining the cohesiveness of the sachemship. Even in the presence of factionalism and competing perspectives, the ideology of the sachemship effectively combined notions of kin and family, of continuity through reproduction and marriage, with the strong emphasis on hierarchy, dependency, and advocacy reflected in economic relationships. Family and kinship, and their role within the sachemship, are further discussed in the following chapters.

6.

Kinship As Ideology

> It is very observable; that they are carefull to preserve the memory of their families, mentioning Uncles, Grand-Fathers, and Grandmothers, &c. and much studying the advancing of their houses and kindred: A thing which had a great tang of, and affinitie to the Jewes care of preserving the memoriall of their Tribes.
>
> —John Davenport, 1649

"They hold the band of brother-hood so deare," wrote Roger Williams about the Narragansett, "that when one had committed a murther and fled, they executed his brother; and tis common for a brother to pay the debt of a brother deceased" (1936:29). Such loyalty, along with the careful itemization of kin relationships, appeared to seventeenth-century English observers to be proof of admirable family feeling among the Ninnimissinuok, and to many modern scholars has seemed another demonstration of the "traditional" nature of Native social organization. Without disputing the importance of kinship in structuring social relations among the Ninnimissinuok, I wish to go beyond these parameters and move toward an understanding of the way it reinforced the sociopolitical relations described in the previous chapters.

The Nature of Descent Systems in Southern New England

The descent systems of Algonquian-speakers of southern New England have been described and interpreted in conflicting ways. As Figure 9 illustrates, lists of kinship terms collected in this region in the seventeenth century were inconsistent with one another and incomplete as well. Most such lists omit terms for cross- and parallel aunts, uncles, and cousins, thus making difficult or impossible a clear identification of terminological systems and their associated social structures. Descriptions of social behavior make no reference to kin groupings other than to "families," although observers did note the presence of some of the characteristics of lineal kin groupings; for example, Roger Williams commented on the obligation of members of a person's "family" to come to his or her aid, to avenge wrongs, or to pay debts or brideprice (1936:29, 148). Such mutual responsibility is generally a feature of lineage or clan organization (Murdock 1949:73).

In the eighteenth and nineteenth centuries, people on the northern borders of this region, especially the Western Abenaki, were said to have been patrilineal, and occasionally further organized into weak totemic clans (Day 1978:156). In contrast, Lewis Henry Morgan suggested, based on interviews with a Narragansett woman in 1862, that those people were matrilineal (1959:135; see also Simmons and Aubin 1975:29), as were the Algonquian-speaking Mahican and Delaware to the south and west. In addition, it is likely that variation in social organization did exist historically within the region and that some descent systems there changed through time. In short, although matrilineal and patrilineal systems appear to have been present in southern New England, determining which if either was characteristic of a given group in the late sixteenth and early seventeenth centuries is unlikely.

However, economic conditions in the late precontact period were compatible with matrilineality, particularly in riverine regions, where horticulture was dominant and well-established. Such an existence, predicated on plenty, is often associated with a matrilineal "ideology," which, according to Poewe, focuses on collective relationships, a multiplicity of kin ties, and lineage or clan affiliation (1981:33, 77). Although the nature of coastal subsistence required only a conditional sedentism, evidence points to a natural abundance of critical resources there. Abundance, when it accompanies shifting cultivation and communal ownership where women supply the labor, is also associated with matrilineality (Goody 1976; Douglas 1971).

The genealogy of women was clearly of significance in determining inheritance of office. Matthew Mayhew observed that "the Blood Royal, being in such veneration among this People that if a prince had issue by divers wives, such succeeded as Heir who was Royally descended by the mother, although the youngest" (1940:7–8). This statement is supported by evidence from the genealogy of the Mohegan sachem Uncas, who claimed sachem's status over the Pequot and Mohegan on the basis of descent from sachem women of both groups (Burton and Lowenthal 1974). One seventeenth-century source even suggested that the office passed to the brother of the sachem, before descending to the "sons" (Hubbard 1815:1, 84), a common pattern of succession in matrilineal societies. A Native witness quoted in a Martha's Vineyard deed also recalled:

> An Indian caled Wannamanhit came from the Masachusets Bay to sd Tisbury, and married with a sachim woman of sd Takemy and some time after he had a son by her caled Nananit, and some time after there was a meeting of the sachems of Takemmy abovesaid at which time they concluded that the said Wannamanhit should have some privelledges in the sd land with them as a guardian to the sd Nananehit his son untill he should come of age to manage it for himself, and as such he should have his voate in the managing of the sachimship so long as he should carry himself orderly. (MVD 1:66)

This testimony states clearly that the son of Wannamanhit inherited his status through his mother, a sachem woman. Those sachem women we know of were related by blood or marriage to powerful male sachems, but we cannot be sure that their own matrilineages (about which we know nothing) were not significant as well.

At the same time, seventeenth-century sources also speak to a strong emphasis on patrilineality. Most sources agree that the position of sachem was passed through the male line, although a female could serve "in defect of a Male of the Blood" (M. Mayhew 1694:7–8). Wood wrote that:

> It is the custome for their Kings to inherite, the sonne always taking the kingdome after his fathers death. If there be no sonne, then the queene rules; if no queene, the next to the blood royall. (1634:79)

Native deeds recorded in the mid-seventeenth century include many references to the inheritance of office and the genealogical reckoning of the sachem's forebears. Deeds involving Natives on Martha's Vineyard also suggest that the office of the sachem passed directly from father to son. For example, in 1701, the ahtaskoaog of Takemmeh noted that they had chosen as sachem the firstborn son of their sachem Josiah, who "in the same manner becomes our sachem by straight succession" (Goddard and Bragdon 1988:135). Ben Able of Nantucket was said to be sachem "succeeding his father and grandfather" (269). Genealogies collected there, as well as on Nantucket, and among the Narragansett, Niantic, Pequot, and Mohegan, detail succession from father to son for several generations, in some cases predating the arrival of Europeans.

Polygyny was practiced, at least among the elite, and there are some descriptions of "royal" sibling marriages among the Massachusett, Narragansett, and Mohegan. The impression that this marriage pattern gives of stratified social organization centering around male lineages is further strengthened by numerous seventeenth-century descriptions of the "monarchical" nature of

Massachusett sociopolitical organization, which revolved around the structure and functions of the sachemship.

Previous interpretations of southern New England kinship have been contradictory. Frank Speck believed the Massachusett to have been patrilineal (1928). Simmons and Aubin, following Morgan, suggested that the Narragansett, at least, were matrilineal (1975). Salwen argues for an ambilocal post-marital residence pattern (1978:167), while Lorraine E. Williams contends that the precontact matrilineal pattern was altered in the seventeenth century to conform to patrilineal English models (1972:23–27). Certainly it is true that after English colonization, conditions altered drastically for the southern New England Indians. Within three decades of colonization, they faced resource scarcity, and were forced to engage in a market economy, as well as to accept Protestantism, all circumstances that would favor patrilineality, individualism, and an emphasis on the nuclear family (Poewe 1981:77). Burton and Lowenthal argue, on the other hand, based on an analysis of marriages among the elite of the closely related Mohegan, Pequot, and Narragansett, that lineality was not a significant factor in political leadership among those people (1974:135).

Massachusett kins terms, in partisular, were consistent with a unilineal mode of organization. However, seventeenth-century descriptions of Native life suggest that both matrilineal and patrilineal principles operated in Massachusett society, as they often do in ambilineal descent systems. In an ambilineal system, one that emphasizes *either* matrilineal or patrilineal principles, flexible rules govern descent, inheritance, and alliance. Such a system is sometimes attributed to unilineal kinship systems undergoing stress during periods of epidemic and/or colonization (Ember and Ember 1990:213). In the case of southern New England, however, such a system is more likely to have arisen along with the importance of the sachemship itself. For the Massachusett, Pokanoket, Narragansett, Mohegan, and Pequot, both matrilineal and patrilineal principles contributed to the construction and maintenance of the sachem's identity. It seems probable that members of chiefly lineages derived status and authority from ties to both matrilineal and patrilineal kin as they were linked to the control of land and of political office respectively. The complexity of these ties is especially evident in the case of such "queen" sachems among the Massachusett as Wunnatukquannumou of Martha's Vineyard, and Askammapoo, eldest daughter of the sachem Nickanoose of Nantucket—both of whom may have been sachems by virtue of their large landholdings, possibly inherited from their mothers (Little 1992:3).

The coalescence of patterns of matrilineal land "ownership" and developing patrilineal chiefly lineages in the seventeenth century apparently reinforced the tendency of high status men and women to marry. Such marriages either created or expanded alliances, as was the case for the Mohegan, or solidified leadership within a small number of lineages or clans, as appears to have been true for the Narragansett (Simmons and Aubin 1975:23; E. S. Johnson 1993:174–83).

The Terms and Their Meanings

The words for kin relationships were recorded very unevenly in three types of sources: contemporary recordings by non-Native speakers, especially the missionary John Eliot (1663); eighteenth-century translations and vocabularies by Englishmen having native control of Massachusett, such as Josiah Cotton of Plymoth (1830) and Experience Mayhew of Martha's Vineyard (1709); and Native writings in the Massachusett language (Goddard and Bragdon 1988). As in other Algonquian languages, most of the kinship terms employed by the Ninnimissinuok were derived from dependent noun stems (that is, those stems that can occur only in inflected forms beginning with personal prefixes indicative of intimate possession,

Figure 9
Kinship Terms in Southern New England Languages
from Early Sources

Term	Massachusett (Eliot 1663)		Pokanoket (Cotton 1707)	Narragansett (Williams 1643)	Pawtucket (Wood 1634)
Fa	n8sh		koosh	nòsh	noeshow
Mo	nokas		wuttookăsin	nókace	
			wútchēhwau	nítchwhaw	nitka
So	nunnaumon		wunnaumonien		naumaunais
				nummúckquáchucks	
Da	nittaunes		wuttonnin	nittaûnis	taunais
Br	neemat	MS	oowemăttin	neémat	
	neetompas	FS	wetompasin		
					netchaw
					towwaw
OBr	nunnohtónugqus				
Si	netukksq	FS		wéticks	
	neetompas	MS	wetompasin		
	nummissesin	MS			
	wetáhtuoh	MS	netat		
				weésummis	
Ysb	wesummussoh	M,FS			
U	8shesoh		ooshesin		
U	n8susses			nissesè	
A	kokummes				
Cou	kadtonkqs		wodtonkqsin	natòncks	
Kin (M)					notonquous
Kin (F)					nenomous
Grm	kukummussit		wutt8kummissīn		
Grf			wutt8chĭkkĭnneasin		
Wife	kummittamus		mittumwŭssis	nummíttamus	
				nowéewo	web
				nullógana	
Hus	nasuk		ouwasĕkkīen	wasick	
					tommaushew

M = Male, F = Female, S = Speaker. The *8* replaces Eliot's digraph ∞, meant to indicate the sound *oo* as in *moody*. Note that most forms are possessed. Forms beginning with *n-* = 'my'; with *k-* = 'your'; and with *w-* or *o-* = 'his/her.' The citations from Wood often omit the possessive prefix. His and her forms sometimes have the *oh-* obviative ending used when two third persons are referred to.

such as *nittaunes*, 'my daughter,' *koosh*, 'your father,' or *oowemăttin*, 'his brother.' All attested terms are listed in Figure 9.

As Figure 9 demonstrates, even within the relatively restricted region of southern New England, there was some variation in such common terms as 'mother' (cf. Massachusett *nokas*, Narragansett *nítchwhaw*, and Pawtucket *nitka*) and 'wife' (cf. Narragansett *mittummwŭssis* and Aberginian *web*). Other terms reflect considerable stability over time, including those for 'father,' all derived from Proto-Algonquian *no:hθa* (Hockett 1964). Like all Algonquian systems, those of southern New England languages embody certain classificatory principles, such as the "lumping" of kin in the ascending generation (e.g., father and father's brother, and mother and mother's sister), and of their offspring (e.g., the use of the same term for siblings and parallel cousins). There is also some indication of classification between generations (e.g. the similarities between the terms for grandmother and mother's sister). Since some crucial terms have not been recorded, it is impossible to label the system, but it appears to share a number of features with terminologies commonly associated with unilineal organization. The use of relative age and sex sets of sibling terms (to be discussed below) is also characteristic of unilineal descent systems (Keesing 1975:111–12).

Beyond Terminology: Kinship As Ideology

The difficulties of categorizing the kinship system in southern New England stem in part from the lacunae and biases of the ethnohistorical record and in part from a lack of consensus among scholars about the relevance of terminology to studies of social relations. While some argue that kinship terminology is a linguistic domain only, others suggest that terminological systems reflect the social order (Hedican 1990:9). In keeping with the latter argument, kinship terminology from southern New England appears to be consistent with an emphasis both on lineality, especially in sibling relationships, as well as on the inheritance of office and the inheritance of land or other property.

One of the most fascinating aspects of Algonquian kinship terminology is the plethora of terms referring to the sibling relationship. Massachusett, Narragansett, and Loup employ a system with two sets of terms for siblings of the same sex, two for siblings of the opposite sex, and another set referring to relative age. Hedican points out that Algonquian sibling terminology revolves around these two principles of relative sex and relative age (1990:4). Many Algonquian languages employ a three-term system specifying relative age (with the term for elder sibling also divided into separate terms for gender, resulting in separate terms for older brother, older sister, and younger sibling). A second feature common to about half the languages is a relative terminology dependent on the identity of the speaker. Examples include terms for *brother*/male speaking; *sister*/male speaking; *sister*/female speaking; and *brother*/female speaking. There is great variety among languages, but along the eastern seaboard "the tendency is to divide both the same-sex and opposite sex categories" yielding as many as seven sibling terms (5–6). Massachusett employed a variation of the terminological system in which terms for siblings of the opposite sex were the same regardless of the sex of the speaker (Bragdon 1981:84). Such sex-relative terminologies are characteristic of eastern Algonquian languages, many of which exhibit "social complexity and focus on gender difference (Hedican 1990:7). In the case of the Massachusett (and by implication, other closely related groups such as the Narragansett and Pokanoket), the relationship between siblings was evidently one of considerable cultural emphasis.

Cross-cutting this terminological emphasis on sibling relationships was the principle of classification in which the offspring of siblings referred to one another as siblings. As a result, some relations that English speakers would call "cousins" were referred to by the Ninnimissinuok with the same terms as those for siblings. A great deal of anthropological literature is devoted to the implications of this aspect of classification. Were these classificatory siblings eligible marriage partners? If so, was "sibling" marriage permitted or encouraged? If the incest taboo was enforced for all relations classed as siblings, the only cousin marriages permitted would be those with cross-cousins.

If, as was common in other groups with unilineal terminological systems, the Ninnimissinuok favored cross-cousin marriage, intergenerational linkages between wife-giving and wife-taking lineages might well have been formed. Although at least in theory the successive exchange of marriage partners in a series of cross-cousin marriages implies a balanced reciprocity between local descent groups (Levi-Strauss 1963a:309), the long-term effects of a preference for cross-cousin marriages can entail the development of asymmetries in local social relations, with wife-giving groups sometimes gaining ascendancy over wife-taking groups, particularly when, as was the case with the Ninnimissinuok, a substantial brideprice was paid (Leach 1971:230–31). High-ranking women were said to command a higher price, "If some great mans daughter *Piuckquompaúgatash*, ten fathome" of wampum was required (R. Williams 1936:148).[1] The terminological system and the marriage rules it reflects can thus be seen to reinforce asymmetries that emerged from diachronic patterns of alliance, and centralization of power and prestige, within a small number of ruling lineages.

The genealogy of Uncas appears to demonstrate some such consolidation involving the "exchange" of high-status women (see Fig. 10). Of the four marriages between relatives recorded, relationships are cross and parallel, matrilateral and patrilateral (sometimes simultaneously), and include an aunt-nephew marriage (Burton and Lowenthal 1974:595). One of the keystones of Uncas's claim to the Mohegan sachemship, nevertheless, was his descent from Kesh-ke-choo walt-ma-kunsh, "chief sachem's squaw of the Mogheags", or sister of the Mohegan chief sachem. This woman

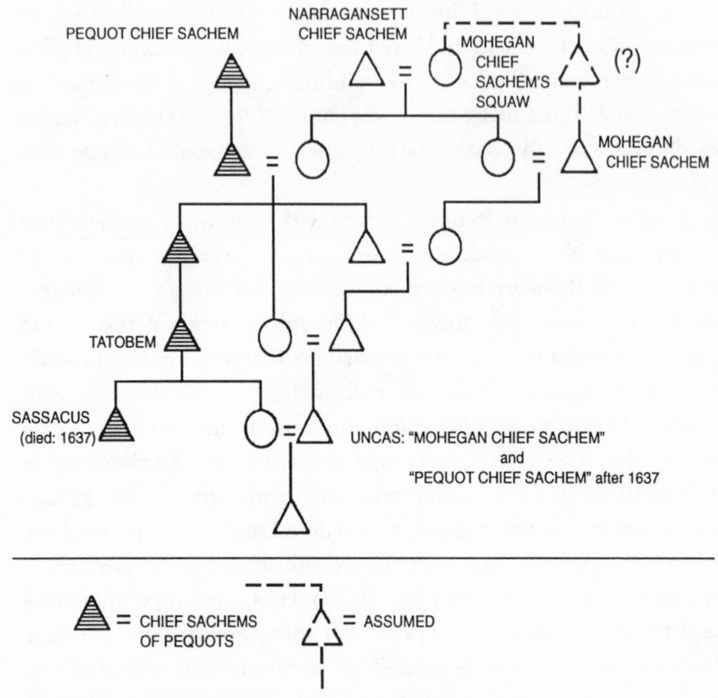

Fig. 10. Genealogy of the Mohegan sachem Uncas. (After Burton and Lowenthal 1974.)

was, in turn, wife of Weeroum, "chief sachem of the Narragansetts." Her daughter married Tamaquawshad, the subsequent chief sachem of the Mohegans, and her matrilateral grandson was Uncas's father (595). While making no claims about the relative importance of matrilineality or patrilineality in determining leadership, this fragmentary genealogy reflects the significance of sibling and maternal relationships in determining rank in subsequent generations, relationships that also served the dominant ideology of the sachemship.

Southern New England languages, especially Massachusett, also had kinship terms that can be loosely translated as referring to "kindreds." These terms fall into two subclasses—those referring to descendants and posterity, and those referring to nonspecific (or unknown) kin. Among the most frequently used of the former terms is *nuppometuonk*, 'my posterity,' employed only on the islands of Martha's Vineyard and Nantucket (Goddard and Bragdon 1988; Bragdon n.d.). *Menoiweankanash*, apparently similar in meaning, was possibly an older term used in the same region. Another term, *ahsuhkouwatuonk*, is translated in a contemporary document as 'succession.' Generalized kinship terms include *auwamochek* and *amn8cummoncheek*, both translated as 'those related to him.' Three terms also translated as 'kindred' may have more specific meanings: *nuttauwaeh, nuttauwam,* and *wuttauwatuonk* sometimes appear in contexts which suggest that they refer to cousins or affines. A number of these terms include the root *auwa*, also found in the word for 'people.'

I suggest that at least for the Massachusett, such terminology demonstrates that lineality and the overarching concept of the sachemship reinforced one another, so that loyalty to the sachem and the sachemship was isomorphic with loyalty to hereditary lineages. Genealogies from Nantucket and Martha's Vineyard document the continued influence of sachem lineages on the islands throughout the first half of the eighteenth century. The ideology of kinship thus functioned to forge consensus and to naturalize inequalities. We cannot know whether it was before the coming of Europeans that the dominant ideology of the Ninnimissinuok was that imposed on social life by the "fundamental group" of the sachems, their families, and advisors, both religious and secular. But Foucault (1980), Bourdieu (1978), and others have amply documented the pervasiveness of power in cultural discourse and compelled us to recognize its presence in previously unexamined domains.

Native testimonies reinforce the view that the notion of the sachemship was "naturalizing" in that it was intimately tied to notions of kin and family, with all their affective associations. So the remark by Martha's Vineyard Native John Ahatun, in the course of a court trial, that he was "often at his sachem's house, for he loved him well" (MVD 1668), can be interpreted as testimony of loyalty to both family and corporate groups, as can the Nantucket documents in which the sachem bestows land-use rights "becayse . . . [he is] greattly akin to me, and I love him, and also he loves me, and hath, formerly, given me, many times, ffive shillings" (quoted in Little 1980:62). The importance of the sachemship community as a focus of identity and affective ties is also suggested in Massachusett kin terminology by the relatively large number of terms referring to "posterity," descendants, and successors. Those terms referring to the descendants or posterity of the group suggest a continued emphasis on the sachemship-community as a source of identity and a reference group for individual members, far beyond the needs and bounds of the nuclear or extended family. By linking kinship to the sachemship in this way, social relations were also justified and reproduced.

7.

Social Relations and Gender Differences

The accounts of both early observers and Natives agree that Native society, particularly in coastal regions, was highly conscious of social distinctions based on status, wealth, age, and gender. To review, of first importance were the sachem families, whose status was marked by differences in dress, comportment, speech, and housing (R. Williams 1936:41, 128, 185; Wood 1977:97–98). Ranking slightly below sachems were the ahtaskoaog, advisors and councilors of the sachem and frequently related to them as well. Following these were the common people, members of the community, but without the distinction of rank or wealth. "Obscure and meane" persons (servants and slaves?) were regarded as occupying an asocial status; like the dead, they had no names (R. Williams 1936:5). Relations between people were structured on the basis of metaphors and habits of sharing and exchange, and of obligation and loyalty. At the same time, however, interactions were ordered along asymmetric lines of dominance and subordination. People looked to sachems as advocates, who in turn protected their interests and "begged" for them when the help of more distant forces was required.

Status and Its Marking

Status was in part a function of age, and as such, was visible in dress and marked by ritual. Transition to adulthood was everywhere commemorated. Boys among the Ninnimissinuok were expected to undergo a severe ordeal wherein each was sent into the wilderness to fast, pray, and seek visions. In some cases, youths were given emetics and forced to drink bitter mixtures until they vomited blood. Among the Pokanoket, they trained the powerful military specialists known as *pniesesok* from youth,

> in great hardness, and make them abstain from dainty meat, observing divers orders prescribed, to the end that when they are of age, the devil may appear to them." (Winslow 1910:345–46)

The guardian spirits or *manitou* encountered during these vigils became the special tutelary guides of each youth, who were then sometimes renamed for these beings. Skills in hunting, sports, and forest lore acquired since their youth were put to the test in enforced solitary adventures, after which, "if they returned fat and sleek, a wife was given them," True adult status for a man was not achieved until he had performed "some notable act, or show forth such courage and resolution as becometh his place" (Winslow 1910:349). Girls were said to undergo a puberty ceremony as well, but no description of it survives. New names marked a transition to adult status for both men and women, "according to their deeds and dispositions" (349).

One of the most potent symbols of age-related status, and of passage from one status to another, was hair. Margaret Holmes Williamson has suggested that for the Powhatan of Virginia, the absence of hair signified an asocial state, or a liminal stage moving towards or away from full human status (1979). Among the Ninnimissinuok newborns were hairless, as were the very old. Youths were not allowed to grow their hair long or to dress it elaborately until they had passed into adult status by virtue of their successful vision quest (Wood 1977:83; Winslow 1910:348). Adult men wore their hair "in a loose and disheveled, womanish manner; otherwise tied up hard and short like a horsetail, bound close with a fillet, which they say makes it grow the faster" (Wood 1977:83). Wood described warriors' hair as "long on one side, the other side being cut short like a screw" (83). Hair was ornamented with ocher and grease, and all manner of feathers, beads, animal fur and hair, bones, and shell (85). Girls of marriageable age among the Narragansett wore their hair in long bangs hanging over their eyes (R. Williams 1936:29). A newly married woman among the Pokanoket cut her hair, and "after weareth a covering on her head, till her hair be grown out" (Winslow 1910:349). Older women wore hairstyles that matched in artistry those of the warriors. Mourners cut their hair as a sign of grief over the death of a loved one.

Clothing too marked status differences. In the early seventeenth century, young boys went naked, while little girls were covered with an apron from their earliest years (R. Williams 1936:118). High-ranking men wore cloaks of moose hide elaborately painted in red or embroidered with shell beads (Wood 1977:84; R. Williams 1936:121). They also wore the remarkable feather cloaks woven by the older men (R. Williams 1936:119). All wore moccasins and simple breechcloths of deerskin tied with snakeskin belts, and the more elderly, according to Wood, wore leggings (1977:84). In cold weather, men also wore an otter or fox skin over their right arm (E. Winslow 1910:350). While many men went unclothed except for the breechcloth or apron indoors, women more frequently kept a loose wrap "ready to gather it up about them" (R. Williams 1936:119). Women also wore longer cloaks with trains that dragged behind them, or mantles crossing under one arm, covering a knee-length skirt.

Fig. 11. Man and woman of the Almouchiquois. (Courtesy of the John Carter Brown Library, Brown University.)

According to Edward Winslow, "women and all of that sex, wear strings about their legs, which the men never do" (1910:350). High-ranking people of both sexes wore elaborate jewelry, the styles and materials of which frequently changed. When Verrazanno met with the Narragansetts in 1524, they were wearing copper breastplates and necklaces of copper beads. Several decades later, Narragansett and "Aberginian" sachems were decked with wampum belts, caps, aprons, necklaces, and bracelets (Wood 1977:85; R. Williams 1936:157).

In addition to their beautiful yet practical clothing, the Ninnimissinuok painted and tattooed their bodies, a practice that both marked status and resonated with cosmological significance. Animals and signs of encounters with manitou (or perhaps totemic figures) were emblazoned on the body and on clothing (Wood 1977:85). People painted themselves red and black for war, black for mourning, and in various colors for "vanity" (Wood 1977:103; R. Williams 1936:165, 191). Team members painted themselves before engaging in sport or gambling, and for dancing at *Nickommo* feasts (Wood 1977:104; Williams 1936). Similarly, and for comparable reasons, warriors also decked themselves with their wampum and other wealth.

Status differences were also marked by deportment and speech. Roger Williams noted that there were two sorts of Native people:

> Some are more rude and clownish, who are not so apt to Salute, but upon salutation resalute lovingly. Others, and the generall, are sober and grave, and yet chearfull in a meane, and as ready to begin a Salutation as to Resalute, which yet the English generally begin, out of desire to Civilize them (1936:1).

Speaking "seldom and opportunely," they rarely laughed, but were nevertheless "naturally cheerful" (Wood 1977:91, 93; Williams 1936:45). The higher ranked person spoke second, and then sparingly (Bragdon 1987). Higher status individuals endeavored to be the last to speak at any encounter or formal parley. Sachems were masters of oratory, and when speaking for the group, employed various rhetorical devices to extol the virtues and power of the groups they represented. They spoke at length, without interruption from their audience, who joined occasionally in group response, like a chorus in a public drama.

These chiefly addresses are examples of "ritual" speech. The distinctive characteristics of such speech give it authority and authenticity, validating both cosmology and social life (Du Bois 1986:324). Such semantically-based "circles of validation" (Hymes 1981: 305– 306) contribute to the experience of life as a seamless whole. This speech style also set the sachem apart from his followers, and validated his own position in the social hierarchy.

Formal terms of address were employed among the high-ranking people, although the "clownish" sort rudely used no greeting, saying merely, "*Keen*, you, *Ewo*, he, &c" (R. Williams 1936:6). Sachems' speech was marked not only by solemnity and rhetorical flourish, but also by archaisms that further emphasized in speech the "authenticity" of the sachem's rule (Wood 1977:92). Different body posture marked status as well. At a parley between the English and the Narragansett sachems Canonicus and Miatonimi in 1637, for example, the older sachem Canonicus "lay along upon the ground, on a mat, and his nobility sate on the ground, with their legs doubled up, their knees touching their chin (E. Johnson 1910[1654]:162).

Definitions of Personhood

From these gleanings it is possible to reconstruct something of the way in which true personhood was defined among the Ninnimissinuok. Young people were expected to defer to their seniors: "The younger sort reverence the elder, and do all mean offices, whilst they are together, although they may be strangers." (E. Winslow 1910:348). Although men smoked great quantities of tobacco, for a boy to do so would be "odious" (349). Men were expected to be brave, to endure pain without flinching or crying out, to be adventurous, brave, dexterous, loyal, and independent (Wood 1977:88, 93; R. Williams 1936:50). They were adjured to speak wisely and with economy, to be generous, to show gratitude for past kindnesses and affection to their children (Wood 1977:88–91; R. Williams 1936:29–30). Loyalty to friends and family, and a quickly kindled pride in community, were valued. (Wood 1977:88). If not of the highest rank, they were to show deference and humility if petitioning for a service or for desired goods. High-ranking men were to act with dignity on all occasions, to show generosity and fairness, to seek consensus, and to act with wisdom and knowledge (R. Williams 1936:142). Unlike their less well-placed followers, however, they were expected to speak with command and authority, to bestow rather than beg, to enjoy closer communication with powerful manitous, and to have their commands carried out without question. English observers called sachems arrogant and "imperious" (Wood 1977:85, 87). Sachems would brook no mockery, it being "a great kindling of Warres amongst them" (R. Williams 1936:186).

Women's Demeanor and Status

Women were "backgrounded" in many of the earliest descriptions of Native people. In one respect only did women's demeanor receive attention. Seventeenth-century observers frequently commented on the "ease" of Native birth and the rapidity with which Native women returned to their regular duties (Wood 1977; R. Williams 1936:149; Winslow 1910:344; Josselyn 1988:91–92; see also Plane 1991). "Most of them count it a shame for a Woman in Travell to make complaint, and many of them are scarcely heard to groane" (R. Williams 1936:149).

In a related way, women were expected to be self-effacing. Marriageable girls were "bashful" and married women were to attend to their husbands' wants without "scolding" (Wood 1977:92; R. Williams 1936:29). "Commendable," wrote Wood, of married women,

> is their mild carriage and obedience to their husbands, notwithstanding all this—their [husband's] customary churlishness and savage inhumanity—not seeming to delight in frowns or offering to word it with their lords, not presuming to proclaim their female

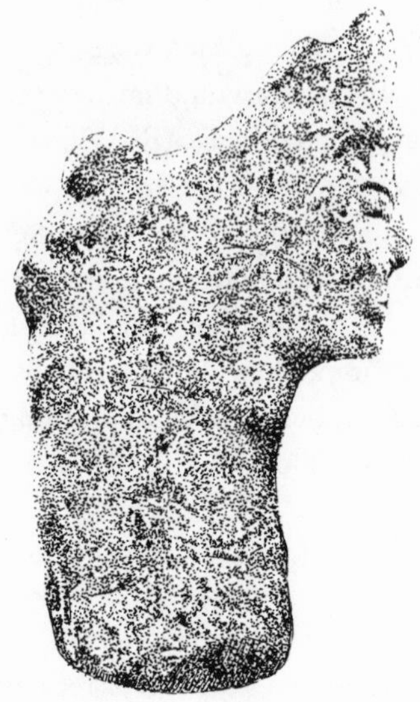

Fig. 12. Mother and child effigy, Annisquam, Massachusetts. (Based on a photograph at the Peabody Museum of Archaeology and Ethnology, Harvard University. Artist: Kimberley Wagner.)

superiority to the usurping of the least title of their husband's charter, but rest themselves content under their helpless condition, counting it the woman's portion. (1977:115)

Women were careful to cover themselves, especially in the presence of strangers (usually men). They were often protected from the notice of such strangers by their male companions (e.g., Verrazzano 1968:17; Brereton 1968:46–47). "Strumpets" among the Ninnimissinuok were shunned (Wood 1977:100). As this epithet suggests, Englishmen were censorious about Native women. Edward Winslow wrote of the Pokanoket that "their women are diversely disposed; some as modest, as they will scarce talk one with another in the company of men, being very chaste also; yet other some light, lascivious and wanton" (1910:349). However, direct reference to women's participation in public activities is relatively unusual in the earliest descriptions of Native life.

The notion of "separate spheres" (e.g., M. Rosaldo 1974) for mens' and women's activities has frequently been employed in modern interpretations of their respective roles among the Ninnimissinuok (e.g., Cronon 1983:44–48). Seventeenth-century Native women were said by contemporary English observers to be entirely responsible for childcare, and for gathering, making clothing, weaving, cooking, and serving meals. Men, on the other hand, were responsible for hunting, fishing. Such divisions were reinforced spatially during women's menstrual separation and their solitary childbirths (R. Williams 1936:149; Plane 1990). Within the house, women stood behind men while they ate (Wood 1977:87). "The womans god" referred to by Williams suggests that some rituals were particular to women. Dietary studies of Native skeletal populations indicate that men consumed more meat than women (Kelley, Barrett, and Saunders 1987:123).

Such separation does not necessarily imply a lower status (Leacock 1978; Lee 1982; McGaw 1989). In fact, some evidence favors an argument for "egalitarian" relations between the genders among the Ninnimissinuok. Premarital sex was permissible (R. Williams 1936:146), and, according to Edward Winslow, divorce was relatively simple:

> if a woman have a bad husband, or cannot affect him, and there be war or opposition between that and any other people, she will run away from him to the contrary party, and there live; where they never come unwelcome, for where are most women, there is greatest plenty. (1910:349).

Men might divorce secondary wives, but "adhere to the first during their lives" (349). Although divorce was not uncommon, Roger Williams wrote that "I know many Couples that have lived twenty, thirty, forty yeares together" (1936:150).

In some parts of southern New England, women could be traders (Grumet 1980:56–57). They could also be sachems and powwaws.

The Narragansett called the sachems' wives *Saunncksquûaog*, and the English called them "Queens" (R. Williams 1936:141). In the latter half of the seventeenth century, women sachems made military alliances, and sought marriage with high-ranking men (E. S. Johnson 1993:80). At least two powerful "queen sachems" ruled on the islands of Martha's Vineyard and Nantucket: Wunnatukquannumou and Askamapoo. These women ruled, not by virtue of their status as sachems' widows, but because they inherited vast territories from their fathers or grandfathers, in spite of the competing claims of male siblings and cousins (Goddard and Bragdon 1988; Little 1990). Saunncksquaog entertained guests in their husbands' absences. There were also some recorded instances of women being sent with important messages or being given dangerous tasks (E. Winslow 1910:283).

Other descriptions imply that women's choices were more limited than those of men. Only men, for example, practiced polygamy, and their wives' status varied according to their rank: A man's first wife was highest in prestige, whereas others were "no better than concubines or servants, and yield a kind of obedience to the principal, who ordereth the family and them in it" (E. Winslow 1910:347). According to Roger Williams, women were valued primarily as sexual partners, and for their role in producing goods for consumption or trade:

> Two causes they generally allege for their many wives. First desire of riches, because the women bring in all the increase of the field, &c, the Husband only fisheth, hunteth, &c. Secondly, their long sequestring themselves from their wives after conception, untill the child be weaned, which with some is long after a yeare old, generally they keep their children long at the breast. (1936:147)

In spite of the sexual freedom women may have had prior to marriage, adultery was a serious offense, and adulterous women were sometimes punished physically, or divorced:

For adultery, the husband will beat his wife and put her away, if he please. Some common strumpets there are, as well as in other places; but they are such as either never married, or widows, or put away for adultery; for no man will keep such an one to wife. (Winslow 1910:349)

The issue of post-marital residence among the Ninnimissinuok is still unresolved; one anecdote concerning the daughter of the Pawtucket sachem Passaconaway suggests that she went to live with her husband's community (T. Morton 1947:27–29), and one could interpret Winslow's remarks about women leaving bad husbands as evidence for their ability to return to their childhood homes. A "price" was paid for wives among the Narragansett (R. Williams 1936:147–48), which Roger Williams confusingly refers to as a "dowrie." It is possible that Wood was using the term in the same way (1977:99). In general, bride-price is paid to compensate the family for the loss of a daughter's labor, and often accompanies patrilocal residence (Murdock 1949:20). Although patrilocality distances women from their natal families, and is hence sometimes linked to the low status of women in societies that practice it, George Peter Murdock points out that "a bride-price is more than a compensation to parents for the loss of a daughter who leaves their home when she marries. It is commonly also a guarantee that the young wife will be well treated in her new home. If she is not, she can ordinarily return to her parents, with the result that her husband forfeits his financial investment in her" (1949:21). Thus, although women were separated from their parents and siblings, their freedom to return to the natal family gave them some power within the context of their marriage.

Ninnimissinuok women, at least in coastal communities, worked very hard. According to Wood, in addition to making mats and constructing houses, planting and tending the cornfields, women had to dry and store the corn, which they then were compelled to hide from their "gourmandizing husbands who would eat up both their allowed portion and the reserved seed if they knew where to find it" (Wood 1977:114). They also caught lobsters for their husbands' use as bait. While not fishing and hunting themselves, they were responsible for carrying home the caught fish, dressing, cooking, and preserving it, and for carrying home the game and processing the animal skins (113–14). They also gathered flags and made mats and baskets, sewed clothing and shoes, and worked hard even while very pregnant (114). Wood claimed women did not eat with men, but served them, and then ate their leftovers. English observers sometimes likened Native women to drudges (Levett 1843:178).

Edward Winslow, writing of the women among the Pokanoket, concurred:

> The women live a most slavish life; they carry all their burdens, set and dress their corn, gather it in, seek to for much of their food, beat and make ready the corn to eat, and have all the household care lying upon them. (1910:348)

Wood also wrote concernedly that

> these ruder Indians . . . scorn the tutorings of their wives [and do not] admit them as their equals—though their qualities and industrious deservings may justly claim the preeminence and command better usage and more conjugal esteem, their persons and features being every correspondent, their qualifications more excellent, being more loving, pitiful, and modest, mild, provident and laborious than their lazy husbands. (1977:112)

Consensus among scholars is that negative reports such as Wood's about the condition of Native women were based on lack of understanding of Native division of labor and on their somewhat jealous perception that Indian men had much in common with English nobility (e.g., Axtell 1985; Salisbury 1982). But while men too worked hard (although more sporadically than women) it would be mistaken to assume that all reports of inequality between men and women were the result of European bias and misunderstanding. Interpretations of Native society in southern New England frequently attribute a primordial egalitarian quality to social relations that at once falsely exaggerates the differences in "complexity" between natives and Europeans, and masks the internal inequalities that had an important impact on many members of Native society, particularly women. The social asymmetry, the hierarchical ideology of the sachemship that characterized the Ninnimissinuok of coastal regions, may well have had its foundation in the growing control of men over the products of their wives' labor and in the fragmentation into nuclear families.

The privileged status of certain women among the Ninnimissinuok does not necessarily negate this argument. Annette B. Weiner argues that in fact the status of certain women is sometimes enhanced as stratification intensifies, not in their roles as wives, but in their roles as *sisters* and *mothers*. Women's contribution to the continuity of ruling groups, Weiner argues, is in actuality a necessity for a truly hierarchical society (1991).

European observers unsurprisingly focused mainly on women as wives, and references to their other activities are scarce. However, limited information concerning sachem women indicates that they served as sachems in the absence of brothers, and that they could and did inherit land, and had the right to distribute it. Male sachems sought women of equal rank as their "principal" wives and claimed jurisdiction over territories and people as a result of such marriages (Winslow 1910:346–47); "otherwise, they say, their seed would in time become ignoble" (347). As may be recalled, sachems claimed the right to rule as the result of the inheritance of rights from their mothers. High-ranking women exercised considerable control over husbands, brothers, and sons. Moreover, the products of high-ranking women's labor, particularly woven wampum belts, held significant symbolic importance, validating not only their family's right to rule, but providing the media of diplomatic exchange, which further increased their family's power.

There may also have been differences in the roles and status of women among inland, coastal, and riverine people. Josselyn's descriptions of the people near the Saco River, and Wood's of the "Aberginians," suggest that women of these regions worked more cooperatively with their husbands, particularly on hunting expeditions, than did women of other regions. Deeds from the 1640s relating to the middle Connecticut indicate that women were more involved with land transactions than were those in coastal regions, and played a more active role in political decision-making (Thomas 1979). Women there were also actively engaged in trade.

The heavy dependence on horticulture in riverine communities undoubtedly influenced womens' work. A passage from Mary Jemison's account of her captivity among the Iroquois in the late eighteenth century gives some sense of the nature of such work:

> Our labor was not severe; and that of one year was exactly similar, in almost every respect to that of others . . . notwithstanding the Indian women have all the fuel and bread to procure . . . their cares certainly are not half as numerous, nor as great [as those of white women]. In the summer season, we planted, tended, and harvested our corn, and generally had all our children with us . . . we could work as leisurely as we pleased . . . (Seaver 1961)

To argue that women's status and roles were universally high, low, or equal, is to assume a homogeneity of cultural knowledge and experience. Evidence from southern New England suggests that people participated differentially in cultural understandings, depending on their status, family position, wealth, and location. Conflicting information about women's status can thus be understood as reflecting in part such differential experience, and the Europeans only partial understanding of it.

If it is true that social meaning is always contested, that symbols and their contents are always vulnerable to redefinition, then the ambivalent status of women, and the contradictory expectations concerning the behavior of high-ranking individuals of both genders, become more than just the product of European misunderstanding or of vagaries in the record, but evidence for the dynamics of cultural process.

8.

Cosmology

The richly spiritual world inhabited by the Ninnimissinuok was not one immediately apparent to those who linked religion to permanent structures of worship, to literacy, or to the existence of a single, all-powerful god. Those English observers who became more familiar with the Ninnimissinuok did come to recognize this spirituality, even if they did not understand it. Edward Winslow wrote, for example,

> Whereas myself and others, in former letters . . . wrote that the Indians about us are a people without any religion, or knowledge of any God, therein I erred, though we could then gather no better; for as they conceive of many divine powers . . . (1910:342)

Manitou Proximate and Distant

These "divine powers" were manifestations of manitou, the impersonal force that permeated the world, observable in anything marvelous, beautiful, or dangerous.

The best information about manitou derives from central Algonquians. Many Algonquian-speaking people believe that the Cosmic Axis, located at the center of the world, serves as a pathway through the openings in the layers of the universe. The Axis, like the World Cedar Tree, which emerges through this same pathway, connects the levels of the cosmos. In many recorded rituals, circular pits, lodges, or other ceremonial structures, placed at the point of intersection between earth and sky, and earth and underworld, represent a symbolic entrance to both worlds. The concept of the Cosmic Axis postulated a connection between various levels of experience, often mediated by manitou. Manitou is a vital force in all things, both natural and supernatural, although for many Algonquian-speaking people the distinction between the two was not clearly drawn. Manitou is not uniformly distributed in the world: some things are more heavily charged with it, while others are infused with negative, dangerous, or harmful force. Manitou is, moreover, a characteristic that inhabits natural phenomena, objects, or people, but is not necessarily a permanent quality.

Beliefs commonly associated with the concept of manitou among Algonquian-speaking peoples are totemism and the theory of guardian spirits. Totemism, which is a system of names for social groupings based on association with eponymous animals, is also frequently marked by the use of images of animals as body decoration or as personal "signs." Some scholars have interpreted the seventeenth-century practice of marking colonial deeds with animal figures or other objects as reflecting a totemic system. Wood also noted that among the Aberginians:

> Many of the better sort [bear] upon their cheeks certain portraitures of beasts, as bears, deers, mooses, wolves, etc,; some of fowls, as of eagles, hawks, etc. . . . whether these be foils to illustrate their unparalleled beauty (as they deem it) or arms to blazon their antique gentility, I cannot easily determine." (1977:85).

A fully operant totemic clan system does not seem to have been present in southern New England, although it was found among the Abenaki to the north and east, and among the Mahican to the west (Brasser 1978; Snow 1978; Day 1978).

Distinct from totemism is the belief in guardian spirits, a widespread notion in the Americas, and closely associated with the concept of manitou. Certain beings, also endowed with manitou, were thought to protect and enhance the well-being of the denizens of the "natural" world. Such guardian spirits, if properly approached, might aid humans as well. Among many Algonquian people, such guardians were represented visually in designs woven into headbands, painted on cloth, or drawn on the human body. The belief in guardian spirits was particularly strong among those people who supported religious practitioners known as *shamans.*

The best descriptions of belief in manitou among the Ninnimissinuok come from Roger Williams, who wrote "there is a generall Custome amongst them, at the apprehension of any Excellency in Men, Women, Birds, Beasts, Fish, &c. to cry out Manittóo A God" (R. Williams 1936:126). Such "excellency" was sometimes more fully realized (or perhaps only more fully described) in a congery of beings (called "gods" or "devils" by the English) with intentions, specific abilities, and associations. These beings, whom Ruth Underhill called "nature persons" (1965:46), included among the Narragansett the children's god and the woman's god. Roger Williams observed,

> I find what I could never heare before, that they have plenty of Gods or divine powers: the Sunn, Moone, Fire, Water, Snow, Earth, the Deere, the Beare etc. are divine powers. I brought home lately from the Nanhiggonsicks the names of 38 of their Gods all they could remember and had I not with feare and caution withdrew they would have fallen to worship O God (as they speake one day in 7). (LaFantasie 1988:146)

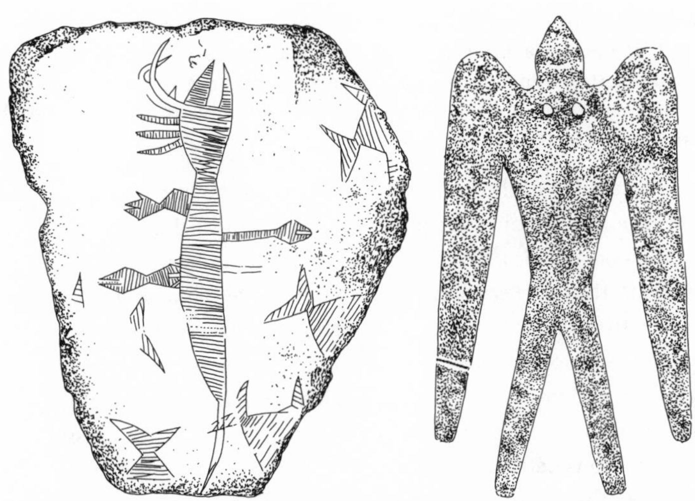

Fig. 13. (left) "Horned serpent" etching, Long Island, New York. (After Matthiessen 1986. Artist: Kimberley Wagner.)
Fig. 14. (right) Thunderbird amulet, Amoskeag, New Hampshire. (Based on a photograph at the Peabody Museum of Archaeology and Ethnology, Harvard University. Artist: Kimberley Wagner.)

Rare or unusual animals were revered as manitou as well. Roger Williams wrote,

> The Indians say they have black Foxes, which they have often seene, but never could take any of them: they say they are Manittóoes, that is, Gods Spirits or Divine Powers, as they say of every thing they cannot comprehend. (1936:103)

Among the manitou known to the Ninnimissinuok was the giant horned or antlered, under(water) world serpent, a being familiar to other Algonquian-speaking people as well. Images of this fearsome underwater dweller sometimes decorated amulets, bowls, and other objects. Its powers were suggested by a curious story told to Josselyn of a sea-serpent or snake, that lay quoiled up like a cable upon a rock at Cape-Ann; a boat passing by with English aboard, and two Indians, they would have shot the serpent, but the Indians dissuaded them, saying that if he were not kill'd outright, they would be all in danger of their lives. (1988:20)

The analog of the underwater serpent in the upper or sky world was the thunderbird, a sacred and beautiful bird in many Algonquian cosmologies. Often the enemy of the underwater panther or serpent, the two were nonetheless halves of the same unity (Vastokas and Vastokas 1973:91). This powerful being is commonly depicted graphically, often as a human figure rendered frontally, with a profiled and prominant beak, or as a human figure with wings (93). Amulets in the same form were worn by the Ninnimissinuok. Associations between birds heard at night and thunder among the nineteenth-century Mohegan seem to reflect the continuity of this belief in southern New England (Speck 1909:203).

In the early seventeenth century these powerful antagonists of the upper and under(water) world were realized as, or symbolically linked to, an analogous pair of other-than-human beings: Cautantouwit (or Keihtan) and Abbomocho (or Hobbomok). Abbomocho may have been called Chepi by some of the Ninnimissinuok or Chepi may have been another powerful nonhuman being included in local cosmology. The descriptions of these beings associate them not only with specific powers, but with sacred directions, colors, and elemental substances such as fire, water, and minerals. Cautantouwit was said to be "the principal and maker of all the rest, and to be made by none" (E. Winslow 1910:342). The Ninnimissinuok stated that "the soules of Men and Women goe to the Sou-west, their great and good men and Women to Cautantouwit his house, where they have hopes (as the Turkes have of carnall Joyes) (R. Williams 1936:130). Cautantouwit was also said to have sent the first kernels of corn to the Ninnimissinuok in the ear of the crow, a belief reflected in the Narragansett refusal to harm crows regardless of the damage they did to their crops (89–90). This being presided in the heavens and "when they would obtain any great matter, [they would] meet together and cry unto him; and so likewise for plenty victory, etc, sing dance, feast, give thanks, and hang up garlands and other things in memory of the same" (E. Winslow 1910:342).

Abbomocho, Hobbomok, or Chepi was the being associated with death, night, the northeast wind, the dark, and the color black (Wood 1977:95; E. Winslow 1910:343; Josselyn 1988:95; Stiles 1916:156; Mayhew 1834:202–204). This being was linked to the underworld as well:

> For their enemies and loose livers, whom they account unworthy of [paradise], they say that they pass to the infernal dwellings of Abamacho, to be tortured according to the fictions of the ancient heathen. (Wood 1977:112)

Abbomocho appeared in many forms, but most often as an eel, snake, or other under(water) world dweller (E. Winslow 1910:343). The powers of this being were large and not altogether benign:

> Him they call upon to cure their wounds and diseases. When they are curable, he persuades them he sends the same for some conceived anger against them; but upon their calling upon him, can and doth help them; but when they are mortal and not curable in nature, then he persuades them Kiehtan is angry, and sends them, whom none can cure; insomuch as in that respect only they somewhat doubt whether he be simply good, and therefore in sickness never call upon him. (Winslow 1910:343)[1]

Abbomocho was sought by (male?) youths who underwent mortifications including sleep avoidance, fasting, and purging. In one such ordeal, initiates drank "juice of sentry and other bitter herbs, till they cast, which they must disgorge into the platter, and drink again and again, till . . . it will seem to be all blood (E. Winslow 1910:360). Among the Pokanoket, young men who survived these ordeals became pniesesok. Although altogether a more fearsome being, Abbomocho was at the same time the more accessible. It was to him that people looked for daily assistance, him whom they blamed for misfortune, and him whose name was sometimes taken by powwaws or pniesesok.

Belief in these paired beings survived in an altered way late into the contact period. In 1674, Daniel Gookin described another pair of beings, markedly similar to Cautantouwit and Abbomocho, of whom he heard while working among the Nipmuck, Massachusett, and Pawtucket:

> Generally they acknowledge one great supreme doer of good; and him they call Woonand, or Mannitt: another, that is the great doer of evil or mischief; and him they called Mattand, which is the devil; and him they dread and fear, more than they love and honour the former chief good which is God. (Gookin 1806:154)

English settlers, and especially missionaries, seized quickly on this pairing as evidence of a rudimentary recognition of the duality of good and evil. Francis Higginson, "a reverend Divine," living by 1629 in Salem, wrote within three months of his arrival that "they do worship two Gods, a good God and an evil God. The good God they call Tantum, and their evil God, whom they fear will do them hurt, they call Squantum" (1970:257). The partial similarities between Native beliefs in Cautantouwit and Abbomocho and the Christian belief in God and the Devil were only that; the opposition of good and evil expressed in the Christian concept had no exact equivalent in the beliefs of the Ninnimissinuok. Cautantouwit's distant benignity was less significant than the more local and powerful, if more ambivalent forces of good and evil embodied in Abbomocho.

The Dual Soul

The goal of many members of Native society was to make contact with manitou and to acquire guardian spirits: through vision quests, the seeking out of sacred spaces, dreams, and induced trance, and through soul travel, accomplished while asleep. The Narragansett belief in the dual soul was related to Native understanding of spirit journeys in search of such encounters. One soul, the dream soul, or *Cowwéwonck*, which traveled in dreams and left the body during illness, was said to roam at night, appearing as a light (Josselyn 1988:95–96) while the body slept. The other, *Míchachunck*, or the "clear" soul, thought to be located in the heart (Simmons 1970:54), was the animating force of every individual (R. Williams 1936:130). As the dream soul sought enlightenment, guardian spirits were entreated for their aid in all manner of human enterprises, and the stronger one's spirit helper(s), the greater one's well-being.

The dream soul was believed to make its way to the southwest, to Cautantowit's house, where

> they hold the immortality of the never-dying soul that it shall pass to the southwest Elysium, concerning which their Indian faith jumps much with the Turkish Alcoran, holding it to be a kind of paradise wherein they shall everlastingly abide, solacing themselves in odoriferous gardens, fruitful corn fields, green meadows, bathing their tawny hides in the cool streams of pleasant rivers, and shelter themselves from heat and cold in the sumptuous palaces framed by the skill of natures curious contrivement. (Wood 1977:111; see also R. Williams 1936:130)

Only the "great and good" among them could expect such rewards, for

> thither bad men go also, and knock at [Kiehtan]'s door, but he bids them *quatchet*, that is to say, walk abroad, for there is no place for such; so that they wander in restless want and penury. (E. Winslow 1910:342)

Spatial Dimensions of the Cosmos

The animated cosmos was, for many Algonquian-speaking people, a tripartite one, including the sky or upper world, the earth or middle world, and the under(water) domains. According to George R. Hamell, "Mythical time and space converge in the furthermost regions from the center . . . real humans have access to mythic time and space and to the powerful man-beings dwelling there, through visions, dreams, and heroic journeys" (1987). Beliefs of the Ninnimissinuok regarding the form of the cosmos were not specifically recorded, but occasional references to the habitual dwellings of sacred beings, and to ritual activities occurring in high places, swamps, and nearby water, suggest the symbolic importance attached to the spatial correlates of manitou. On the arrival of the Pilgrims, for example, Massasoit was said to have called together his shamans, or *powwaws*, "for three days together in a horrid and devilish manner, to curse and execrate them with their conjurations, which assembly they held in a dark and dismal swamp" (Bradford 1970:84). The Ninnimissinuok retreated to deep swampy places in times of war, where they were not only harder to find but had stronger links to their other-than-human protectors (R. Williams 1936).

Hamell's research has focused on those sacred places where the powerful denizens of the other-than-human world could be met. Such places, according to Hamell, are metaphorical thresholds between this world and other worlds, the crossing of which entails physical, spiritual, and social transformation. Thresholds might, he argues, be coterminous for farming people with the village clearing. Among coastal dwellers, the ocean marked an equivalent dividing place. Anomalous watery places, springs, whirlpools, swamps, and marshes were thought to be the customary dwelling places of powerful manitou, many identified with amphibious animals such as salamanders, lizards, turtles, frogs, and snakes, as well as water-dwelling mammals such as beavers and otters (1987: 67–69).

The thresholds of the three realms were regularly crossed by humans in dream-soul form, powwaws in nonhuman form, the souls

Fig. 15. Carved bowl, Nipmuck or Mohegan. (Courtesy of the Haffenreffer Museum of Anthropology, Brown University.)

of the dead, and beings-other-than-human seeking entry into the (real) social world. Humans seeking greater power employed intermediaries to these realms, who acted as advocates and as channels of power, and as sources of wealth and well-being in the human realm. Edward Winslow wrote, "so have I heard them call upon some as if they had their residence in some certain places, or because they appeared in those forms in the same" (1910:344). The boundaries between the world of humans and beings other than human were fluid, just as the boundaries between physical states were illusory. The Massachusett term *hogk*, 'body,' for example, meant only "that which *covers* a man or animal" (Trumbull 1903:27; emphasis added).

Origin Tales

Origin tales were also linked to spatial realms and the beings associated with them. In northerly sections of southern New England, people spoke of ancient floods:

> a great while agon their countrey was drowned, and all the people and other creatures in it, only one powaw and his webb foreseeing the flood fled to the white mountains carrying a hare along with them and so escaped; after a while the powaw sent the hare away, who not returning emboldened thereby they descended, and lived many years after, and had many children, from whom the countrie was filled again with Indians. Some of them tell another story of the beaver, saying that he was their father. (Josselyn 1988:96–97)

Thomas Morton, who lived among the Massachusett, was told:

> God made one man and one woman, and had them live together, and get children . . . and that their posterity was full of evill, and made God so angry; that hee let in the sea upon them, & drowned the greatest part of them . . . And they went to Sanaconquam who feeds upon them, pointing to the Center of the Earth: where they imagine is the habitation of the Devill. (1947:34–35)

Water's common association with fertility is also suggested by an origin tale recorded by Daniel Gookin describing two girls wading in the water when some of its foam "touched their bodies, from whence they became with child" (1806:146).

Ninnimissinuok in the southerly, coastal regions attributed their creation to Cautantowuit, located in the skyworld and in the sacred southwest:

> At first, they say, there was no sachim or king, but Kiehtan, who dwelleth above in the heavens. . . . Never man saw this Kiehtan; only old men tell them of him, and bid them tell their children, yea to charge them to teach their posterities the same, and lay the like charge upon them . . . (Winslow 1910:342)

The Narragansett also averred that

> Kautántowwit made one man and woman of a stone, which disliking, he broke them in pieces, and made another man and woman of a Tree, which were the Fountaines of all mankind (R. Williams 1936:135)

The shape of the physical landscape and the appearance of animals and plants were attributed in sacred stories to giant culture heros or tricksters:

> They have many strange relations of one Wétucks, a man that wrought great miracles amongst them, and walking upon the waters, &c. with some kind of broken resemblance to the sonne of God (R. Williams 1936:A4)

The Gay Head Indians recounted many stories of Mausop, a giant culture hero, who created landscape features and transformed living creatures (Bassett 1806:139). Mohegans in the late nineteenth century also spoke of dwarfs of the forest and of spirits who were active at night—one carrying a light and the other appearing raucous and malevolent (Speck 1909:201).[2]

The cosmos of the Ninnimissinuok was a crowded one, pervaded by manitou and various mythical heros. The likelihood that animals in the dark woods or deep waters were transformations of even more powerful beings, and the certainty that the "natural" world was imbued with power, structured and made sacred hunting and collecting. The Narragansetts, for example, were "very tender of their traps where they lie, and what comes at them; for they say, the Deer, (whom they conceive have a Divine power in them) will soone smell and be gone" (R. Williams 1936:173). The people with whom Josselyn lived appeased their prey with prescribed butchering practices. Upon killing a moose,

> the victors, who having cut the throat of the slain take off his skin, their young webbs by this time are walking towards them with heavie

> bags and kettles at their backs, who laing down their burdens fall to work upon the carkass, take out the heart, and from that the bone, cut off the left foot behind, draw out the sinews, and cut out his tongue, &c. (1988:98)

As Bird-David suggests, such practices and beliefs endow the experiences of hunting, trapping, gathering, collecting, and farming with richly elaborated social meaning. These activities are ways to "keep in touch" with supernatural helpers. To seek and take food is to experience directly with the supernatural the kind of "demand exchange" often conducted with human beings (1992).

Purity, Danger, and Liminality: Avoidances among the Ninnimissinuok

The widespread belief in the elemental power of women, a power inherent in their ability to conceive and give birth, a power unsought, and therefore all the more dangerous, particularly during the reproductive years, was frequently reflected among the Ninnimissinuok in the separation of women during their menstrual period, and in the various restrictions placed on their activities and on the objects they could use during their seclusion. Among the Narragansett,

> they constantly separate their Women (during the time of their monthly sicknesse) in a little house alone by themselves foure or five dayes, and hold it an Irreligious thing for either Father or Husband or any Male to come neere them. (R. Williams 1936:A4)

This belief was also manifest in the customs and restrictions placed upon pubescent or marriageable women, who, as in many parts of Native North America, were shielded from light, the sun, and, sometimes, from fire (Underhill 1965:58). For example, unmarried women at the northern boundaries of the region wore fringed or beaded caps that hung down, obscuring their faces (T. Morton 1947). Among the Narragansett, "their virgins are distinguished by a bashful falling downe of their haire over their eyes" (R. Williams

1936:29). After marriage, a woman's head could again go uncovered (Winslow 1910:349). Women's regenerative powers, indexed in these restrictions on "virgins," were recognized as dangerous, but they had not become, as they had for the Englishman, "uncleane" (Douglas 1966).

As mentioned in chapter 7, childbirth was also carried out in solitude, perhaps to protect the community from the powerful forces unleashed when a woman gave birth to a child (Underhill 1965:59). Other avoidances of widespread and presumably ancient origin were associated with the dead. The dream soul Cowwewonck, described previously, was in many parts of North America believed to linger after death, and had sometimes to be avoided by the living. The fact that this soul was thought to be lodged in the head might explain the custom of taking heads in battle to prevent enemies from completing their journey to the afterworld (Simmons 1970:59). Roger Williams wrote of several customs among the Narragansett that seem to suggest an avoidance of the dead:

> they abhorre to mention the dead by name, and therefore, if any man beare the name of the dead he changeth his name; and if any stranger accidentally name him, he is checkt, and if any wilfully name him he is fined; and and [*sic*] amongst States, the naming of the dead Sachims, is one ground of their warres . . . (1936:202)

Furthermore,

> after the dead is laid in grave, and sometimes (in some parts) some goods cast in with them, they have then a second great lamentation, and upon the Grave is spread the Mat that the party died on, the dishe he eat in, and sometimes a faire coat of skin hung upon the tree next to the grave, which none will touch, but suffer it there to rot with the dead (203).

According to Edward Winslow, the houses of the deceased among the Pokanoket were avoided as well:

> If it be the man or woman of the house, they will pull down the mats, and leave the frame standing, and bury them in or near the same, and either remove their dwelling or give over house-keeping. (1910:348)

Mourners were under additional restrictions. Close relatives lamented over the graves for extended periods, and all the subjects of a deceased sachem were required to undergo a protracted period of mourning (R. Williams 1936:43). During the period of mourning, the bereaved were to abstain from play (gambling?), from wearing decorative body paint, and were adjured to avoid arguments (43). On February 28, 1637/8, Roger Williams wrote of Miantonimi's mourning:

> in case his Father in law, Caunounicus his brother, (whome I saw neere death with above a thoughsand men mourning and praying about him) in case he recover, otherwise it is unlawfull for them (as they conceave) to goe farr from home till toward midsomme. (LaFantasie 1988:145)

The fetal position of the body at birth and in burials, the blackening of the heads of mourners and the bodies of newborns, the hairlessness of babies and the shaved heads of mourners, naming avoidances at death and the delay in naming babies, and sexual abstinence practiced by mourners and nursing mothers appear to have been in recognition of the liminal and quasi-social status of both the newborn and the newly dead. The crow, linked with Cautantowit, at once life-giver and guardian of the afterlife, was also associated with dreams and visions, with death, and with children (Simmons 1970:62).

Health, Wealth, and Well-Being

Spiritual power, manifest in action and appearance, in dream-soul travel and transformation, and in liminal states and sacred encounters, was inextricably linked to ideas of health and well-being among the

Ninnimissinuok. Hamell has argued that such well-being was isomorphic with "wealth," and was embodied, among other things, in objects, especially those colored white (or crystal), sky blue-green, red, and black (1987a:75). These objects were associated with the sky and underwater realms, and with the beings who inhabited them. To engage in proper demeanor toward, and ritual "exchange" with, these beings was to be healthy, and acquisition of sacred objects linked to them was a form of "insurance and assurance of physical, spiritual, and social well-being" (75). The motivations for seeking spiritual power were not merely personal, however, but were tied to deep concerns about community health as well. The use, payment, or sacrifice of these objects to religious specialists and in ritual, the subjects of the following chapters, was to promote both personal and community well-being, making the social and the sacred a seamless whole.

9.

Religious Specialists Among the Ninnimissinuok

Although Ninnimissinuok had the power to attain spiritual and social health through trance, soul flight, sacrifice, and encounters with manitou, they were also able to employ intermediaries in their relations with the other-than-human. The intermediaries were religious specialists of remarkable skill, whose role in Native society is less than perfectly understood. In spite of the tendency in the literature on the Ninnimissinuok to refer to all religious practitioners as members of a homogeneous category, there appear to have been distinctions in their function and status. Roger Williams recorded several terms for religious practitioners, including *powwaw*, "their priest," *maunêtu*, "a conjurer," *nanouwétea*, "an over-seer and orderer of their worship," and the *mockuttásuit*, "who winds up and buries the dead," (1936:128; 198; 203). On occasion, sachems experienced qualifying visions, and also became powwaws. Such sachems, like Tispaquin, the "Black Sachem" of Assawomset, and Passaconaway of the Pawtucket, were both feared and respected (E. Winslow 1910; Wood 1977).

No seventeenth-century accounts clearly describe the differences between these practitioners or their roles within a given community. Ezra Stiles was told by the Niantics in 1761 that there might be ten or twelve powwaws in a community of three or four hundred people (Sturtevant 1975:440). The Narragansett made further divisions between overseers of worship and what appears to have been a learned body of ritual leaders, whose roles complemented one another. Williams remarked that they had

> an exact forme of King, Priest, and Prophet . . . their Kings or Governours called *Sachimaüog*, Kings, and *Atauskowaũg* Rulers doe govern: Their priests, performe and manage their worship: Their wise men and old men of which number the priests are also, whom they call *Taupowaüog* they make solemne speeches and orations, or Lectures to them, concerning Religion, Peace, or Warre and all things. (R. Williams 1936:128)

The Powwaws

English descriptions of the most common sort of religious specialists among the Ninnimissinuok, the powwaws, were filled with contempt, and fear:

> There are among them certain men and women, whom they call powows. These are partly wizards and witches, holding familiarity with Satan, the evil one; and partly are physicians, and make use, at least in show, of herbs and roots, for curing the sick and diseased. (D. Gookin 1806:154)

The powwaws were separated from ordinary vision seekers by the extreme power of their visions and the fact that their manitou was unsought. Otherwise fully functioning members of their communities (they could marry and have children [Eliot and Mayhew 1834:258–59]), powwaws were involuntarily summoned by Abbomocho or Chepi, who appeared to them in dreams in the form of a snake or some other sacred being. Powwaws told Eliot, for example, that

> if any one of the Indians fall into any strange dreame wherein *Chepian* appears unto them as a serpent, then the next day they tell the other Indians of it . . . [who] dance and rejoyce for what they tell them about this Serpent, and so they become their Powwows. (A. Eliot 1834:19–20).

The beings encountered in dreams imparted particular powers to their human clients. A Martha's Vineyard powwaw recalled that he had encountered four beings in one of his dreams:

> one was like a man which he saw in the Ayre, and this told him that he did know all things upon the island, and what was to be done; and this he said had its residence over his whole body. Another was like a Crow, and did look out sharply to discover mischiefs coming towards him, and had its residence in his head. The third was like to a pidgeon, and had its place in his breast, and was very cunning about any businesse. The fourth was like a serpent, very subtile to doe mischief, and also to doe great cures, and these he said were meer Devills, and such as he has trusted to for safety, and did labour to raise up for the accomplishment of any thing in his diabolicall craft. (Whitfield 1834:186)

The powers of brass, iron, and stone also lent their aid to powwaws (187).

Strong links between people so aided and their tutelary spirits was marked in their mutuality of appellation. Thomas Mayhew, for example, called the spirit helpers of the powwaws, *powwaunnomas*, or "imps" (Whitfield 1834:187). At least two men known to the English in the early seventeenth century were named *Hobbomok*: one a *pniese*, and a follower of Massasoit, and the other a man described by William Wood (1977). Tisquantum (Squanto), the Patuxet advisor to the Pilgrims, likewise was linked to the manitou or "god" bearing the same name as his. In 1761 Stiles visited two Native women near Niantic, Connecticut, and learned that "the Nehantics named their Pawawen, Mondtu" and that "By this Name they call themselves & the Supreme Diety" (quoted in Sturtevant 1975:440).

These links were so strong that spirit-helpers were said to "torment" those hosts who rejected them (Whitfield 1834b:205–206).

Powwaws As Shamans

Southern New England pawwaws shared many characteristics with a class of individuals known to anthropologists as *shamans*, who in many cultures were prophets, "sucking doctors," and wonder-workers (Underhill 1965:85). Shamans are men and women who through extraordinary visionary experiences and the acquisition of powerful spirit-helpers, are able to influence, tap, or control unseen powers of the world for the benefit or ill of mankind. Such visionary experiences are achieved through "ecstatic" trance, assisted by drumming, dancing, and sometimes the use of hallucinogens and other substances. Shamans are able to perform extraordinary feats, communicating with spirits, harnessing world energy, transcending barriers of space and time. Their power is sometimes directed toward curing the sick, whose illness might have been caused by loss of the soul, which only the shaman has the power to restore.

In some areas of North America shamans were divided into three separate groups. The first was associated with prophecy, used to predict the outcome of a battle or hunting expedition. These shamans practiced for a fee and formed no larger fraternity. Such shamans were in some groups assisted by turtles and thunderbirds, and practiced in a small round roofless "tent," in which the shaman would sit and act as a "channel" for the manitou present. The second group consisted of curers, specializing in herbal knowledge and hunting and fertility magic. These shamans also practiced alone and were feared as sorcerers. The third group, a more organized "priesthood," preserved religious and cultural lore.[1]

Transformation, and human/animal metamorphoses, are central to shamanistic belief and practice (Furst 1976:6), and are intimately connected to a widespread belief in dual souls. Among Algonquian-speaking people, including the Ninnimissinuok, it was thought that such metamorphoses occurred during sleep or trance when the dream soul left the body. Shamans had especially powerful dream souls that took on other forms and traveled to supernatural realms. Encounters with and instruction from tutelary spirits or manitou occurred when soul flight took place.

Trance, vision, dreams, and the use of hallucinatory drugs such as tobacco, are parts of a shamanistic repertoire designed to achieve transformation or sensitivity to those beings who are themselves transformed. In many parts of the world, shamans are linked through a multiplicity of symbols to birds, or to those animals who shift between environments or mediate between disparate states. Birds are likewise linked to the experience of drug-induced "flight," a linkage marked by the common association in Native North America between birds, tobacco, and smoking pipes (Hall 1977:503–504; Springer 1981:229).

In much of the Northeast, beings endowed with manitou are thought to be "addicted" to tobacco, and smoking thus attracts and appeases them (Von Gernet and Timmons 1987:40). Shamans often relied on manitou who took the form of birds; in some cases, a remarkable fusion of guardian spirits and dream soul resulted in a being known as a "guardian soul." Sometimes shamans identified so strongly with these guardian souls that they became their alter-egos (39–40). Among the Penobscot, for example, shamans were said to be able to transform themselves into their guardian souls (Hultkrantz 1979:72–3), and Ojibwe vision questers were thought to be able to transform themselves into birds (Hallowell 1966:284).

The curing function of the powwaws in southern New England, which involved the "sucking" out of sickness, was frequently remarked on by English observers:

> The powah is eager and free in speech, fierce in countenance, and joineth many antic and laborious gestures with the same, over the

party diseased. If the party be wounded, he will also seem to suck the wound. (Winslow 1910:343; see also Wood 1977:101)

Powwaws worked in exchange for goods of several sorts. Observers mention wampum, beads, and other "wealth" as payment for cures and divinations. Payment of symbolically charged objects did not enrich the powwaw, however, as he was required to "sacrifice" wealth to attain a cure. Edward Winslow wrote that

In the powah's speech, he promiseth to sacrifice many skins of beasts, kettles, hatchets, beads, knives, and other the best things they have to the fiend, if he will come to help the party diseased. (1910:343–44).

The powwaw's skills as a healer were linked with his or her ability to summon the aid of spirit-helpers to discern the cause of illness, and to use his or her power to draw sickness out of the body. According to Winslow, "if they be curable (as they say) he toucheth it not, but *askooke*, that is the snake, or *wobsacuck*, the eagle, sitteth on his shoulder, and licks the same" (1910:343). Powwaws were also thought to shoot a "bone" into the ill person and to make use of serpents in their curing (Eliot and Mayhew 1834:202–204). The role of powwaws in mourning and burial is not well known, however. Although prominent in curing rituals, powwaws did not figure in descriptions of mourning and burial practices. As dream-travelers and consorts of manitou, they may well have been forced to avoid the places where the "dream soul" began its journey to the afterworld.

Pawwaws performed shamanic divinatory rituals during periods of crisis such as before battle (Ward 1905:67; Stiles 1916:232). Their "repertoire" included induced visions read as good or bad omens, dream-soul journeys, and looking, with the help of their guardian spirits, at events in the past, future, or at a distance. Powwaws' skills in discerning the causes of illness were also linked to their abilities to predict the future and even to identify thieves and murderers (M. Mayhew 1694:12; Hopkins 1911:35–36). Pawwaws and pniese with such powers may have been sought out by sachems, as was true among the Powhatan (Williamson 1993). Hobbomok, a pniese who lived with the Pilgrims for many years, may have been employed by Massasoit as an agent with superior powers of divination and insight (Shuffelton 1976:111–12; Nanepashemet 1993a). Divining and prophesizing, often associated with spirit possession (Underhill 1965:85), are commonly practiced by shamans among Algonquian-speaking people. Powwaws were also wonder-workers. Wood wrote that

> if we may believe the Indians who report of one Passaconaway that he can make the water burn, the rocks move, the trees dance, and metamorphise himself into a flaming man. (1977:101)

Shamans/powwaws embodied and wielded the power of the forces of the other-than-human worlds that bounded those of true humans. Shamans were closely associated with water and beings of the under(water) world (Speck 1919:281). The great Penobscot shaman John Neptune, for example, had seven spirit helpers, but the principle one was an eel (Snow 1976:284). Several seventeenth-century accounts note that southern New England powwaws included snakes or eels and other water-dwellers among their "familiars" (Wilson 1834:19–20; Whitfield 1834:186). Wood recounted an eyewitness' story about a powwaw's curing:

> he wrapped a piece of cloth about the foot of the lame man [and] upon that wrapping a beaver skin through which he—laying his mouth to the beaver skin—by his sucking charms he brought out the stump which he spat into a tray of water. (1977:101)

In this cure, the skin of a water-dweller, the beaver, is employed, and the sickness-causing wooden stump is vitiated in water as well. Other water-dwelling species, fish and shellfish, recur in stories of Mausop, the giant shaman-like culture hero of southern New England. He, and the culture hero known as Wetucks, could walk on water and sometimes transformed humans into water-dwelling creatures. A Pequot shaman is said to have planned to swim underwater to destroy English pinnaces on the eve of the Pequot war (LaFantasie 1988:54). Powwaws often sought to make rain: "if the yeere proove drie . . . They have great and solemne meetings at one high place, to supplicate their gods; and to beg raine (Williams 1936:67; see also Winslow 1841:366).

Shamanic associations with the under(water) world thus existed not only with snakes, eels, fishes, and other water-dwellers, but with water itself. The powerful powwaw/sachem Passaconaway

> would goe under water to the further side of a river to broade for any man to undertake with a breath & deluding the company with casting a mist before their eies that see him enter in and come out . . . likewise by our English in the heat of all summer to make Ice appeare in a bowle of faire water. (Morton 1947:25–26)

Water, serpents, and their associations with the underworld, were also closely tied to Abbomocho or Chepi, and thus were sources of great power. Substances derived from water or water-dwellers, particularly shell, were likewise symbolically significant. Gifts and "payment" to powwaws for curing, divination, and protection were often comprised of this substance, and shells and shell beads frequently appeared as grave goods as well (Hamell 1987:75) (see chapter ten). The connection between shamanism, serpents, and shell was so compelling as to survive in southern New England folklore well into the nineteenth century. A tradition recorded on Nantucket recounts that the body of a malicious sorcerer would not stay buried until a whelk shell was placed in each of its hands (Jenks 1827, cited in Little 1986:51; see also Simmons 1986).

Also among the powwaw's spirit-helpers were denizens of the upper or sky world, particularly the crow and the eagle. As Simmons has pointed out, the crow had strong affiliations with Cautantouwit, a sky-being associated with light, life, warmth, agricultural products, and the southwest (1970:61). "Wealth" objects used by powwaws additionally included substances associated with the sky world such as blue trade beads and naturally occurring crystals, thought to be the products of thunderbolts (R. Williams 1936). The rich polyphony of sky symbols employed and embodied by powwaws were also linked to the strong association, previously mentioned, between birds, pipes, and tobacco smoking among shamans (Von Gernet and Timmons 1987:38). Perhaps powwaws painted themselves with bird designs (Wood 1977:85). They certainly called upon manitou/birds for their cures and prophesies (eg., Whitfield 1834:186), and their soul flights made shaman/powwaws birdlike as well. Domesticated birds, like dogs, were also associated with shamanic and transformative ritual since at least the Middle Woodland period (eg., Kerber et al. 1989:165; Butler and Hadlock 1949). Throughout southern New England, birds, especially the Thunderbird, also figured prominently in shamanic-inspired pictographs, which appear on petroglyphs, and in amulets.

Pictographs and Shamanic Practice

Pictographic art has been interpreted as a "record" of the visions of shamans, although it apparently has no sequential order and cannot be "read" as are similar images on birchbark scrolls, for example. Vastokas and Vastokas argue that special sites were chosen for such significant images, including rocky cliffs, boulders, and outcroppings with clefts, holes, or crevices, associated with the haunts of guardian spirits and mythological beings and with their emergence from the underworld or sky world (1973). Pictographic motifs from all Algonquian-speaking areas appear to reflect shared shamanic practice and experience, and, perhaps, shared underlying cosmologies. Images include "haloed" heads, associated with the solar deities or "ecstatic" shamanistic experience; snakes; shaman figures with outstretched hands or carrying objects such as bags or rattles; thunderbirds; and various animal representations including turtles and deer (Vastokas and Vastokas 1973:62–65; 92–103; 113).

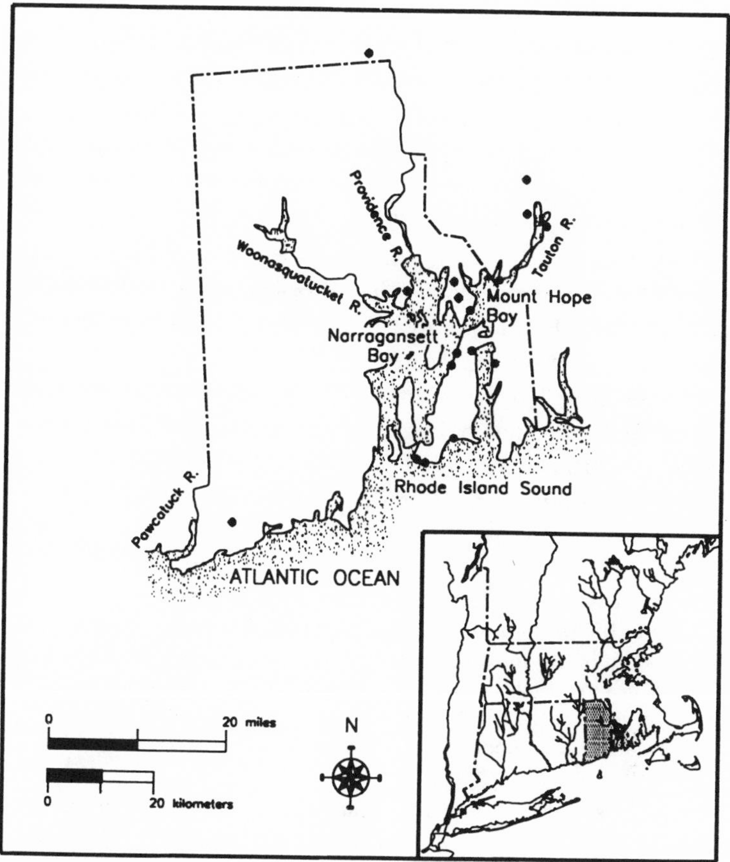

Map 12. Map of petroglyph sites, southern New England. (After Delabarre 1928.)

Pictographs in southern New England have received little scholarly attention. Their age is unknown, and no ethnographic accounts survive that explain their meaning or creation. It seems clear, however, that the pictographs are strongly associated with shamanic practice and provide evidence for a long history of such practice in southeastern New England. Widespread "visual literacy," and a generalized knowledge of the meaning of these signs during the Late Woodland period, no doubt provided a source of shared understanding between otherwise separated polities, and underlay the practice of ritual as well.

Images from southern New England petroglyphs, most of which are located on rocks jutting out into water, support the argument for strong shamanistic ideology in this region during the Woodland period, particularly in the area historically occupied by the Narragansett and Pokanoket. (Map 12)

The most well-known of these, the Dighton Rock petroglyphs, attracted the attention of English observers as early as 1680, when John Danforth, minister at Dorchester, drew an illustration and wrote a description of them now preserved in the British Museum. It reads:

> the uppermost of the Engravings of a Rock in the river Assoonet six miles below Taunton in New England. Taken out sometime in October 1680 by John Danforth. It is reported from the Tradition of old Indians, that there came a wooden house, (& men of another country in it) swimming up the river Asonet, that fought the Indians & slew their Saunchem, &c . . . (quoted in Delabarre 1928:30)

Ezra Stiles, close to a century later, recorded similar markings throughout southern New England (Stiles 1916; Delabarre 1928:204ff.). (Fig. 16)

Images recorded at the Solon, Maine petroglyphs (Snow 1976), include many with sexual connotations, including ithyphallic males, sexually receptive females, and abstract male and female genitalia. Representations of female genitalia may be depicted on the Dighton rock, Among the Portsmouth, Rhode Island, petroglyphs, or at Mark Rock in Warwick, Rhode Island (Figs. 18–19). Snow attributes the marked prominence of sexual motifs at Solon to the strong asso-

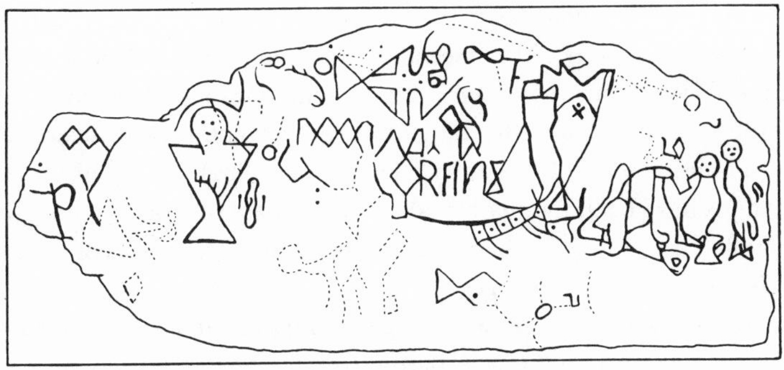

Fig. 16. Dighton Rock. (After Delabarre 1928.)

ciations between shamanism and eroticism (1976). In a like manner, Vastokas and Vastokas also argue that at the Peterborough, Ontario petroglyphs,

> the female images . . . might be interpreted as materializations of the manitous or spirits of nature and the male figures as representations of shamans in their capacity as phallic creatures . . . the Algonkian shaman is capable of penetrating other worlds, of entering and making communication with the spiritual world in order to foster the fertility and well-being of animals and of men . . . the site itself, a pierced and perforated rock, may be read as an ideal feminine symbol; it is a symbolic uterus and a means of access for the shaman to the hidden power or sexual energy of nature upon which he can draw for the benefit of mankind. (1973:89)

Several of the markings on the Dighton Rock might have a similar interpretation.

At the Solon petroglyph, one of the phalli has wings, and fifteen other birds are depicted as well—some with human-like forms or triangular-shaped torsos (Snow 1976:287). A number of petroglyphs and amulets, reported from sites in Maine, southern New England, and Long Island, also depict this "anthropomorph with birdlike attributes" (Hedden 1991:42), and are said to be "Thunderbirds" or shamans with special connections to Thunderbirds in Algonquian belief (Schoolcraft 1853). Similar representations have been located throughout the region stretching from Holt's Point, New Brunswick, to Thunder Bay, Michigan (Cleland et al. 1984). Many of these designs have been found on shale disks, some well-worn as though handled frequently. Such disks are often found near bodies of water (Hedden 1991:47) (Fig. 17).

In several of these depictions, patterning in the chest area corresponds with many images dating from at least 1200 A.D. in the Great Lakes area (Cleland et al. 1984), which show the cosmic tree that connects the heavens and the deeps to the plane of the earth. These hatched lines are also thought to represent the concept, present in but not limited to Algonquian cosmology, of several ranked tiers of progressively more powerful and distant spiritual powers in the heavens (1984).

In Maine, triangular bodied anthropomorphs with bird-like attributes appear ca. 1000 A.D. and become more frequent through time. In the earliest phase, they are "semi-naturalistic" but become increasingly abstract and abbreviated (Hedden:1991:43–44). These "later" abstract images appear in southern New England on amulets, pendants, shale disks, and as part of ceramic designs—such as the figure incised on a ceramic sherd from Martha's Vineyard dating from 800 A.D. to 1300 A.D. (Petersen, cited in Hedden 1991:44). Two thunderbird amulets recovered from sites in northern Massachusetts and New Hampshire are made of imported metals, and thus are evidence of the persistence of the thunderbird motif into the contact period.

The Thunderbird is always associated with, and structurally opposed to, the horned serpent, underwater serpent, or underwater "panther." The horned serpent, also common in pictographs, has numerous associations, not simply with the powers of evil and darkness, but also with the energy of life and the powers of

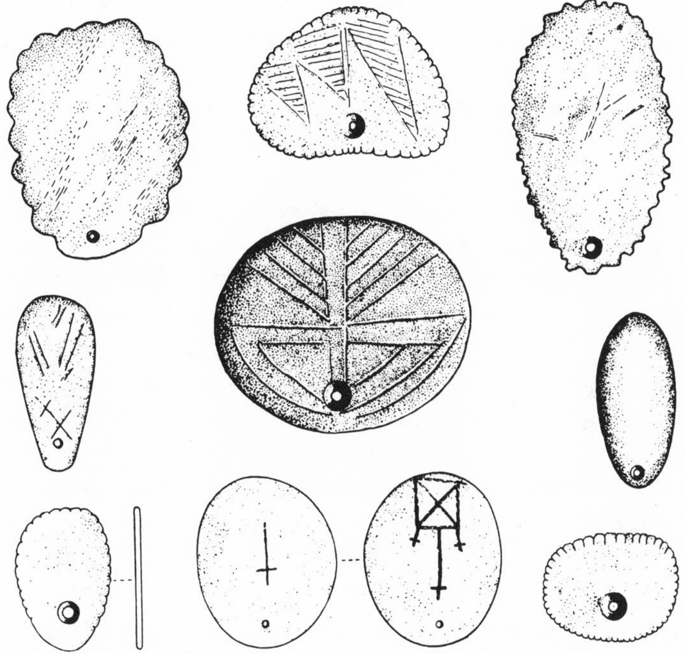

Fig. 17. Amulets, southern New England. (After Willoughby 1935.)

regeneration, cunning, and subtlety. At the Peterborough petroglyphs, some of the carved snakes appear with "eggs," also symbolic of fertility, (Vastokas and Vastokas 1973:97), and several images of serpents "emerge" from natural fissures in the rock, as do those at Dighton rock that were illustrated by Delabarre. As Mundkur (1983:276) eloquently demonstrates, the serpent is a nearly universal symbol of supernatural forces almost always associated with water, a connection clearly made in Algonquian cosmology as well. Other portable images of horned or underwater serpents have also been recovered from Cape Cod and Long Island (see Fig. 13).

Another sacred reptile was the turtle, often a symbol of earth, motherhood, and fertility, and found in many pictographs in Algonquian territories. Turtles appear in several plastic media in southern New England: on petroglyphs, on pendants and charms, ornamenting wooden bowls, and even forming a seventeenth-century button-mold.

If pictographic images were indeed associated with shamanic activities, they communicate something of the complexity of cosmological beliefs and the embodiment of those beliefs in the social world. Powwaws served their communities as advocates and champions in relations with the supernatural and in their connections with the manitous who appeared in animal or anthropomorphic form. Pictographs are not so much a "record" of their role and function as they are a "conversation" to which other-than-human powers, the powwaws as intermediaries, and those who "read" the pictographic signs, all contributed.

The Pniese and the Overseer of Worship

The ancient, widespread, and comprehensive ideology and practice of shamanism was complemented, especially in coastal southern New England, by the development of other classes of religious specialists. According to Edward Winslow there were three classes of people to whom powerful manitou appeared:

> [Abbomocho] appeareth most ordinary and is most conversant with three sorts of people. One, I confess I neither know by name nor office directly; of these they have few, but esteem highly of them, and think that no weapon can kill them; another they call by the name powah, and the third pniese. (1910:343).

A Pniese was also said to be invulnerable to ordinary attack (E. Winslow 1910). Invulnerability is often thought to be a characteristic of those individuals whose quest for sacred knowledge has progressed through a series of stages, sometimes marked with secret ceremonies,

Figs. 18 and 19. Drawings by Ezra Stiles of the Portsmouth petroglyphs, 1767. (Courtesy of the Beinecke Rare Book and Manuscript Library, Yale University.)

or by membership within an elite society of adepts. The Midewiwin society of the Ojibwe was one such graded, secret society in which shamans who advanced through a fourth grade were believed to be supernaturally potent, combining all the abilities of the shaman: healing, wonderworking, use of herbals, soul flight, and transformation (Underhill 1965:93). Perhaps the pniese and those other, unnamed practitioners represented a similar society of highly skilled shamans among the Ninnimissinuok.

It is likely that at least among the coastal people there were additionally religious practitioners whose skills were more priestly than shamanic, those individuals who were "proprietors of a memorized ritual passed down by inheritance and not received directly by vision" (Underhill 1965:93). These included the Narragansett *taupowaüog*, or wise men, as well as the previously described nanouwetea and mockuttasuit. Never described as a *powwaw*, the mockuttasuit was a man of the 'the chiefest esteeme' who wrapped and buried the bodies of the dead (R. Williams 1936:203).

Differences between groups may also have been reflected in the variety of religious practitioners and the rituals over which they presided. Edward Winslow was told of one ceremony typical of Narragansett religiosity occuring in

> a great spacious house, wherein only some few (that are, as we may term them, priests) come. Thither, at certain known times, resort all their people, and offer almost all the riches they have to their gods, as kettles, skins, hatchets, beads, knives etc., all which are cast by the priests into a great fire that they make in the midst of the house, and there consumed to ashes. (1910:345)

As Winslow pointed out, these customs were not universal, although the Pokanoket of his day wished "their sachems would appoint the like" (345).

The panoply of religious specialists mirrored a hierarchy of spiritual powers, ranging from the most familiar and proximate to the most distant and disinterested. The spatial hierarchy of proximity and distance was paralleled by a hierarchy of power and prestige, reinforced by symbolically potent objects of wealth given as gifts to powwaws, or "sacrificed" to their guardian spirits and helpers. The notion of sacrifice, with its strong associations with wealth and health, was also linked to the rituals of the Ninnimissinuok. It is ritual that forms the subject of the following chapter.

10.

Ritual

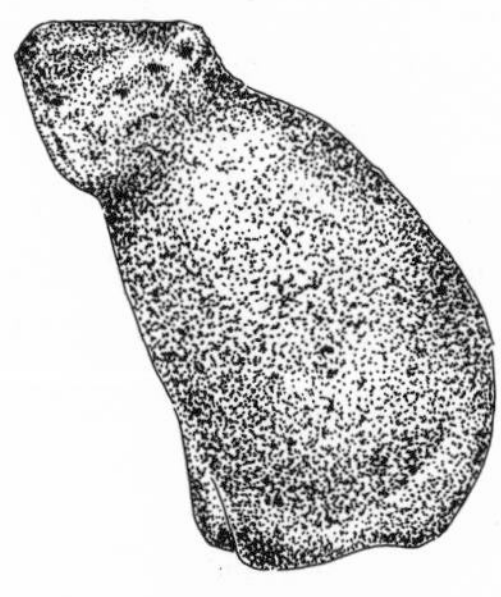

In ritual, the beliefs and symbolic relations that made sense of the world for the Ninnimissinuok were played out in public contexts. Ritual condensed and celebrated all that was to them significant, reaffirming the social order, and society's relations with the supernatural as well. Rituals of many sorts were performed by them according to season and need. These included calendrical rituals, life-cycle rituals, and critical rites (enacted during plagues, droughts, war, and famine). Through motion, sound, the creation of sacred space, and an elaborated use of symbols, ritual embodied and interpreted daily experience, and reflected cosmological principles also expressed in social and economic relations. In structure, process, and in the symbols employed, rituals functioned both to reproduce cultural forms, and in some cases, to transform those relationships on which they were phenomenologically based.

The Physical Correlates of Communitas: Sound and Motion in Ritual

Basic elements of ritual among the Ninnimissinuok included repetitious sound and vigorous body motion (see also Underhill 1965:107, 111). Through these actions powwaws and their audiences sought the aid of manitou. Sound and motion played an important role in all ritual activities, including curing. William Wood wrote:

> the parties that are sick or lame being brought before them, the powwow sitting down, the rest of the Indians giving attentive audience to his imprecations and invocations, and after the violent expression of many a hideous bellowing and groaning, he makes a stop, and then all the auditors with one voice utter a short canto. (Wood 1977:101)

Other rituals were marked by the constant repetition of words or short phrases. Sacred gambling games, for example, were accompanied by a monotonous repetition of words such as *hub, hub, hub* ('come, come, come') such that "They may be heard play[ing] at this game a quarter of a mile off" (104).

Dance was also basic to a wide range of activities whose sacred quality was invisible to many English observers. The Nipmuck were said to

> delight much in their dancings and revellings; at which time he that danceth (for they dance singly, the men and not the women, the rest singing, which is their chief musick) will give a way in his frolick, all that ever he hath, gradually, some to one, and some to another, according to his fancy and affection. And then, when he hath stripped himself of all he hath, and is weary, another succeeds and doth the like: so successively, one after another, night after night, resting and sleeping in the days; and so continue sometimes a week together. (Gookin 1806:153)

Gookin added, "they use great vehemency in the motion of their bodies, in their dances; and sometimes the men dance in greater numbers in their war dances." (153)

The emotional and psychological purpose of repetitious sound and body motion in ritual, well documented in other cultures, was to create or reinforce the experience of *communitas*, the ties that bind social groups together and lend cosmic justification to those social ties (Turner 1969).

Ritual and the Creation of Sacred Space

Other diffuse symbols contributed to the cosmological significance of ritual. The formation of sacred circles of spectators, or the construction of special circular or oblong houses or "arbors," marked the celebration of many types of ritual. Among the Narragansett, a ritual lodge or *qunnèkamuck*, sometimes two hundred feet long, was constructed near the "court," or *kittcickaũick*, during the harvest feast, wherein people danced and gave away goods. In addition, an arbor or playhouse, the *puttuckquapúonck*, oblong and nearly twenty feet high, was set up for gambling, a structure on which people hung goods staked on the players (R. Williams 1936:179; 180). Ritual structures were also associated with first fruit and green corn ceremonials throughout the area (Witthoft 1949). Special mourning houses were built (LaFantasie 1988:323), and other activities of sacred significance, including the sweat house and the menstrual lodge, may have been variations on this theme. These structures represented symbolic "thresholds," as did the ritual lodges of central Algonquian speaking people: those places where the boundaries between the three separate worlds of the cosmos intersected and where passage from one world to the other was facilitated. All of these structures marked the passage of players and audience alike from a state of profanity to that of the sacred.

The use of "arbors" and the practice of "lying among the trees," recorded for one or more rituals among the Narragansett, suggest that trees contributed to the sacred landscape. A Narragansett origin myth links people with trees, and the dreaded Mohawks to the west were known both as "tree-eaters" and "men-eaters" (R. Williams 1936:13, 16, 49). Trees linked the three realms of the underworld, the surface world, and the sky world, and places where they grew were likely spots for encounters with the powerful other-than-human beings who dwelt there. Like the sacred spaces created to mark significant historical or mythical events (see chapter four), these trees created or marked spaces resonating with cultural meanings that contributed to the power and cohesive function of rituals as they reaffirmed the cosmic order.

Consumption and Its Transformations in Ritual

Feasting and fasting too were actions redolent with meaning within the ritual context. The significance of food, eating, and intimate ownership discussed in chapter four "fed" an enhanced sense of membership within the social group. Most of the rituals described for the Ninnimissinuok included descriptions of feasting, often for days on end (e.g., R. Williams 1936; Wood 1977; D. Gookin 1806). Food has clear associations with abundance, health, and life; fasting with sacrifice, loss, and death. The shared and joyous consumption of food, as well as its avoidance, marked equally the prodigality of spiritual relations and their cyclical renewal.

Sacred Smoke

The symbolic and shamanic associations of smoking described in chapter 9 endowed ritual and everyday practice with sacred qualities. Roger Williams mentions that people were "joyfull in meeting of any in travell, and will strike fire either with stones or stickes, to take Tobacco, and discourse a little together" (1936:14, 45, 73). Newcomers were offered tobacco, and smoking accompanied all lengthy and solemn orations. In the eighteenth century, Native Christian services on Nantucket ended with the passing of a smoking pipe (Bragdon 1989). (Fig. 20).

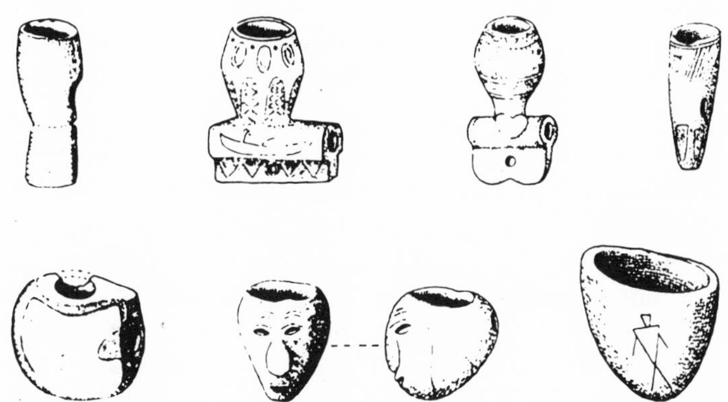

Fig. 20. Effigy smoking pipes, southern New England. (After Willoughby 1935.)

Health, Wealth, and Well-being

Wealth was linked to ideas of well-being among the Northeastern Woodlands people. The act of giving away wealth ensured future gifts, and was not only an exchange, but a contract and a reaffirmation of ties between realms or with the powerful denizens of those realms. Such reciprocal relationships were consonant with relations within the social world as well. The correlation between wealth and health was furthermore one that linked individuals to their communities. The well-being of each member was intimately tied to that of the community of which she or he was a part.

Cyclicity and the Alternations between Death and Renewal

Underlying much ritual activity was the Ninnimissinuok sense of time, which was cyclical, rather than linear. Passing time was experienced as alternating between two opposed, but structurally linked, periods of death and renewal. Such oppositions were expressed within specific rituals, and in the sequence of major rituals throughout the calendrical cycle. Crucial ceremonies took place in winter, mid-summer, and autumn, each reflecting various stages of passage from death to regeneration.

Risking the Cosmos

Gambling, commonly mentioned as part of ritual events, took three forms: the "dice" game *hubhub*; the counting game played with rushes called *puim*; and placing bets on players in football or sidebets on the outcome of *puim* or *hubhub* games played by another pair of players. Puim was a game with rules "like unto the English cards" using fifty to sixty shortened reeds distributed among the players (Williams 1936:177). The reeds were somehow shuffled in the players' hands and assigned value according to "a kind of arithmatick" (Wood 103–104). Hubhub was a game in which peach stones painted black on one side and white on the other were tossed in a shallow basket, and the players gambled on how many of each color would "show." A remarkably similar game was also played among the agricultural Iroquois, who linked success in the game to successful harvest. The color symbolism of black (death, cold, winter, frost) and white (light, life, warmth, summer) was central to a game "propitiatory to the force vital to the successful growth of crops" (Blau 1967:36). According to Ceci (1978:310), "The game may be seen as a replay of an environmental versus human drama of critical importance, a ritual structured by the same planes of crisscrossing binary oppositions inherent to the Pleiades annual schedule, that is east: west, summer: winter, light: darkness, warmth: frost, health: deformity, life: death, and of course, Pleiades: maize." This, she argues, explains the "tension" and "excitement" with which the game was played, emotions also noted among the Natives of southern New England playing the similar game of hubhub.

Gambling also took place at meetings for "play." At these meetings a ball game that pitted "town against town" was commonly accompanied by the construction of an arbor wherein gambling took place. Teams vied for rich "goals" of money, jewelry, furs, and other goods (R. Williams 1936:179–80). Geertz's classic analysis of Balinese gambling argues that the cockfight is an arena in which social categories are contested and status is symbolically "risked" (1973). For the people of southern New England it was also the continuity of life that was "at risk."

The sacred quality of gambling was marked by the gain and loss of wealth objects, and the use of charms and invocations to guardian spirits or manitou. Roger Williams wrote that during games of chance:

> The chiefe gamesters amongst them much desire to make their gods side with them in their Games . . . therefore I have seene them keepe as a precious stone a piece of Thunderbolt, which is like unto a Chrystall, which they dig out of the ground under some tree. (1936:178)

Private Rituals with Public Meaning

Participants in rituals and sacred activities observed special customs of dress and body decoration. Wood observed:

> When they go to their wars, it is their custom to paint their faces with diversity of colors, some being all black as jet, some red, some half red and half black, some black and white, others spotted with diverse kinds of colors, being all disguised to their enemies to make them more terrible to their foes, putting likewise their rich jewels, pendants, and wampompeag, to put them mind they fight not only for their children, wives, and lives, but likewise for their goods, lands, and liberties. (1977:103)

It seems equally likely that the symbolic significance of colors, and of wealth in the form of wampum, crystal, red, blue, and white stones, bone, and metal, made this dress both a source of power and protection, and a reference to the cosmic implications of war as part of the cycle of death and renewal. In a similar manner, gamblers and players in the sacred "football" games bedecked themselves with jewelry and painted their faces and bodies as if for war (104).

Shamanic Rituals of Divination and Transformation

Cross-cutting the sensory dimensions of scent, sound, and motion, the symbolic references to time, space, and the role of human intervention in cosmic alternations between death and renewal with which rituals among the Ninnimissinuok resonated were the purposes for which the rituals were intended. Rituals were public or private, divinatory or propitiatory, celebratory or despairing. Powwaws generally presided over those "darker" rituals associated with illness.

In these rituals, wealth was also linked to recovery and health. When curing was accomplished, both the people of northern Massachusetts Bay, described by William Wood, and the Natives of the middle Connecticut River had a similar ritual. According to de Laet:

> it appears that the Sickanames before mentioned, make a sort of sacrifice. They have a hole in a hill in which they place a kettle full of all sorts of articles that they either have by them or can procure, as a part of their treasures. Then a snake comes in, then they all depart, and the *Manittou*, that is the devil, comes in the night and takes the kettle away, according to the statement of the Koutsinacka, or devil-hunter, who presides over the ceremony. (1909:87)

Josselyn too noted that

> if the sick recover, they send rich gifts, their Bowes and Arrowes, Wompompers, Mohacks, Beaver-skins or other rich furs to the eastward, where there is a vast rock not far from the shore, having a hole in it of an unsearchable profundity, into which they throw them. (1988:96)

Sometimes the powwaw received gifts or wealth "if they recover, then because their sickness was chargeable, they send corn and other gifts unto them, at a certain appointed time, whereat they feast and dance, which they call commoco (Winslow 1910:348). Indeed, much wealth might be expended in curing, causing debtors to plead poverty (R. Williams 1936:).

Powwaws also presided over those rites intended to predict the outcome of events, especially those preparatory to war. Mary Rowlandson, captured during the attack on Deerfield by Metacom or King Philip's forces in 1675, recorded the following ritual prior to a raid on Sudbury:

Before they went to that fight, they got a company together to Powaw; the manner was as followeth. There was one that kneeled upon a Deerskin, with the company round him in a ring who kneeled, and striking upon the ground with their hands, and with sticks, and muttering and humming with their mouths; besides him who kneeled in the ring, there also stood one with a Gun in his hand: Then he on the Deer-skin made a speech, and all manifested assent to it; and so they did many times together. Then they bade him with the Gun go out of the ring, which he did, but when he was out, they called him in again; but he seemd to make a stand, they called the more earnestly, till he returned again; Then they all sang. Then they gave him two Guns, in either hand one: And so he on the Deerskin began again; and at the end of every sentence in his speaking, they all assented, humming or muttering with their mouthes, and striking upon the ground with their hands. Then they bade him with the two Guns go out of the ring again; which he did, a little way. Then they called him in again, but he made a stand; so they called him with greater earnestness; but he stood reeling and wavering as if he know not whither he should stand or fall, or which way to go. Then they called him with exceeding great vehemency, all of them, one an another; after a little while he turned in, staggering as he went, with his arms stretched out, in either hand a gun. As soon as he came in, they all sang and rejoyced exceedingly a while. And then he upon the Deer-skin, made another speech unto which they all assented in a rejoicing manner: and so they ended their business, and forthwith went to Sudbury-fight. (Rowlandson 1913:152–153)

If, through the aid of trance and dream, powwaws determined that success was unlikely, war parties were disbanded or raids delayed (Simmons 1976:234).

Other ritual actions associated with war referenced the sacred alternation between death and renewal, particularly in the treatment of prisoners, and of the slain bodies of honored enemies. Torture of prisoners was described by Josselyn only for the "eastern" Indians (1988:104), although it is possible that the Englishman Captain Stone, whose execution by the Pequots in 1633 was said by contemporaries to have been one cause of the Pequot war, was "roasted" alive (Clap 1970:363). If torture was uncommon, however, the taking of war trophies was not:

all that are slaine are commonly slain with great Valour and Courage: for the Conquerour ventures into the thickest, and brings away the Head of his Enemy. (R. Williams 1936:189)

According to Wood,

if they return conquerors, they carry the heads of their chief enemies that they slay in the wars, it being the custom to cut off their heads, hands, and feet to bear home to their wives and children as true tokens of their renowned victory. (1977:103)

Ritual cannibalism may have occurred occasionally as well. Uncas of the Mohegan ate a piece of the shoulder of his newly slain enemy Miantonimi (DeForest 1964:198). Yet others of the Ninnimissinuok were said to despise and fear the Iroquoians, particularly the Mohawks, for their cannibalistic practices (Gookin 1806:162; Williams 1936:13, 16, 49; Salisbury 1993).

Public Rituals and the Health of the Body Social

The aforementioned rituals can be generally characterized as personal or unstructured, and associated with what was probably an ancient and widespread shamanic ideology. Another class of rituals was also common among the Ninnimissinuok of coastal regions, community rituals that were presided over by sachems and other high-status "overseers" of religion. Although formalized, these rituals encompassed and referenced those general and cosmic principles previously discussed, in the service of community well-being.

A major Narragansett ritual took place around harvest time, an event that Roger Williams called "their chiefest Idoll of all for sport and game" (1936:180). At that ritual, which occurred in times of peace, the Indians erected an arbor

> upon a plaine neer the Court where many thousands, men and women meet, where he that goes in danceth in sight of all the rest and is prepared with money, coats, small breeches, knifes, or what hee is able to reach to, and gives these things away to the poore, who yet must particularly beg and say *Cowequetúmmous*, that is, I beseech you. (180)

Daniel Gookin noted a similar harvest ritual among the Nipmuck, and added darkly that "much impiety is committed at such times" (1806:153).

Another feast occurred "especially" in winter "for then (as the Turke saith of the Christian, rather the Antichristian, they run mad once a yeare) in their kind of Christmas feasting" (R. Williams 1936:127). Finally there was "*Keesaqúnnamun*, a kind of solemne publike meeting, wherein they lie under the trees, in a kind of Religious observation, and have a mixture of Devotions and sports." Williams does not say when Keesaqúnnamun was held, but it may have been that "most Sollemne meeting for play" observed by him among the Narragansett in June of 1638 (LaFantasie 1988:160). Another ceremony that may have been Keesaqúnnamun was enacted in August of 1637 when the Narragansett sachems Conanacus and Miantonimi refused an English demand because "[they were] busy ten or twelve days together . . . in a strange kind of solemnity, wherein the sachims eat nothing but at night, and all the Natives round the country were feasted." To another correspondent Williams wrote of the same ceremony, saying "Miantunnomu . . . replies they have bene this fortnight busie that is keeping a kind of Christmas" (La Fantasie 110–11). Hints at additional calendrical rituals include references to spring "games" at fishing camps (T. Morton 1947) and to green corn ceremonies, conducted in mid-to-late summer (Witthoft 1949:9–11).

Interspersed among these seasonal, annually recurring rites, were privately sponsored ceremonies of public importance and sacred significance. In particular, high status Pokanoket and Narragansett men and women sponsored the *Nickommo*, or 'feast,' performed "after harvest, after hunting, when they enjoy a caulme of Peace, health, Plenty, Prosperity." Nickommo feasts were hosted by men and women who provided lavishly for all guests,

> he or she that makes this *Nickòmmo* feast or dance, besides the feasting of sometimes twenty, fifty and hundreth, yea I have seene neere a thousand persons at one of these feasts, they give I say a great quantity of money, and all sort of their goods (according to and sometimes beyond their Estate) In severall small parcells of goods, or money to the value of eighteen pence, two Shillings, or thereabouts, to one person; and that person that receives this gift, upon the receiving of it goes out, and hollowes thrice for the health and prosperity of the party that gave it, the Mr. or Mistris of the Feast. (R. Williams 1936:128–29)

Of themselves, the sponsors said *Nowemausitteem*, "I give away at the Worship" (128)

The distribution of important rituals and privately sponsored feasts throughout the seasonal cycle marks the transition from death to rebirth and renewal while underlining their essential unity; so too each ritual within itself marked that same sublime relationship. Loss, generally represented by "sacrifice" of goods to guests, in gambling or to members of an opposing team, was balanced by the gains of future well-being. For renewal is achieved only through loss, and vice-versa; one implies and requires the other. The public nature of these events ensured that all people shared in the general gains associated with sacrifice and loss, all had such losses explained and justified, and all participated in the effort to maintain the balance of life.

The cycle of death and regeneration was also referenced in rituals marking changes in life course, particularly revolving around birth, puberty, sickness, and death. Black ashes smeared on the faces of shamans, mourners, those tending the terminally ill, newborn babies, and those preparing for war signified the liminality of these states of being that involved crossing the thresholds of human (social) life. Soon after birth, babies were washed as well as "sooted," and there is some evidence to suggest that Native women sought locations near water in which to give birth (Plane 1990:21). Van Gennep was the first to point out the significance of washing as a transition ritual at birth (1960:52), one way of marking the threshold between life and death.

In summary, rituals among the Ninnimissinuok were either personal and shamanic, aimed at tapping the powers of manitou or public and calendrical, and only diffusely directed toward supernatural forces. Underlying both were cosmological principles of the cycle of renewal and the role of wealth in promoting group and individual health and well-being. Both sorts of rituals also marked a hierarchy of forces, nearby and distant, personal and disinterested. The intermediary role of religious specialists also gave them special prominence as advocates and emissaries to the realms of manitou, to whom ordinary people must go for help, just as guests at Nickommo feasts became supplicants to their hosts. In this way ritual confirmed and justified both cosmological principles and social relations. Yet rituals were not static, nor did they simply cement already existing relationships. Ritual, during which the meanings of symbols are constantly revised, also serves as a "litmus test" of change—of symbolic transformation (Turner 1969; Geertz 1973; Sahlins 1985). In the concluding section, I review the rituals associated with burial as evidence for the dynamism of social experience among the Ninnimissinuok and the way in which ritual reflected the increasingly marked social differentiation characteristic of their society in the early seventeenth century.

Conclusions

It seems appropriate to end this analysis where it began, with archaeological evidence, evidence for the nature of Native life following the establishment of English colonies in southern New England by the middle of the seventeenth century. The fact that available documents were written by Europeans does not obviate the necessity for archaeology, but rather makes archaeology a valuable corrective to the bias of their observations. Through the lens of archaeological data, the details of each documented "contact" event give way to regularities in patterns of ritual behavior after European colonization was well entrenched, patterns which were consistent with those recognizable in daily practice, in social relations, governance, and cosmology that obtained in the earliest years of colonization.

At the same time, mortuary ritual, and its implied behavioral correlates, can be placed within the broader context of theories of culture change, many of which have been advanced to explain such ritual practice in New England. Mortuary ritual is well suited to this task because it is partially reflected in archaeological remains, which form an independent source of data concerning response to "contingent" events. The archaeology of ritual demonstrates that the Ninnimissinuok were in fact a people whose post-contact history was in large part independent of that of the English settlers who attempted to subdue, marginalize, and reinvent them.

Woodland Parsimony Transformed

Late Woodland primary burials generally are of flexed, randomly oriented, unadorned, and unaccompanied bodies. They are located in shallow pits near large camps, and rarely occur in clusters. Examples of such burials have been recorded at Nantucket (Leudtke 1980a) and Deerfield (Johnson and Bradley 1987). While their poverty of grave furnishings is frequently interpreted as evidence for the ephemeral and "simple" nature of Native life prior to contact (e.g., Lavin 1988; Ceci 1990), their simplicity may have other explanations. Some burials may have involved only the preliminary treatments of corpses destined for more elaborate secondary burials; alternatively, it is possible, even likely, that only certain of the deceased received specialized treatment. It is also conceivable that people of the Late Woodland period did not employ mortuary ritual to express social differentiation, a not uncommon decision among chiefly people (Earle 1987:291).

By the mid-1500s A.D., however, primary burials were uniformly oriented with the heads of the deceased pointing west or southwest, and were accompanied by grave goods of both Native and European origin (although European tools and other "useful" objects were not prominent). These included glass beads, iron objects, ceramics, and especially copper and brass ornaments, wampum beads, and blanks (Tuma 1985:74; Hamell 1987). In the early historic period, such interments were sometimes surrounded by palisades or placed in burial grounds of upwards of two hundred graves (of which five are known) (e.g., Gibson 1980; Simmons 1970; Robinson et al. 1984; McBride 1993).

By the early seventeenth century, while still marking a community consciousness seen earlier in ossuary burials, mortuary practices apparently began to focus on individual qualities and status. In the cemeteries dating to the second and third quarter of the seventeenth century, although all corpses were accompanied by some grave goods, some individuals seem to have been singled out for especially elaborate treatment. In particular, children and adolescents were often buried with what appear to have been the most valuable objects (McBride 1993). In addition, the presence of European goods in graves was more marked. Added to Native-made effigy stone pestles, stone or clay pipes, shell beads, and wampum, were brass and copper kettles and iron axes, as well as European clay pipes. The trend of adding European goods in graves was to increase throughout the seventeenth century (Tuma 1985:75).

Mortuary Ritual: Practice and Premise

According to the earliest written descriptions of mortuary practice among the Ninnimissinuok of the coastal regions, the rituals surrounding the dead were highly elaborated. Thomas Morton said that the Massachusett

> make some monuments, over the place where the corps is interred: But they put a greate difference between persons of noble, and of ignoble, or obscure, or inferior descent . . . For indeed in the grave of the more noble, they put a planck in the bottom for the corps to be layed upon and on each side a plancke, and a plancke upon the top in form of a chest, before they cover the place with earth. This done, they erect some thing over the grave in forme of a hearse cloath . . . they hold impious, and inhumane to deface the monuments of the dead . . . They themselves esteeme of it as piaculum, and have a custome amongst them, to keep their annals: & come at certaine times to lament, & bewaile the losse of their friend. (1947:35–36)

Among the Pokanoket:

> When they bury the dead, they sew up the corpse in a mat, and so put it in the earth. If the party be a sachim, they cover him with many curious mats, and bury all his riches with him, and enclose the grave with a pale. If it be a child, the father will also put his own most special jewels and ornaments in the earth with it; also will cut his hair, and disfigure himself very much, in token of sorrow. (Winslow 1910:348)

The rituals marking the transition from life to death were public, and involved tne construction of visible markers—reminding all who passed that death had occured.

The very burial of bodies (there are, after all, many other ways of disposing of corpses) was also a reminder of the cyclical nature of death and renewal, just as the "burial" of stored foods in underground burial pits was representative of the renewal of life during periods of winter "death." The disposal of the dead in pits, wrapped in mats, shows parallels with storage pits (e.g., compare illustrations in Mills 1991:53 and Bendremer et al. 1991:331). It is possible that storage pits were reused as burial pits as well. Other associations between food storage, food discard, and human remains include the frequent one of burials with shell-midden refuse (Ceci 1990). Claassen (1991) argues that shell middens may in fact have ceremonial and symbolic associations, a plausible idea based on a well-established ritual use of shell.

Constance A. Crosby also links burial and the planting of seed corn:

> there was a continuous flow between the world of the living and the land of Cautantowwit. . . . the physical and the spiritual were joined in a dynamic relationship through the mediation of corn and earth-mother. According to their traditions, the body was planted in the ground from whence corn and other plants sprang, and the soul traveled to the southwest from whence corn originated. The body entered the womb of earth-mother via the grave and enriched her, bringing forth more corn, which the soul returned to the

southwest and joined Cautantowwit and the ancestors, thus enriching the group's tradition. Thus the relationship between birth and death was a cycle of continuous renewal for both the community of the living and the community of the ancestors in Cautantowwits house. (1988:191)

The connection between spiritual power and physical corruption is further marked in the Massachusett word for death, *anit*, which means more precisely 'he who exceeds, or goes beyond, rots,' and is closely associated with *m'anit*, 'sacred, spiritual force, god' (Trumbull 1903:49).

Burial ritual was linked to daily life experience in other ways as well. The fiery destruction, described as a feature of Narragansett chiefly burials, consumed in order to renew. A Narragansett ritual in which all manner of wealth was cast into a fire and burnt (Winslow 1910:344–45), the burning of a Narragansett sachem's house and wealth after the death of his son, are reflections of the same concept of renewal through burning. Like the burning of fields in preparation for planting, or to encourage the return of game and other edible plants, burning corpses and their possessions emphasized the regenerative power of fire (Williamson 1993). The sachem/powwaw Passaconnaway reminded his followers of this with a "conjuring trick": "in winter when there is no greene leaves to be got, [Passaconnaway] will burne an old one to ashes, and putting those into the water, produce a new greene leafe" (Morton 1947).

The southwestern orientation of the body in the grave reflected cosmological notions of directionality. Hamell identifies seven symbolically important directions in the Northeast: centerness, above, below, and north, south, east, and west (1987:68). Each of these was associated with a particular manitou (R. Williams 1936). The southwest was significant among the Ninnimissinuok for it was the direction of Cautanntowit's house (Simmons 1970). Archaeological evidence also demonstrates that the great majority of Late Woodland and early contact period graves and "grave yards" in southern New England were located near or within sight of water (Tuma 1985:101–102), and therefore associated with Hobbomok, the manitou most closely linked to the underworld.

Local and exotic materials derived from water or associated with water-dwellers and used as grave furniture embodied cosmic principles, making them a kind of medicine (Hammell 1987a:67–68). This was also the case for objects associated with the sky world, particularly crystal (R. Williams 1936), blue/green colored metal, stone, and shell. There is ample evidence for the use of such wealth objects endowed with color symbolism in southern New England mortuary ritual. Grave goods in southern New England include white shell beads and ornaments, blue trade beads and purple wampum, and red-gold copper (e.g., Simmons 1970, Gibson 1980; Robinson et al. 1985).

Mortuary Ritual, Social Relations, and Cultural Change

A basic assumption of most interpretations of burial ritual is that bodies were buried with objects appropriate to their "role and status" (e.g., Simmons 1970:44). Another common argument states that those European objects which appeared with greater frequency as burial goods because they were "deemed to be in great favor and short supply" (44). Mortuary remains thus reflect the social organization of the living population and a utilitarian evaluation of trade goods, both of which are thought to be reproduced in the afterlife (Binford 1972; Brenner 1988:148). The patterns of the distribution of grave furniture therefore mark social facts such as the division of labor between men and women, reflected in the types of goods buried with each. Such contrasts in gendered grave furniture are most marked in early seventeenth-century graves in southern New England (e.g., Simmons 1970; Tuma 1985).

A contrasting approach, employed by Ian Hodder (1982:10), argues that burial patterns do not directly reflect social patterns, but instead are ordered ideologically, and can thus reflect the legitimization, masking, or marking of political relations of inequality (Brenner 1988:148). Elise M. Brenner, for example, suggests that at a time of "political instability," such as that which developed in southern New England in the early decades of the seventeenth century as a result of European settlement, "social advertisement in death ritual was expressly overt owing to changing relations of domination, that resulted in status re-ordering and consolidation of new social positions" (150). Political actors and entrepreneurs, in her view, sought status and power through the possession and strategic manipulation of European commodities (see also Thomas 1979, 1985:139, 148). These so-called "big men" (Thomas 1979, 1985; Sahlins 1963) were forced to redistribute wealth to maintain and add to their following (Brenner 1988:152). According to a number of authors, when a community distributes goods in graves "as a strategy to mark political differentiation," it prevents the prestige of certain scarce items from becoming "diluted" (152). In opposition to Simmons (1970), Brenner suggests that wealth was put out of circulation not to provide people with status in the afterlife, or merely to mark their status among the living, but rather to maintain "changing relations of power" within the living community (1988:152).

Another approach to understanding the relationship between mortuary ritual and culture change has been to interpret seventeenth-century burial remains as reflecting resistance to European presence and domination. Basing his argument on documentary sources, Axtell suggests that burial ritual became increasingly important as an expression of Northeastern Native identity vis à vis the European invaders. As the most private of rituals, burials came to represent all that was important about Native culture, and the rights to Native style burial were among those most energetically defended by Native people in southern New England (1985). Robinson et al. have also suggested that the inclusion of Native manufactured goods, beads, wampum, and other symbolically significant objects was a further reflection of resistance to the European presence (1985).

The increasing number of grave goods found in burial grounds in southern New England in the mid-seventeenth century has in a related way been attributed to an increasing need for the "social marking" associated with ethnicity. Ethnicity, commonly associated with the intrusion of a state society (Comaroff and Comaroff 1992), becomes marked as social boundaries harden and as cultural values are contested. Robinson suggests that Narragansett burials dating to before 1640 show less evidence of "social marking" than graves dating 1640–1675—a period when Narragansett assertions of hegemony were challenged and in many cases, ignored (1990:108).

Rejecting the foregoing interpretations as both polarized and politicized, Michael Nassaney suggests that culture contact situations are often subject to conflicting modern interpretations. Most scholars agree, for example, that Native American life changed drastically as a result of contact, yet many modern ethnographers and historical treatments also stress the persistence of Native American ethnic identity and society (Nassaney 1989:84; see also Berkhofer 1976: 102–103). He further suggests that recent interpretations of Native mortuary practices are colored by Native American retribalization in the twentieth century. A more reasonable approach, in his view, is to interpret mortuary ritual in light of the complementarity of accommodation and resistance. He suggests that burial goods be understood "from the point of view of cultural accommodation—that is, that Native people such as the Narragansett chose to incorporate European elements in their world view to rationalize a changing social order" (86). Like Brenner (1988), and following Wolf (1982), he suggests that European goods "provided individual Native Americans with new opportunities for socio-economic mobility outside of their traditional economic roles.

At the same time, Nassaney argues that the economic processes of uneven accumulation within class societies are mediated through a "hegemonic ideology." Accordiong to Eugene Genovese such ideologies are hegemonic because they compel segments of society to define themselves within the ruling system even while resisting it (1974:77). Changes in the way identity was expressed were also accompanied by changes in group identity maintenance through affiliation with the English monarchy, or with Roger Williams (in opposition to the Pilgrims and their allies the Pokanoket) (Nassaney 1989:87; see also Weinstein 1983:81; Little 1981; Grumet 1978; and Robinson 1990). Such processes would have been reflected in the organization of burial grounds and in the grave furniture itself, marking at once the impact of European control, the rise of Native "entrepreneurs," and resistance in the form of symbolically charged objects of Native origin or import.

Other explanations have focused on the ways in which people respond to disastrous events such as the epidemics that ravaged southern New England in 1616–1619 and in 1633. One response to such disasters, which has been well documented cross-culturally, is a florescence of ritual (Starna 1992:515). The increasing quantities of grave goods found in seventeenth-century burial grounds are evidence for such an increasing emphasis on ritual, associated with the effects of European disease and the perceived lack of efficacy of Native curing techniques (Robinson et al. 1984). The systematization and intensification of mortuary ritual are also interpreted as means of revitalizing a rapidly changing (perhaps declining) set of beliefs (Nassaney 1989:88).

However, burial goods also reflect the ideological aspects of Late Woodland period belief systems, which appear to have remained intact. As Hamell argues, the Indians' response to Europeans and European trade goods was both ideationally premised and aesthetically motivated. It appears that traditional "mythical reality" and its dependent social, exchange, mortuary, and ritual subsystems were initially reified by European contact and European trade goods (1987:71). Native people were not childlike in their desire for baubles, and did not universally accept the technological superiority of European goods. According to Hamell, "the preferential disposal of European trade goods in protohistoric mortuary contexts and the differential distribution of European trade goods within a cemetery . . . suggests that European trade goods functioned not only as traditional status . . . goods, but also as substantial metaphors of traditional cultural value" (71). In support of this argument, Hamell notes that analogous Native goods frequently accompany such European trade goods in these mortuary contexts. He concludes that Native shell, stones, and metals, comprise the greater part of Middle Woodland mortuary ceremonialism, and that "the quantitatively significant reappearance of these goods in protohistoric mortuary contexts along with analogous European trade goods, further suggests that European contact initially reified the native mythical reality of which this mortuary behavior was an empirical expression, and energized and/or reactivated other interrelated cultural subsystems, which had been relatively dormant since the end of the Middle Woodland" (1987:82).

Burial goods may also have functioned, I would argue, as "sacrifices" that were designed to promote renewal, particularly in light of the obvious changes taking place in the Native world. Burial of goods was an offering consistent with notions of destruction and renewal—and with the Native conception that the greater the sacrifice, the greater the social gain of the individual and his or her family. The families of those people buried with large amounts of goods were seen to act in a socially beneficial way—and their sacrifices were greater as the perceived crisis in the human world intensified. These burial acts would add to their prestige in the same way that the Nikommo feast created differences among living people.

Thus, burial remains reflect the daily concerns and structural principles of the Ninnimissinuok. Gender differences in grave goods mark the habitual division of labor, the dualism of male and female, so central of every day experience. The cyclicity of death and renewal, marked in the seasonal round, is also found in mortuary ritual. Hierarchy is marked in the differential distribution of goods as well. Cosmological links to the underworld and the afterlife are referenced in the directionality of the burials and in the grave furniture accompanying them. The links between wealth and health are marked in the grave goods. Through these goods community well-being is sought, with the help of intermediaries both living and deceased.

Reproduction and Transformation

A result of this intensified use of wealth in ritual, however, was the ultimate destabilization of cultural systems in southern New England. As Marshall Sahlins has eloquently demonstrated, the application of "traditional" principles in the context of "contingent" historical events can serve to alter irrevocably an established cultural trajectory (1985). According to Hamell, contact energized existing rituals promotive of the reciprocal exchange relationship between humans and game animals. He argues that peoples of the Northeast also sought greater numbers of goods, in part as the means to well-being in the face of disease, spiritual malaise, and social disruption (1987:84). The increasing need for such goods altered social relations, affected the organization and evaluation of labor, and polarized lineages now competing for wealth.

The competition for wealth between lineages exacerbated inequalities already present in Late Woodland coastal societies. The quality and quantity of grave goods found with adolescents and children in the mid-seventeenth century coastal burial grounds supports such an argument, as cross-cultural studies of mortuary practices often link the burial of wealth objects with children and adolescents to ascribed, rather than achieved status (but see Brenner 1988:152). The increase in differentiation in grave goods through time suggests that this process intensified during the early contact period. Finally, the distribution of the cemeteries is closely associated with the centers of wampum manufacture and trade, arguing for a link between chiefly lineages and the control of wealth, another characteristic of chiefdoms (Map 13). The focus on ascribed status and on control over wealth in the late sixteenth and early seventeenth centuries suggests a dynamic relationship between ritual and social relations, ideology and economics. The consistency with which notions of wealth, and health and reciprocity, supported a reality in which some individuals and lineages enjoyed a higher standard of living and access to more power and prestige than others, demonstrates the inextricability of ideology and economic relations in situations of developing inequality, without favoring one over the other (Earle 1987:300).

At the same time, the marking of social boundaries and the developing territoriality reflected in burial grounds and other archaeological remains continued to be expressed in mortuary ritual, just as it was reflected in historically documented competition for control of wampum production and distribution. The consistency of the archaeological record with the reports from the early contact period indicates that the processes evident in accelerated form during the contact period were well established prior to the arrival of Europeans.

In the ordered forms of their ritual, in the sacred grip of manitou, the Ninnimissinuok expressed and experienced those principles that gave structure and meaning to experience, structure phenomenologically linked in turn to that experience. This recursiveness, which emerged out of long familiarity with one another, was a conversation enriched and interlaced with themes born out of the ecological and social complexity of the region. In the seventeenth century, the colonizing English, French, and Dutch contributed their voices as well.

The vague outlines of this conversation appeared in the period conventionally labeled *prehistoric*, marked in large part by differences

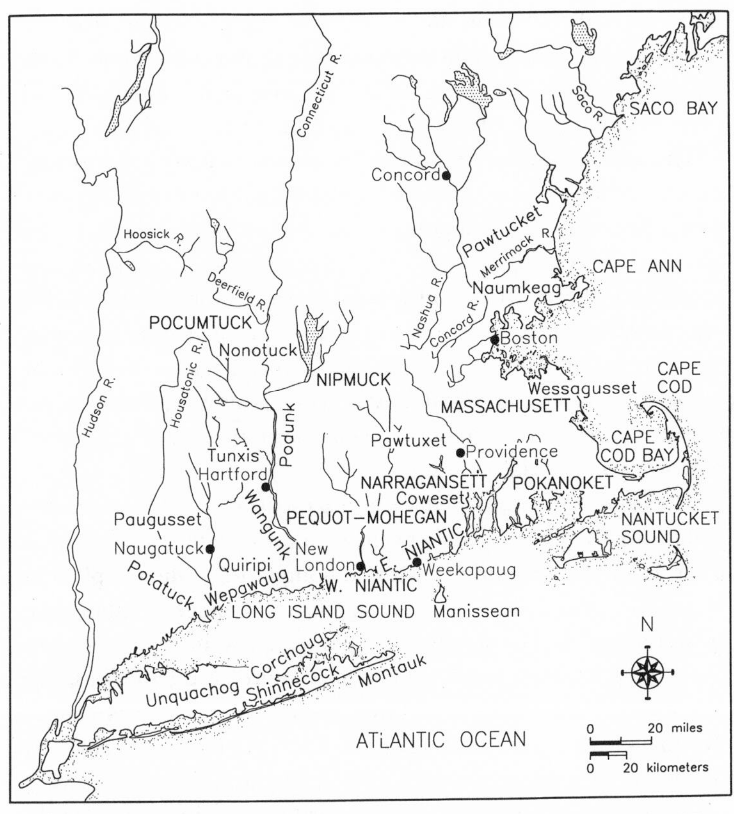

Map 13. Historic forts, burial grounds, and trading posts in southern New England. (Artist: Sondra Jarvis.)

FORTS: (1) Fort Island, (2) Fort Ninegret, (3) Fort Mystic, (4) Fort Shantok, (5) Fort Corchaug, (6) Montauk Fort, (7) Fresh Pond Fort, (8) Shinnecock Fort, (9) Manhasset Fort

BURIAL GROUNDS: (10) West Ferry, (11) Long Pond, (12) Crescent Beach, (13) RI 1000, (14) Burr's Hill

TRADING POSTS: (15) Dutch Island, (16) Kenposybald, Block Island, (17) Fort Ninegret, (18) East Hartford, (19) unnamed fort north of Hartford, (20) Roger William's post in patterns of settlement and subsistence among coastal, riverine, and uplands peoples, in the evidence for cultural contact and trade, and in the rise or re-emergence of color and shell symbolism, and elaborate mortuary ritual, particularly in coastal regions.

The reality coming to expression in such patterns was recognizable in daily practice, in gendered, habitual work, in obligatory comportment, and in generous giving and calculated trade. Interactions between peoples of differing eco-social modalities contributed in turn to a larger, regional reality. It was in the context of this regional setting that structural asymmetry flourished, consistent with the premises of habitual action in coastal regions, a cosmology that modeled hierarchy, and a ritual that was not only dependent upon intermediaries, but also made direct links between social well-being, health, and material wealth.

The response to contingent historical events reflected in mortuary ritual was also phenomenologically explicable in terms of habitual patterns of thought and behavior, although these, when applied in altered circumstances, led to significant changes among the Ninnimissinuok. The adoption of European tools increased productivity of agricultural fields, and enabled more productivity as well for those artisans already inclined to specialize (Weinstein 1982; Turnbaugh 1976). In coastal regions, such specialization, allied as it was to the wampum and fur trades, required the restructuring of daily and yearly work cycles, further skewing the already unbalanced work load within communities (R. Williams 1936). Increasing competition for agricultural lands in coastal southern New England led to the consolidation of many Native communities in the most defensible or remote parts of their territories, putting further pressure on land (Weinstein 1982). In these circumstances, the "managerial" role of the sachem became increasingly important (Brasser 1971, 1978; Little 1980; Bragdon 1981). Members of the sachem's family or lineage shared in this added power and prestige, exacerbating social divisions already sharply drawn. At the same time, the inflationary tendencies of the wampum industry spurred greater production, placing strain on the producers. Yet even as wampum was produced in greater volume, its status declined among Native people, especially when it became available to "commoners" among the Ninnimissinuok (Cronon 1983:96).

The new sachems and those "big men" taking their place celebrated a renewed "cultural emphasis on individual achievement and demonstrated ability," which was marked by, among other things, an elaborate costume, worn in life and accompanying its owner in death (Brenner 1988:150). In contrast to the Late Woodland pattern in which "the living group had little need for outward objectification of its collective identity," historic graves reflected a newly developed hierarchy and increased sense of community identity (Brenner 1988:154–56). At the same time, their authority was placed in jeopardy by their increasing demands for tribute (E. S. Johnson 1993:242).

On the Connecticut River, negotiations with English settlers or threats from hostile Mohawks and Mahicans from the west led some communities to relocate altogether (Thomas 1979). The contrast between the riverine peoples and those of the coast was marked by their continued mobility, associated with their lack of centralized authority (E. S. Johnson 1993:256), a mobility that allowed them a greater flexibility than that of coastal groups. Those riverine peoples who remained, however, became increasingly tied to the fur trade and constricted by their role as "buffers" to hostile westerners and fur-producers to the north. As their access to furs was limited, their clientage to English entrepreneurs eventually served as the engine of their dispossession, as many trading debts were paid off with their one remaining asset—land (Thomas 1985).

Competition for land and resources, as well as for powerful English allies, led to increased territorial and ethnic marking as well. Narragansett leaders such as Miantonimi, in local contests of hegemony exacerbated by the English presence, attempted to assert

Narragansett authority through the manipulation of symbols of wealth and through control over ritual form and sequence (Robinson 1990:29). Material culture begins to reflect such "ethnic" distinctions as well (E. S. Johnson 1993:272–74). The ideological aspects of this transformation can be seen in an increased concern for representing the existing social order as something that had always existed: in the words of the Narragansett sachem Pessicus (1643–1676), since "time out of mind." Here, as Marshall Sahlins has argued, changes in Narragansett society involved social reproduction, with new meaning becoming attached to old forms (1985:ix).

In August of 1641, Miantonimi appealed to the Montauks to join with the Narragansetts against the English

> for so are we all Indians, as the English are, and Say brother to one another, so must we be one as they are, otherwise we shall be all gone shortly , for you know our fathers had plenty of deer and skins, our plains were full of deer, as also our woods, and full of turkies, and our coves full of fish and fowl. (Gardiner 1859:26)

Miantonomi's appeal to the past in his well-known speech also speaks to the increasing "historicity" and "deroutinization" characteristic of southern New England Native communities in the 1630s and 1640s (Giddens 1990:222). Elaborated formal ritual and historicity alike register an altered perception of time and of group identity.

At the same time, and in spite of the tremendous pressures toward transformation, the Ninnimissinuok by the same process retained old patterns of thought in new guises. The concept of manitou was extended to English material culture, which was incorporated into ritual and contributed to a continuation of Native ideas about health and well-being (Hamell 1987; Crosby 1988:88). Men continued to hunt, fight, conduct diplomacy, and trade; women continued to farm and gather. Sachems continued to represent their communities, adjudicate disputes, lead war parties, and "appoint" rituals. Manitou was still sought, through the advocacy of powwaws or the sacrifice of wealth. As interference from English colonists increased, the contest of cultures continued to be played out in intimate contexts of dress, language, local political relations, and in ritual. In these contexts, the structural relations between men and women, advocates and petitioners, the proximate and the distant, the human and the other-than-human, and the constant alternation between growth and decay that shaped existential experience for the Ninnimissinuok, remained the same.

Notes

Preface

1. Eastern Algonquian languages such as Massachusett pluralize animate nouns by using variations of the suffix *-ak* (or *-og*, *-ag*, *-ogk*, *-ok*). Inanimate nouns are pluralized by adding the suffix -ash (Goddard and Bragdon 1988:490). Except where terms are quoted directly from seventeenth-century sources, *-ok* and *-ash* are used. For some words, which have common usage in English, such as *sachem* or *powwaw*, I use English pluralization.

Introduction

1. For a discussion of the history of the search for the mythical Northwest Passage see Quinn 1975:369–84; and Allen 1987.

2. Aside from Goddard's work on pidgins (1978b, 1979), very little research has been done on multilinguistic interaction in seventeenth-century New England, but see Hagedorn 1988 on interpreters to the Iroquois in the early eighteenth century.

3. Both terms are from Proto-Algonquian **sa:kima:wa*, 'leader.' The differences between the terms reflect linguistic rather than organizational differences. Native names provided to John Smith were subsequently altered in his published map (Krim 1980:73).

4. Estimated total population figures are drawn from Snow and Lanphear 1988.

5. The dates associated with these periods, as well as their cultural/historical parameters, are inconsistently presented in the archaeological literature, in part because of a conflation the concepts of period and stage (Snow 1980:261–62). Snow's substitution of the terms *Early Horticultural* (combining *Early* and *Middle Woodland*) and *Late Prehistoric* (replacing *Late Woodland*) to describe periods addresses the difficulty of distinguishing Early from Middle Woodland culturally, but implies a reliance on horticulture in most areas of southern New England far earlier than the evidence warrants. In order to avoid repetitious strings of dates, I too conflate stage and period, and employ the stage names to refer to mean dates and time periods as follows: Terminal Late Archaic (mean date 2700 B.P.), Early Woodland (mean date 2200 B.P.), Middle Woodland (mean date 1100 B.P./950 A.D.), Late Woodland (950–400 B.P./1000–1550 A.D.), Contact period (400 B.P.–330 B.P./1550–1620 A.D.), Historic period (330 B.P.–present/1620 A.D.–present). All refer to calibrated radio-carbon dates. These dates are based on McBride (1984) and Bernstein (1990).

6. Ironically, one of the few interpretations that stresses innovation in plant domestication assigns the innovative role to men. Guy Prentice (1986) suggests that Archaic period (male) shamans were responsible for the cultivation of gourd-like cucurbits for ritual purposes.

Chapter 1.

1. I am indebted to Kevin McBride, James Peterson, Barbara Luedtke, Fred Dunford, Deborah Cox, Stephen Mrozowski, Lucianne Lavin, Paul Robinson, and James Bradley for discussing their research and ideas with me as I prepared this section. Any errors of interpretation are my own.

2. Nantucket and outer Cape Cod have no true estuaries, having no freshwater rivers.

3. Little cautions that fish bones from species such as scup, bluefish, tautog, cunner, striped bass, and sturgeon, generally caught in summer from shore or boat and sometimes found in shell middens, may reflect use of dried fish during winter, rather than year-round use (1988:79). She also argues that no large interior sites without shell middens have been tested for seasonality (80).

4. Carbon isotope "signatures" identified in archaeologically recovered bone differ for certain types of plants, allowing for a determination of which plants were present in a particular individual's diet. For example, nitrogen isotopes can help to determine whether marine resources were important (Medaglia et al. 1990:52). The study of modern fauna shows varying signatures depending on habitat, with deep-water fish contrasting with tidal-creek and harbor-dwelling fish and shellfish. These contrasts should also appear in human populations (55)

5. The Sapowet Marsh area, near Tiverton, Rhode Island has also yielded a number of assemblages that indicate a wide range of subsistence activities and the use of an impressive variety of plant and animal resources associated with the saltmarsh and nearby river, along with numerous burials (Leveille, cited in Kerber 1988:68). Likewise, extensive study of prehistoric remains from North Kingstown and Narragansett, Rhode Island, revealed Woodland period sites encompassing a "vast array of features, including large storage pits of oak, hazelnut, hickory and carbonized beans" (Morenon, cited in Kerber 1988:70). Both Leveille (in Kerber 1988:69) and Morenon (in Kerber 1988:70) argue for semi-sedentary occupation during at least the summer and fall seasons of the Late Woodland period in Rhode Island. Kerber found evidence for summer, fall, and possibly winter occupation of the Potowomut River estuary in the Late Woodland period (1984:152–55; 1988:69). Leveille and Van Coughyen (1990:51), based on surveys of the Taunton River drainage, the Sakonnet River, and the Pettaquamscutt River, suggest that Woodland occupation of the coast was more dense. They argue, following Cox, Thorbahn, and Leveille (1983), that intense coastal use in the Late Woodland period may have been in response to environmentally dry episodes where inland watertables were low.

6. Hickory was a particularly important resource throughout the Archaic and Woodland period in southern New England (Bernstein 1992:8), as attested not only by ubiquitous charred remains on archaeological sites, but by the presence of storage and roasting pits (8). Acorns also have great antiquity and wide distribution as a food resource. The popularity of these two nuts must have been due in part to their ease of collection, seasonal abundance, and high protein yield, as well as to their widespread distribution. Oak and hickory woodlands encompass much of central, eastern, and coastal New England, growing

even where other species cannot thrive (Thomson 1958:101–102). Bernstein cautions, however, that the marked presence of hickory in the archaeological record may also be due to its good preservational qualities and to the possibility that the shells were used for fuel (1992:9).

7. McBride's (1984) analysis of numerous sites in central and coastal Connecticut is by far the most comprehensive and detailed examination of late prehistoric settlement in southern New England. He characterizes the early Late Woodland (what he calls the Selden Creek phase) as one with increased use of nonlocal lithic materials and a variable ceramic assemblage within the context of "semi-sedentary villages located along the Connecticut River with associated temporary camps and task-specific locations uplands" (1984:139). The lack of large nonriverine interior sites during the Selden Creek phase suggests to McBride that if groups were moving seasonally, it was within the estuarine zone (141). McBride notes that although no evidence for maize use has been found on Selden Creek sites, settlement pattern did change at the beginning of the phase (144).

Chapter 2.

1. Riley et al. suggest that eight-row northern flint entered the southeast through Florida from South America or Mexico's Gulf coast around 200 A.D. The distribution of beans suggests two routes of entry as well (1980:528). Chenopods and possibly other plants, on the other hand, may have been locally domesticated in eastern North America (1990:117; Chomko and Crawford 1978:405, 407).

2. But see Snow 1980:19.

3. No mention of fish fertilizer is made in the Connecticut Valley sources (D. Gookin 1806:100–101).

Chapter 3.

1. The overall impact of Native people on the landscape was both systematic and extensive, due not only to their ecological intervention, but to their population density as well. Snow (1980) and Snow and Lanphear (1988) estimate that population density in southern New England was somewhere between 1.93 and 2.6 people per square kilometer in coastal regions (Snow 1980:39) and .2 people per square kilometer in the upland interior regions (39). Thomas also argues for dense populations along the middle and upper Connecticut, where an arbitrary community population of 400 people would have required

80–100 acres of agricultural lands per year (Thomas 1976:12). Taking fallow periods into account, that same community would in reality require between 990 and 2320 acres (13). Additional lands needed to support the entirely undomesticated fauna, and dependence on dispersed resources such as nuts, berries, and anadromous fish, meant that each Native community had to control the lands extending several miles around their central village locations. Thomas argues that the settlement pattern of the Connecticut River valley, with villages occurring every 25 miles or so, was determined by these land-base requirements. A similar calculation for coastal groups would yield a minimum of 1500 acres cleared for farming and hunting per community.

Chapter 4.

1. See for example, Cronon (1983), Salisbury (1982), Axtell (1985), and Crosby (1988). Both Cronon and Salisbury draw upon Sahlins's insightful *Stone Age Economics* (1972) in their analyses of southern New England Native economy.

2. According to Gudeman, a model may be built upon several primal metaphors or contain elements that are not strictly metaphors. These usually receive some form of "external" justification, ranging from "as if" to "as being" formulations (that is, schemes that are seen as convenient fictions or those seen as identical with the thing described). Such validation can take the form of everyday experience, or knowledge of myth or history (1986:44).

3. John Eliot was the first to note that the locative, third person singular form, *weekuwout*, 'in his house,' was the basis for the English word 'wigwam,' (Eliot 1896:12).

4. I am indebted to Richard Rhodes for this comparison.

Chapter 6.

1. According to Ceci (1990a:63), a fathom of wampum consisted of approximately 330 beads, each worth from 3 to 6 English pence in the early 1630s when Williams's *Key* was written. Williams himself prices 10 fathoms at 50 shillings (1936:155), although he noted that a few years earlier it was worth twice that. If the payment included the purple wampum *suckauhock*, the value would be considerably more, as each purple bead was worth twice that of the white (152).

Chapter 8.

1. It should be noted that the purported sexual gender of these manitou is probably an artifact of the English language. Algonquian languages, it will be recalled, do not specify sexual gender grammatically, but most English writers automatically assigned male gender to beings (human and other than human) of importance in the Ninnimissinuok world.

2. For a complete collection of these sacred tales, and an analysis of their content and meaning, see Simmons (1986).

Chapter 9.

1. The latter, practitioners of the Midewiwin among the central Algonquians, may have been a postcontact phenomenon (Vastokas and Vastokas 1973:38).

References

Allen, John L. 1987. The Illy-Smelling Sea: Indians, Information, and the Early Search for the Passage. *Man in the Northeast* 33:127–35.

Andrews, J. Clinton. 1986. Indian Fish and Fishing Off Coastal Massachusetts. *Bulletin of the Massachusetts Archaeological Society* 47(2):42–46.

Axtell, James. 1985. *The Invasion Within: The Contest of Cultures in Colonial North America.* New York: Oxford University Press.

Bailey, Alfred Goldsworthy. 1969. *The Conflict of European and Eastern Algonkian Cultures, 1504–1700: A Study in Canadian Civilization.* Toronto: University of Toronto Press.

Banks, Charles Edward. 1966. [1911]. *History of Martha's Vineyard.* 3 vols. Reprint, Dukes County Historical Society.

Barber, Russell J. 1979. Human Ecology and the Estuarine Ecosystem: Prehistoric Exploitation in the Merrimack Valley. Ph.D. diss. Department of Anthropology, Harvard University.

———. 1982. *The Wheeler's Site: A Specialized Shellfish Processing Station on the Merrimac River.* Peabody Museum Monograph 7. Cambridge, Mass.: Harvard University Press.

Basset, Benjamin. 1806. Fabulous Traditions and Customs of the Indians. *Collections of the Massachusetts Historical Society* 1:139–40.

Basso, Keith. 1984. "Stalking with Stories": Names, Places, and Moral Narratives among the Western Apache." Pp. 19–55 in *Text, Play and Story*, edited by Edward Brunner. Washington, D.C.: American Ethnological Society Publications.

Bellantoni, Nicholas F. 1993. Animal Exploitation Patterns from Prehistoric Shell Midden Sites on Block Island, Rhode Island. Paper presented at the annual meeting of the Northeastern Anthropological Association, 27 March, Danbury, Conn.

Bendremer, Jeffrey C. M., and Robert E. Dewar. 1994. The Advent of Prehistoric Maize in New England. Pp. 369–94 in *Corn and Culture in the Prehistoric New World*. Edited by Sissel Johanessen and Christine A. Hastorf. Boulder: Westview Press.

Bendremer, Jeffrey C. M., Elizabeth A. Kellogg, and Tonya Baroody Largy. 1991. A Grass-Lined Maize Storage Pit and Early Maize Horticulture in Central Connecticut. *North American Archaeologist* 12(4):325–49.

Berkhofer, Robert F., Jr. 1976. The Political Context of a New Indian History. Pp. 101–26 in *The American Indian*, edited by N. Hundley. Santa Barbara, Calif.: Clio Press.

———. 1978. *The White Man's Indian: Images of the American Indian from Columbus to the Present*. New York: Knopf.

———. 1987. Cultural Pluralism Versus Ethnocentrism in the New Indian History. Pp. 35–45 in *The American Indian and the Problem of History*, edited by Calvin Martin. New York: Oxford University Press.

Bernstein, David J. 1990. Trends in Prehistoric Subsistence on the Southern New England Coast: The View from Narragansett Bay. *North American Archaeologist* 11(4):321–52.

———. 1992. Prehistoric Use of Plant Foods in the Narragansett Bay Region. *Man in the Northeast* 44:1–13.

———. 1993. *Prehistoric Subsistence on the Southern New England Coast: The Record from Narragansett Bay*. San Diego: Academic Press.

Biard, Pierre. 1897 [1616]. *Relation*. Vol. 3 in *The Jesuit Relations and Allied Documents*, edited by Reuben G. Thwaites. Cleveland: Burrows Brothers.

Binford, Lewis R. 1972. Mortuary Practices: Their Study and Their Potential. Pp. 208–43 in *An Archaeological Perspective*, edited by L. Binford. New York: Seminar Press.

———. 1980. Willow Smoke and Dogs' Tails: Hunter-Gatherer Settlement Systems and Archaeological Site Formation. *American Antiquity* 45(1):4–20.

Bird-David, Nurit. 1992. Beyond "The Original Affluent Society": A Culturalist Reformulation. *Current Anthropology* 33(1):25–47.

Black, David W., and Ruth Holmes Whitehead. 1988. Prehistoric Shellfish Preservation and Storage on the Northeast Coast. *North American Archaeologist* 9(1):17–30.

Blau, Harold. Notes on the Onondaga Bowl Game. Pp. 35–49 in *Iroquois Culture: History and Prehistory*, edited by Elisabeth Tooker. New York: New York State Museum Science Service.

Bloomfield, Leonard. 1941. Proto-Algonquian—i:t—'Fellow.' *Language* 75(4):292–97.

Bock, Philip K. 1978. Micmac. In Trigger, ed., *Northeast*, pp. 109–12, *Handbook of North American Indians*, vol. 15.

Boserup, Ester. 1965. *The Conditions of Agricultural Growth*. London: Allen and Unwin.

Bourdieu, Pierre. 1978. *Outline of a Theory of Practice*. Richard Nice, trans. New York: Cambridge University Press.

Bourque, Bruce J. 1975. Comments on the Late Archaic Populations of Central Maine: The View from the Turner Farm. *Arctic Anthropology* 12(2):35–45.

Bourque, Bruce J., and Ruth H. Whitehead. 1985. Tarrantines and the Introduction of European Trade Goods in the Gulf of Maine. *Ethnohistory* 32:327–41.

Bowen, Joanne. 1990. A Study of Seasonality and Subsistence in Eighteenth Century Suffield, Connecticut. Ph.d. diss., Department of Anthropology, Brown University.

Bradford, William. 1970. *Of Plymouth Plantation, 1620–1647*. Edited by Samuel Eliot Morison. Reprint, New York: Alfred A. Knopf.

Bradley, James W. 1983. Blue Crystals and Other Trinkets: Glass Beads from Sixteenth and Early Seventeenth Century New England. Pp. 29–39 in *Proceedings of the 1982 Glass Trade Bead Conference*, edited by C. F. Hayes, III. Research Records 16, Rochester Museum and Science Center, Rochester, N.Y.

———. 1987. Native Exchange and European Trade: Cross-Cultural Dynamics in the Sixteenth Century. *Man in the Northeast* 33:31–46.

———. 1987a. *Evolution of the Onondaga Iroquois: Accommodating Change, 1500–1655*. Syracuse: Syracuse University Press.

———. 1989. The Grove Field Ossuary. *Bulletin of the Massachusetts Archaeological Society* 50(1):19–23.

Bradley, James, Arthur E. Spiess, Wayne E. McFee. 1991. Mass Strandings of the Long-finned Pilot Whale on Cape Cod: Implications for Native American Subsistence and Settlement. Poster display, American Anthropological Association Meeting, Washington, D.C.

Bragdon, Kathleen. 1981. "Another Tongue Brought In": An Ethnohistorical Study of Native Writings in Massachusett. Ph.D. diss., Department of Anthropology, Brown University.

———. 1987. Emphattical Speech and Great Action: An Analysis of Speech Events Described in Seventeenth Century Sources. *Man in the Northeast* 33:101–11.

———. 1987a. The Sachemship and Its Defenders. Paper presented at the annual meeting of the American Historical Association, Washington, D.C., December, 1987.

———. 1991. Native Christianity in Eighteenth Century Massachusetts: Ritual as Cultural Reaffirmation. Pp. 117–26 in *New Dimensions in Ethnohistory*, edited by Barry Gough and Christie Laird. *Papers of the Second Laurier Conference on Ethnohistory and Ethnology*. Canadian Museum of Civilization.

———. n.d. Language and Cultural Identity in Southern New England. In *Collected Papers of the Second Mashantucket Pequot History Conference*, edited by William Starna and Jack Campisi. Norman: University of Oklahoma Press, in press.

Brasser, Ted J. C. 1971. The Coastal Algonkians: People of the First Frontiers. Pp. 64–91 in *North American Indians in Historical Perspective*, edited by Eleanor B. Leacock and Nancy O. Lurie. New York: Random House.

———. 1978. Early Indian-European Contacts. In Trigger, ed., *Northeast*, pp. 78–88, *Handbook of North American Indians*, vol. 15.

Braun, David P. 1980. On the Appropriateness of the Woodland Concept in Northeastern Prehistory. Pp. 93–108 in *Proceedings of the Conference on Northeastern Anthropology*. Research Report 19. University of Massachusetts, Amherst.

Brenner, Elise M. 1988. Sociopolitical Implications of Mortuary Ritual Remains in 17th-Century Native Southern New England. Pp. 147–82 in *The Recovery of Meaning: Historical Archaeology in the Eastern United States*, edited by Mark P. Leone and Parker B. Potter, Jr. Washington D.C.: Smithsonian Institution Press.

References

Brereton, John. 1968 [1602]. A Briefe and True Relation of the Discoverie of the North Part of Virginia. Reprinted in *Sailors' Narratives of the Voyages along the New England Coast 1524–1624*, edited by George Parker Winship. New York: B. Franklin.

Brumbach, Hetty Jo. 1975. "Iroquoian" Ceramics in "Algonquian" Territory. *Man in the Northeast* 10:17–28.

Bullen, Ripley P. 1949. *Excavations in Northeastern Massachusetts. Papers of the Robert S. Peabody Foundation for Archaeology* 1(3), Andover, Mass.

Burgess, Edward. 1970. [1926] The Old South Road of Gay Head. Reprint, *Dukes County Intelligencer* 12(1):1–25.

Burke, Kenneth. 1962 [1945]. *A Grammar of Motives and A Rhetoric of Motives.* New York: World Publishing. Reprint, New York: Meridian Books.

Burling, Robbins. 1974. *The Passage of Power: Studies in Political Succession.* New York: Academic Press.

Burrage, Henry S., ed. 1930. *Early English and French Voyages Chiefly from Hakluyt, 1534–1608.* New York: Charles Scribners Sons.

Burton, M. L., Brudner, L. A., and White, D. R. 1977. A Model of the Sexual Division of Labor. *American Ethnologist* 4:227–51.

Burton, William. 1976. "Hellish Fiends and Brutish Men": Amerindian-Euroamerican Interaction in Southern New England: An Interdisciplinary Analysis, 1600–1750. Ph.D. diss., Department of Anthropology. Kent State University. Ann Arbor, Mich.: University Microfilms.

Burton, William, and Richard Lowenthal. 1974. The First of the Mohegans. *American Ethnologist* 1(4):589–99.

Butler, Eva L. 1948. Algonkian Culture and the Use of Maize in Southern New England. *Bulletin of the Archaeological Society of Connecticut* 22:3–39.

Butler, Eva L., and Wendell S. Hadlock. 1949. Dogs of the Northeastern Woodland Indians. *Bulletin of the Massachusetts Archaeological Society* 10(2):17–35.

Byers, Douglas S., and Irving Rouse. 1960. A Re-examination of the Guida Farm. *Bulletin of the Archaeological Society of Connecticut* 30:5–39.

Carlson, Catherine C., George J. Armelagos, and Ann L. Magennis. 1992. Impact of Disease on the Precontact and Early Historic Populations of New England and the Maritimes. Pp. 141–53 in *Disease and Demography in the Americas*, edited by John W. Verano and Douglas H. Ubelaker. Washington, D.C.: Smithsonian Institution Press.

Carneiro, Robert L. 1968. Slash-and-burn Cultivation Among the Kiukuru and Its Implications for Cultural Development in the Amazon Basin. Pp. 131–44 in *Man in Adaptation: The Cultural Present*, edited by Yehudi Cohen. Chicago: Aldine.

———. 1970. A Theory of the Origin of the State. *Science* 169(3947): 733–38.

Cassedy, D., P. Webb, T. Millis, H. Millis, and Garrow and Associates. 1993. New Data on Maize Horticulture and Subsistence in Southwestern Connecticut. Paper presented at the annual meeting of the Northeastern Anthropological Association, Danbury, Connecticut, 27 March.

Ceci, Lynn. 1975. Fish Fertilizer: A Native North American Practice? *Science* 188(4183):26–30.

———. 1977. The Effect of European Contact and Trade on the Settlement Pattern of Indians in Coastal New York, 1524–1665: The Archaeological and Documentary Evidence. Ph.D. diss., Department of Anthropology, City University of New York.

———. 1978. Watchers of the Pleiades: Ethnoastronomy and Native Cultivators in Northeastern North America. *Ethnohistory* 25:301–17.

———, 1979–1980. Maize Cultivation in Coastal New York: The Archaeological, Agronomical, and Documentary Evidence. *North American Archaeologist* 1(1):45–74.

———. 1982. Method and Theory in Coastal New York Archaeology: Paradigms of Settlement Pattern. *North American Archaeologist* 3(1):5–36.

———. 1990. Radiocarbon Dating "Village" Sites in Coastal New York: Settlement Pattern Changes in the Middle to Late Woodland. *Man in the Northeast* 39:1–28.

———. 1990a. Wampum as a Peripheral Resource in the Seventeenth-Century World System. Pp. 48–63 in *The Pequots in Southern New England: The Fall and Rise of an American Indian Nation*, edited by Laurence M. Hauptman and James O. Wherry. Norman: University of Oklahoma Press.

Chamberlain, Barbara Blau. 1964. *These Fragile Outposts—A Geological Look at Cape Cod, Martha's Vineyard, and Nantucket*. Garden City, N.Y.: Natural History Press.

Champlain, Samuel de. 1922 [1613]. *Les Voyages du Sieur de Champlain*. Vol. 1 of *The Works of Samuel de Champlain*, edited by H. P. Biggar. Toronto: Champlain Society.

———. 1968 [1613]. Voyage. Reprinted in *Sailors' Narratives of the Voyages along the New England Coast 1524–1624*, edited by George Parker Winship. New York: B. Franklin.

Childs, Terry. 1984. Prehistoric Ceramic Analysis, Technology and Style. Vol. 2 in *Chapters in the Archaeology of Cape Cod*, edited by Francis P. McManamon. Division of Cultural Resources, North Atlantic Regional office, National Park Service, Boston, Massachusetts.

Chomko, Stephen A., and Gary W. Crawford. 1978. Plant Husbandry in Prehistoric Eastern North America: New Evidence for Its Development. *American Antiquity* 43(3):405–408.

Claassen, Cheryl P. 1991. Gender, Shellfishing, and the Shell Mound Archaic. Pp. 276–300 in *Engendering Archaeology*, edited by Joan M. Gero and Margaret W. Conkey. London: Basil Blackwell.

Clap, Roger. 1970 [1731]. Memoirs of Capt. Roger Clap. Reprinted in *Chronicles of the First Planters of the Colony of Massachusetts Bay 1623–1636*, edited by Alexander Young. New York: De Capo Press.

Cleland, Charles E., Richard D. Clute, and Robert E. Haltiner. 1984. Naub-cow-zo-win Discs from Northern Michigan. *Midcontinental Journal of Archaeology* 9(2):235–49.

Clifford, James. 1986. Introduction. Pp. 1–26 in *Writing Culture: The Poetics and Politics of Ethnography*, edited by James Clifford and George E. Marcus. Berkeley: University of California Press.

Collier, Jane F. 1987. Rank and Marriage: Or, Why High Ranking Wives Cost More. Pp. 197–200 in Collier and Yanagisako, *Gender and Kinship: Essays Toward a Unified Analysis.*

Collier, Jane F., and Michelle Z. Rosaldo. 1981. Politics and Gender in Simple Societies. Pp. 275–329 in *Sexual Meanings: The Cultural Construction of Gender and Sexuality*, edited by Sherry Ortner and Harriet Whitehead. Cambridge: Cambridge Univerisity Press.

Collier, Jane F., and Sylvia J. Yanagisako, eds.. 1987. *Gender and Kinship: Essays Toward a Unified Analysis.* Stanford: Stanford University Press.

———. 1987a. Introduction. In Collier and Yanagisako, eds., *Gender and Kinship: Essays Toward a Unified Analysis*, pp. 1–13. Stanford: Stanford University Press.

Comaroff, Jean, and John Comaroff. 1991. *Of Revelation and Revolution: Christianity, Colonialism, and Consciousness in South Africa.* Vol. 1. Chicago: University of Chicago Press.

———. 1992. Of Totemism and Ethnicity. In *Ethnography and the Historical Imagination*, eds. Comaroff and Comaroff, pp. 49–68. Boulder: Westview Press.

Conkey, Laura E., Ethel Boissevain, and Ives Goddard. 1978. Indians of Southern New England and Long Island: Late Period. In Trigger, ed., *Northeast*, pp. 198–212, *Handbook of North American Indians*, vol. 15.

Connole, Dennis A. 1976. Land Occupied by the Nipmuck Indians of Central New England. *Bulletin of the Massachusetts Archaeological Society* 38(1–2)14–20.

Cook, Sherburne F. 1976. *The Indian Population of New England in the Seventeenth Century.* Berkeley: University of California Press.

Coontz, Stephanie, and Henderson, Peta. 1986. Property Forms, Political Power and Female Labor in the Origins of Class and State Societies. Pp. 108–55 in *Women's Work, Men's Property: The Origins of Gender and Class*, edited by S. Coontz and P. Henderson. London: Verso Press.

Cotton, Josiah. 1830. Vocabulary of the Massachusetts (or Natick) Indian Language. *Collections of the Massachusetts Historical Society.* 3rd ser. 2:147–257.

Cox, Deborah. 1982. Prehistoric Site Summary for Bay Street 1 Site. I-495 Archaeological Data Recovery Program, vol. 2. Public Archaeology Laboratory, Brown University, Providence, R.I.

Cox, Deborah, Ann Davin, and Alan Leveille. 1985. *Archaeological Data Recovery at the Jamestown Bridge Site.* Conanicut Island, Narragansett Bay. The Public Archaeology Laboratory, Inc. Report no. 37-1. Rhode Island Historic Preservation Commission, Providence, R.I.

Cox, Deborah, Peter Thorbahn, and Alan Leveille. 1983. *An Archaeological Assessment Survey of the Pettaquamscutt River Basin.* The Public Archaeology Laboratory, Report no. 12-1. Rhode Island Historic Preservation Commission, Providence, R.I.

Cronon, William. 1983. *Changes in the Land: Indians, Colonists, and the Ecology of New England.* New York: Hill and Wang.

Crosby, Constance A. 1988. From Myth to History, or Why King Philip's Ghost Walks Abroad. Pp. 183–210 in *The Recovery of Meaning: Historical Archaeology in the Eastern United States*, edited by Mark P. Leone and Parker B. Potter, Jr. Washington D.C.: Smithsonian Institution Press.

Custer, Jay. 1986. Late Woodland Cultural Diversity in the Middle Atlantic: An Evolutionary Perspective. Pp. 143–68 in *Late Woodland Cultures of the Middle Atlantic Region*, edited by Jay Custer. Newark: University of Delaware Press.

Day, Gordon M. 1953. The Indian as an Ecological Factor in the Northeastern Forest. *Ecology* 34(2):329–46.

———. 1965. The Identity of the Sokokis. *Ethnohistory* 12(3):237–49.

———. 1975. *The Mots Loups of Father Mathevet. National Museum of Man, Publications in Ethnology* 8. Ottawa.

———. 1978. Western Abenaki. In Trigger, ed., *Northeast*, pp. 148–59, *Handbook of North American Indians*, vol. 15.

DCHS = Dukes County Historical Society. 1650-present. Collections. Dukes County Historical Society, Edgartown, Massachusetts.

De Forest, John W. 1964 [1851]. History of the Indiant of Connecticut from the Earliest Known Period to 1850. Reprint, Hamden, Conn.: Archon Books.

Delabarre, Edmund Burke. 1928. Dighton Rock: A Study of the Written Rocks of New England. New York: Walter Negle.

Delabarre, Edmund Burke, and Harris H. Wilder. 1920. Indian Corn-Hills in Massachusetts. *American Anthropologist* 22(3):203–25.

Delaney, C. 1986. The Meaning of Paternity and the Virgin Birth Debate. *Man* 21:494–513.

Demeritt, David. 1991. Agriculture, Climate, and Cultural Adaptation in the Prehistoric Northeast. *Archaeology of Eastern North America* 19:183–202.

Denny, Peter. 1989. Algonquian Connections to Salishan and Northeastern Archaeology. Pp. 86–107 in *Papers of the Twentieth Algonquian Conference*, edited by William Cowan. Ottawa: Carleton University.

DePaoli, Neil. 1984. Patterns of Settlement and Land Use: Contact Period (1500–1620), Plantation Period (1620–1675). Pp. 46–76 in *Historic and Archaeological Resources of the Connecticut River Valley*, edited by James Bradley. Boston: Massachusetts Historical Commission.

De Rasieres, Isaack. 1909 [1628]. Letter of Isaack de Rasieres to Samuel Blommaert, 1628. Pp. 97–116 in *Narratives of New Netherland 1609–1664*, edited by J. Franklin Jameson. New York: Charles Scribner's Sons. Reprint, New York: Barnes and Noble, 1967.

Dermer, Thomas. 1968 [1619]. To His Worshipfull Friend M. Samuel Purchas, Preacher of the Word, at the Church a Little Within Ludgate, London. Reprinted in *Sailor's Narratives of the Voyages along the New England Coast 1524–1624*, edited by George Parker Winship. New York: B. Franklin.

Dincauze, Dena F. 1973. Prehistoric occupation of the Charles River Estuary. *Archaeological Society of Connecticut Bulletin* 38:25–39.

———. 1974. An Introduction to Archaeology in the Greater Boston Area. *Archaeology of Eastern North America* 2(1):39–67.

———. 1993. Centering. *Northeast Archaeology* 46:33–37.

Dincauze, Dena F., and Robert J. Hasenstab. 1987. Explaining the Iroquois: Tribalization on a Prehistoric Periphery. Pp. 67–87 in *Centre and Periphery*, edited by T. C. Champion. *Proceedings of the World Archaeological Congress*, September, 1986, Pt. 4. London: Unwin Hyman.

Douglas, Mary. 1966. *Purity and Danger: An Analysis of the Concepts of Pollution and Taboo.* London: Routledge and Kegan Paul.

———. 1970. *Natural Symbols: Explorations in Cosmology.* London: Barrie and Rockliff.

———. 1971. Is Matrilineality Doomed in Africa? Pp. 123–37 in *Man in Africa*, edited by Mary Douglas and Phyllis M. Kaberry. Garden City, N.Y.: Anchor Books.

Dowd, Anne S. 1988. Prehistoric Ceramics in Rhode Island: An Overview. *Bulletin of the Archaeological Society of Connecticut* 49:71–79.

DuBois, John W. 1982. Self-Evidence and Ritual Speech. Pp. 313–36 in *Evidentiality: The Linguistic Coding of Epistemology*, edited by Wallace Chafe and Johanna Nichols. Norwood, N.J.: Ablex.

Dudley, Thomas. 1970 [1630]. Letter to the Countess of Lincoln. In Young, ed., *Chronicles of the First Planters of the Colony of Massachusetts Bay 1623–1636*, pp. 304–41.

Dunford, Frederick J. 1992. Conditional Sedentism: The Logistical Flexibility of Estuarine Settlements in Circumscribed Environments. Paper presented at the fifty-seventh annual meeting of the Society for American Archaeology, 8–12, April, Pittsburg, Pa.

———. 1993. Territory and Community: The Spatial Dimensions of Ceramic Design Variability on Cape Cod, Massachusetts (1000–400 Years B.P.). Ph.D. dissertation prospectus, Deptartment of Anthropology, University of Massachusetts.

Dyson-Hudson, Rada, and Eric Alden Smith. 1978. Human Territoriality: An Ecological Reassessment. *American Anthropologist* 80(1):21–41.

Earle, Timothy K. 1987. Chiefdoms in Archaeological and Ethnohistorical Perspective. *Annual Reviews in Anthropology* 16:279–308.

Eliade, Mircea. 1959. *The Sacred and the Profane.* New York: Harcourt.

Eliot, John. 1663. The Holy Bible. Containing the Old Testament and the New. Cambridge, Mass.: Samuel Green and Marmaduke Johnson.

———. 1896 [1666]. The Indian Grammar Begun; or, An Essay to Bring the Indian language into Rules for the Help of Such as Desire to learn the Same for the Furtherance of the Gospel Among Them. Reprint, Cambridge, Mass.: Samuel Green and Marmaduke Johnson.

———. 1834 [1647]. The Day-Breaking, If Not the Sun-Rising of the Gospell with the Indians in New England. Reprint, *Collections of the Massachusetts Historical Society,* 3rd ser., 4:1–23.

Eliot, John and Thomas Mayhew. 1834 [1653]. Tears of Repentance: or, A further Narrative of the Progress of the Gospel Amongst the Indians in New-England. London: Peter Cole. Reprinted in *Collections of the Massachusetts Historical Society,* 3rd ser., vol. 4, pp. 197–287.

Ember, Carol and Melvin Ember. 1990. *Cultural Anthropology.* Englewood Cliffs, N.J.: Prentice-Hall.

Erickson, Vincent O. 1978. Maliseet-Passamaquoddy. In Trigger, ed., *Northeast,* pp. 123–36, *Handbook of North American Indians,* vol. 15.

Fabian, Johannes. 1986. *Language and Colonial Power: The Appropriation of Swahili in the Former Belgian Congo 1880–1938.* Cambridge: Cambridge University Press.

Feder, Kenneth L. 1990. Late Woodland Occupation of the Uplands of Northwestern Connecticut. *Bulletin of the Massachusetts Archaeological Society* 51(2):61–68.

Feinman, Gary, and Neitzel, Jill. 1984. Too Many Types: An Overview of Sedentary Prestate Societies in the Americas. *Advances in Archaeological Method and Theory* 7:39–102.

Fenton, William. 1951. Symposium on Local Diversity in Iroquois Culture. Bureau of American Ethnology, Bulletin 149. Washington, D.C.

Fiedel, Stuart J. 1987. Algonquian Origins: A Problem in Archaeological-Linguistic Correlation. *Archaeology of Eastern North America* 15:1–11.

Fitzhugh, William, ed. 1985. *Cultures in Contact: The European Impact on Native Cultural Institutions in Eastern North America,* A.D. *1000–1800.* Washington, D.C.: Smithsonian Institution Press.

Flannery, Regina. 1939. *An Analysis of Coastal Algonquian Culture.* The Catholic University of America, Anthropological Series no. 7, Washington D.C.: Catholic University of America Press.

Foucault, Michael. 1980. *Power/Knowledge: Selected Interviews and Other Writings, 1972–1977.* Edited and translated by Colin Gordon. New York: Pantheon Books.

Fried, Morton. 1967. *The Evolution of Political Society: An Essay in Political Anthropology.* New York: Random House.

———. 1975. *The Notion of Tribe.* Menlo Park: Cummings.

Furst, Peter. 1976. *Hallucinogens and Culture.* Novato, Calif.: Chandler and Sharp.

Garman, James C. 1991. Prehistoric Maize at Riverside, Gill. *Bulletin of the Massachusetts Archaeological Society* 52(1):1–7.

Gardiner, Leift Lion. 1660. Gardener's Pequot Warres. *Collections of the Massachusetts Historical Society,* 3rd ser., 3:131–60.

———. 1652. Lion Gardiner to John Winthrop, Jr. *Collections of the Massachusetts Historical Society,* 4th ser., 8:62–65.

Geertz, Clifford. 1973. Deep Play; Notes on a Balinese Cockfight. Pp. 412–53 in *The Interpretation of Cultures. Selected Essays.* New York: Basic Books.

Genovese, E. D. 1974. *Roll, Jordan, Roll: The World the Slaves Made.* New York: Pantheon.

Gero, Joan M., and Margaret Conkey, eds. *Engendering Archaeology: Women and Prehistory.* Oxford and Cambridge, Mass.: Basil Blackwell.

Gewertz, D. 1984. The Tchambuli View of Persons: a Critique of Individualism in the Work of Mead and Chodorow. *American Anthropologist* 86:615–29.

Gibson, Susan. 1980. *Burr's Hill: A 17th Century Wampanoag Burial Ground in Warren, Rhode Island.* Providence, R.I.: Brown University Press.

Giddens, Anthony. 1990. *Central Problems in Social Theory: Structure and Contradition in Social Analysis.* Berkeley: University of California Press.

Goddard, Ives. 1973. Delaware Kinship Terminology. *Studies in Linguistics* 23:39–55.

———. 1978. Eastern Algonquian Languages. In Trigger, ed., *Northeast,* pp. 70–77, *Handbook of North American Indians,* vol. 15.

———. 1978a. Central Algonquian Languages. In Trigger, ed., *Northeast,* pp. 583–87, *Handbook of North American Indians,* vol. 15.

———. 1978b. Some Early Examples of American Indian Pidgin English from New England. *International Journal of American Linguistics* 43(1):37–41.

———. 1979. Further Examples of American Indian Pidgin English from New England. *International Journal of American Linguistics* 44(1):73.

Goddard, Ives, and Kathleen Bragdon, eds. and trans. 1988. *Native Writings in Massachusett.* Memoirs No. 185. American Philosophical Society, Philadelphia, Pa.

Goffman, Erving. 1959. *Presentation of Self in Everyday Life.* New York: Doubleday.

Goodby, Robert G. 1992. Diversity as a Typological Construct: Understanding Late Woodland Ceramics from Narragansett Bay. Paper presented at the annual meeting of the Northeastern Anthropological Association, 11–14 March, Bridgewater, Mass.

Goody, Jack. 1976. *Production and Reproduction.* Cambridge: Cambridge University Press.

Gookin, Daniel. 1806 [1674]. Historical Collections of the Indians in New England. Reprinted in *Collections of the Massachusetts Historical Society,* 3rd ser., vol. 1, pp. 141–229.

———. 1972 [1836]. *An Historical Account of the Doings and Sufferings of The Christian Indians in New England in the Years 1675, 1676, 1677.* Reprint, New York: Arno Press.

Gookin, Frederick William. 1912. *Daniel Gookin, 1612–1687.* Chicago: R. R. Donnelley and Sons.

Gramly, R. M., and Gretchen Gwyne. 1979. Two Late Woodland Sites on Long Island Sound. *Bulletin of the Massachusetts Archaeological Society* 40(1):5–19.

Grumet, Robert. 1978. "We Are Not so Great Fools": Changes in Upper Delawaran Sociopolitical Life, 1630–1758. Ph.d. diss., Department of Anthropology, Rutgers University.

———. 1980. Sunksquaws, Shamans, and Tradeswomen: Middle Atlantic Coastal Algonkian Women During the 17th and 18th Centuries. Pp. 43–62 in *Women and Colonization: Anthropological Perspectives,* edited by Mona Etienne and Eleanor Leacock. New York: Praeger.

Gudeman, Stephen. 1986. *Economics As Culture: Models and Metaphors of Livelihood.* London: Routledge and Kegan Paul.

Hall, Robert L. 1977 An Anthropocentric Perspective for Eastern United States Prehistory. *American Antiquity* 42(4):499-518.

Hallowell, A. Irving. 1928. Recent Changes in the Kinship Terminology of the St. Francis Abenaki. Pp. 97-145 in *Proceedings of the 22nd International Congress of Americanists.* 2 vols. Rome, 1926.

———. 1943. The Nature and Function of Property as a Social Institution. *Journal of Legal and Political Sociology* 1(3-4):115-38.

———. 1955. *Culture and Experience.* Philadelphia: University of Pennsylvania Press.

———. 1966. The Role of Dreams in Ojibwa Culture. Pp. 267-92 in *The Dream and Human Societies*, edited by Gustave Edmund von Grunebaum and Roger Caillois. Berkeley: University of California Press.

Hamell, George R. 1987. Mythical Realities and European Contact in the Northeast during the Sixteenth and Seventeenth Centuries. *Man in the Northeast* 33:63-87.

———. 1987a. Strawberries, Floating Islands, and Rabbit Captains: Mythical Realities and European Contact in the Northeast During the Sixteenth and Seventeenth Centuries. *Journal of Canadian Studies* 21(4):72-94.

Hare, Lloyd C. 1932. *Thomas Mayhew Patriarch to the Indians 1593-1682.* New York: D. Appleton and Co.

Heath, Dwight, ed. 1963 [1622]. *A Journal of the Pilgrims at Plymouth: Mourt's Relation.* Reprint, New York: Corinth Books.

Heckenberger, Michael J., James B. Petersen, and Nancy Asch Sidell. 1992. Early Evidence of Maize Agriculture in the Connecticut River Valley of Vermont. *Archaeology of Eastern North America* 20:125-49.

Hedden, Mark H. 1991. A Winged Figure Incised on a Slate Pebble. *The Maine Archaeological Society Bulletin* 31(1):41-50.

Hedican, Edward J. 1990. Algonquian Kinship Terminology: Some Problems of Interpretation. *Man in the Northeast* 40:1-15.

Helms, M. 1981. Succession to High Office in Pre-Columbian Circum-Carribbean Cheifdoms. *Man* 15:718-31.

Henretta, James. 1979. Social History as Lived and Written. *American Historical Review* 84(5):1293-1331.

Higginson, Francis. 1970 [1629]. Francis Higginson's New England Plantation. In Young, ed., *Chronicles of the First Planters of the Colony of Massachusetts Bay 1623-1636*, pp. 239-68.

Hirsch, Adam J. 1988. The Collision of Military Cultures in Seventeenth-Century New England. *Journal of American History* 74:1187–1212.

Hocart, A. M. 1970. *Kings and Councilors. An Essay in the Comparative Anatomy of Human Society.* Edited by Rodney Needham. Chicago: University of Chicago Press.

Hockett, Charles F. 1964. The Proto-Central Algonquian Kinship System. Pp. 239–57 in *Explorations in Cultural Anthropology: Essays in Honor of George P. Murdock*, edited by Ward H. Goodenough. New York: McGraw-Hill.

Hodder, Ian. 1982. Theoretical Archaeology: A Reactionary View. Pp. 1–16 in *Symbolic and Structural Archaeology*, edited by Ian Hodder. Cambridge: Cambridge University Press.

Hoffman, Curtiss. 1989. Figure and Ground: The Late Woodland Village Problem as Seen from the Uplands. *Bulletin of the Massachusetts Archaeological Society* 50(1):24–28.

Hopkins, Samuel. 1911. Historical Memoirs relating to the Housatonic Indians (1693–1755). The Magazine of History, Extra Number 17.

Hubbard, William. 1815 [1677]. *The Present State of New England. Being a Narrative of the Troubles with the Indians in New-England, from the First Planting Thereof in the Year 1607, to this Present Year 1677* [. . .] Reprint, Boston: John Foster.

———. 1865 [1677]. *The History of the Indian Wars in New England from the First Settlement to the Termination of the War with King Philip, in 1677.* 2 vols. Reprint. Edited by Samuel G. Drake. Roxbury, Mass.: W.E. Woodward.

Hultkrantz, Ake. 1979. *The Religions of the American Indians.* Berkeley: University of California Press.

Humins, John H. 1987. Squanto and Massasoit: A Struggle for Power. *The New England Quarterly* 60(1):54–70.

Hymes, Dell. 1981. *"In vain I tried to Tell You": Essays in Native American Ethnopoetics.* Philadelphia: University of Pennsylvania Press.

Jaworski, Carole. 1990. 2500-year-old Village Predates Agriculture. *Nor'easter* 2(2):32–37.

Jenks, Samuel. 1827. The Tradition of the Taumkhods. *New England Galaxy* 10(486), 2 February.

Jennings, Francis. 1975. *The Invasion of America: Indians, Colonialism, and the Cant of Conquest.* Chapel Hill: University of North Carolina Press.

Jirikowic, Christine. 1990. The Political Implications of a Cultural Practice: A New Perspective on Ossuary Burial in the Potomac Valley. *North American Archaeologist* 11(4):353–74.

Johnson, Edward. 1910 [1654]. *Johnson's Wonder-Working Providence, 1628–1651.* Edited by J. Franklin Jameson. Reprint, New York: Charles Scribner's Sons.

Johnson, Eric S. 1991. Released from Thraldom by the Stroke of War: Coercion and Warfare in Native Politics of Seventeenth-Century Southern New England. Paper presented at the Dublin Seminar for New England Folklife, Boston University, 29 and 30 June.

———. 1992. Community and Confederation: A Protohistoric Political Geography of Southern New England. Paper presented at the Northeastern Anthropological Association Meeting, Bridgewater, Mass., 11–14 March.

———. 1993a. "Some by Flatteries and Others by Threatenings": Political Strategies among Native Americans of Seventeenth Century New England. Ph.D. diss., Department of Anthropology, University of Massachusetts.

Johnson, Eric S., and James W. Bradley. 1987. The Bark Wigwams Site: An Early Seventeenth-Century Component in Central Massachusetts. *Man in the Northeast* 33:1–26.

Johnson, G. A. 1978. Information Sources and the Development of Decision-Making Organizations. Pp. 87–112 in *Social Archaeology*, edited by C. L. Redman, M. J. Berman, E. V. Curtin, W. T. Langhorne, Jr., N. M. Versaggi, and J. C. Wanser. New York: Academic Press.

Josselyn, John. 1988 [1674]. John Josselyn, Colonial Traveler: A Critical Edition of Two Voyages to New England. Edited by Paul J. Lindholdt. Hanover, N.H.: University Press of New England.

Juet, Robert 1912 [1609]. The Third Voyage of Master Henry Hudson, Written by Robert Juet, of Lime-House. Reprinted in *Forerunners and Competitors of the Pilgrims and Puritans*, edited by Charles Herbert Levermore, pp. 389–426. New York: The New England Society.

Keesing, Roger M. 1975. *Kin Groups and Social Structure.* New York: Holt, Rinehart and Winston.

Kellaway, William. 1961. *The New England Company, 1649–1776: Missionary Society to the American Indians.* New York: Barnes and Noble.

Kelley, Marc A., T. Gail Barrett, and Sandra D. Saunders. 1987. Diet, Dental Disease, and Transition in Northeastern Native Americans. *Man in the Northeast* 33:113–25.

Kelley, Marc A., Paul S. Sledzik, and Sean P. Murphy. 1987. Health, Demographics, and Physical Constitution in Seventeenth-Century Rhode Island Indians. *Man in the Northeast* 34:1–25.

Kerber, Jordon E. 1984. Prehistoric Human Occupation and Changing Environment of Potowomut Neck, Warwick, Rhode Island: An Interdisciplinary Approach. Ph.D. diss., Department of Anthropology, Brown University.

———. 1988. Where Are the Woodland Villages in the Narragansett Bay Region? *Bulletin of the Massachusetts Archaeological Society* 49(2): 66–71 [preface pp. 44–45].

Kerber, Jordan E., and Barbara Luedtke. 1981. Technical Report on a Prehistoric Survey of Prudence Island. Rhode Island Historic Preservation Commission.

Kerber, Jordan E., Alan Leveillee, and Ruth L. Greenspan. 1989. An Unusual Dog Burial Feature at the Lambert Farm Site, Warwick, Rhode Island: Preliminary Observations. *Archaeology of Eastern North America* 17:165–74.

Kohl, P. L. 1981. Materialist Approaches in Prehistory. *Annual Review of Anthropology* 10:89–118.

Krim, Arthur J. 1980. Acculturation of the New England Landscape: Native and English Toponymy of Eastern Massachusetts. Pp. 69–88 in *New England Prospect: Maps, Place Names, and the Historical Landscape*, edited by Peter Benes. Boston: Boston University.

Kuper, Hilda. 1972. The Language of Sites in the Politics of Space. *American Anthropologist* 74:411–25.

Kupperman, Karen Ordahl. 1980. *Settling with the Indians: The Meeting of English and Indian Cultures in America, 1580–1640.* Totowa, N.J.: Rowman and Littlefield.

Laet, Joannes de. 1909. From the "New World," by Johan de Laet, 1625, 1630, 1633, 1640. Pp. 29–60 in *Narratives of New Netherland 1609–1664*, edited by J. Franklin Jameson. New York: Charles Scribner's Sons. Reprinted, New York: Barnes and Noble, 1967.

LaFantasie, Glenn W., ed. 1988. *The Correspondence of Roger Williams, Volumes I (1629–1653) and II (1654–1682).* Hanover: University Press of New England.

Lavin, Lucianne. 1988. Coastal Adaptations in Southern New England and Southern New York. *Archaeology of Eastern North America* 16:101–20.

———. 1988a. The Morgan Site, Rocky Hill, Connecticut: A Late Woodland Farming Community in the Connecticut River Valley. *Bulletin of the Connecticut Archaeological Society* 51:7–22.

Lavin, Lucianne, and Harold Juli. 1987. Aboriginal House Structures in Southern New England and Southern New York. Paper presented at the Annual Meeting of the Conference on New England Archaeology, Amherst, Mass., 21 March.

Lavin, Lucianne, Fred Gudrian, and Laurie Miroff. n.d. Pottery Production and Cultural Process: Prehistoric Ceramics from the Morgan Site. Feschrift for Bert Salwen. Edited by Nan Rothschild and Diana Wall. *Man in the Northeast*, In press.

Leach, Edward. 1971 [1951]. The Structural Implications of Matrilateral Cross-Cousin Marriage. *Journal of the Royal Anthropological Institute* 81:24–29; 51–53. Reprinted in *Readings in Kinship and Social Structure*, edited by Nelson Graburn, pp. 223–31. New York: Harper and Row.

Leacock, Eleanor. 1954. The Montagnais "Hunting Territory" and the Fur Trade. *Memoirs of the American Anthropological Association* 78. Menasha, WI.

———. 1978. Women's status in egalitarian society: Implications for social evolution. *Current Anthropology* 19:247–55, 268–75.

———. 1982. Relations of Production in Band Society. Pp. 159–70 in *Politics and History in Band Societies*, edited by Eleanor Leacock and Richard Lee. Cambridge: Cambridge University Press.

———. 1983. Ethnohistorical investigation of Egalitarian Politics in Eastern North America. Pp. 17–31 in *The Development of Political Organization in Native North America*, edited by Elisabeth Tooker. Philadelphia: The American Ethnological Society.

Leacock, Eleanor, and Richard Lee. 1982. Introduction. Pp. 1–20 in *Politics and History in Band Societies*, edited by Eleanor Leacock and Richard Lee. Cambridge: Cambridge University Press.

Lechford, Thomas. 1833 [1642]. Plaine Dealing: Or Nevves from New England. Reprint. *Massachusetts Historical Society* 35(3): 53–128.

LeClerq, Chrétien. 1910 [1691]. *New Relation of Gaspesia, with the Customs and Religion of the Gaspesian Indians*, edited and translated by W. F. Ganong. Reprint. Toronto: The Champlain Society.

Lee, Richard. 1982. Politics, Sexual and Non-sexual, in an Egalitarian Society. Pp. 37–60 in *Politics and History in Band Societies*, edited by Leacock and Lee. Cambridge: Cambridge University Press.

Lescarbot, Marc. 1907-1914 [1618]. *The History of New France*, edited and translated by W. L. Grant. Reprint. Toronto: The Champlain Society.

Leveille, Alan and Renee Van Coughyen. 1990. The Hoskins Park and South Wind Sites: A Program of Archaeological Data Recovery in Rhode Island's Coastal Zone. Vol. 1. The Public Archaeology Laboratory, Pawtucket, R.I.

Levett, Christopher. 1843 [1628]. *Voyage to New England.* Collections of the Massachusetts Historical Society. 3rd ser. 8:159–90.

Levi-Strauss, Claude. 1963. *Structural Anthropology*, translated by Claire Jacobson and Brooke Grundfest Schoepf. New York: Basic Books.

Lightfoot, Kent, Robert Kalin, Owen Lindauer, and Linda Wicks. 1985. Coastal New York Settlement Patterns: A Perspective from Shelter Island. *Man in the Northeast* 30:59–82.

Lindholdt, Paul J. 1988. *Introduction to John Josselyn, Colonial Traveler: A Critical Edition of Two Voyages to New England*, edited by Paul J. Lindholdt. Hanover, N.H.: University Press of New England.

Little, Elizabeth A. 1980. Three Kinds of Indian Land Deeds at Nantucket, Massachusetts. Pp. 61–70 in *Papers of the Eleventh Algonquian Conference*, edited by William Cowan. Ottawa: Carleton University Press.

———. ed. 1981. The Writings of Nantucket Indians. *Nantucket Algonquian Studies* 3. Nantucket Historical Association.

———. 1983. Locus Q-6, Site M52/65, Quidnet, Nantucket, Massachusetts. *Nantucket Archaeological Studies* 2. Nantucket Historical Association.

———. 1986. Observations on Methods of Collection, Use and Seasonality of Shellfish on the Coasts of Massachusetts. *Bulletin of the Massachusetts Archaeological Society* 47(2):46–59.

———. 1988. Where are the Woodland Villages on Cape Cod and the Islands? *Bulletin of the Massachusetts Archaeological Society* 49(2):72–82.

———. 1990. *Bibliography for Historic and Prehistoric Nantucket Indian Studies.* Nantucket: Nantucket Historical Association.

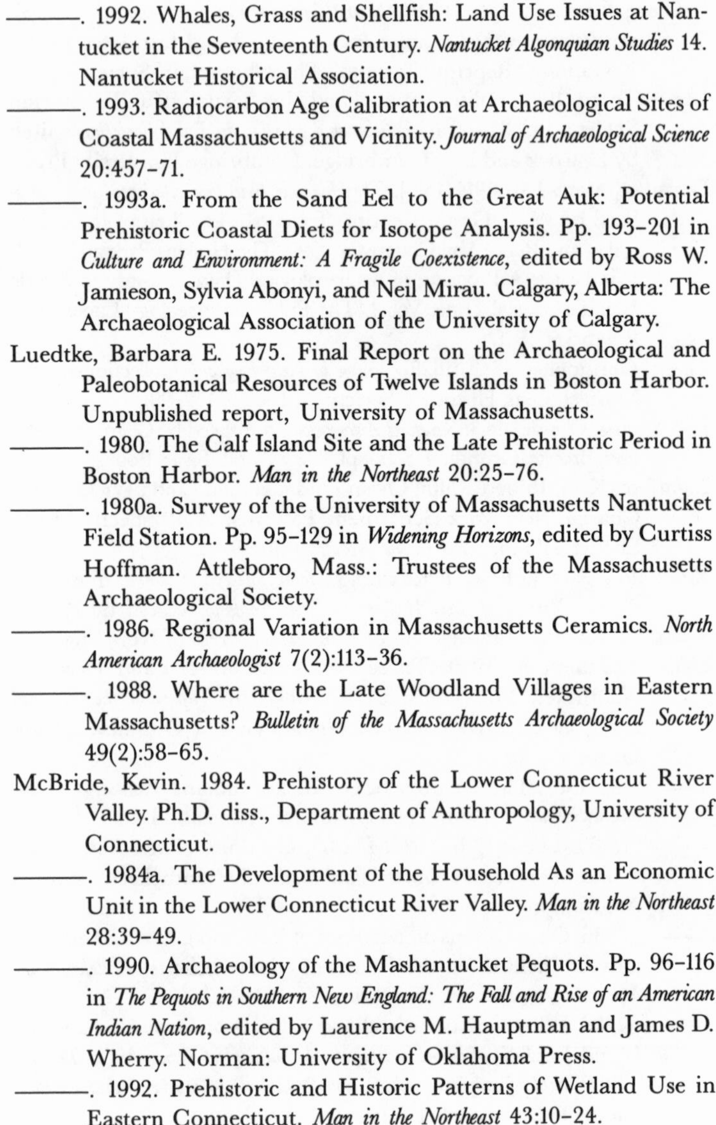

———. 1992. Whales, Grass and Shellfish: Land Use Issues at Nantucket in the Seventeenth Century. *Nantucket Algonquian Studies* 14. Nantucket Historical Association.

———. 1993. Radiocarbon Age Calibration at Archaeological Sites of Coastal Massachusetts and Vicinity. *Journal of Archaeological Science* 20:457–71.

———. 1993a. From the Sand Eel to the Great Auk: Potential Prehistoric Coastal Diets for Isotope Analysis. Pp. 193–201 in *Culture and Environment: A Fragile Coexistence*, edited by Ross W. Jamieson, Sylvia Abonyi, and Neil Mirau. Calgary, Alberta: The Archaeological Association of the University of Calgary.

Luedtke, Barbara E. 1975. Final Report on the Archaeological and Paleobotanical Resources of Twelve Islands in Boston Harbor. Unpublished report, University of Massachusetts.

———. 1980. The Calf Island Site and the Late Prehistoric Period in Boston Harbor. *Man in the Northeast* 20:25–76.

———. 1980a. Survey of the University of Massachusetts Nantucket Field Station. Pp. 95–129 in *Widening Horizons*, edited by Curtiss Hoffman. Attleboro, Mass.: Trustees of the Massachusetts Archaeological Society.

———. 1986. Regional Variation in Massachusetts Ceramics. *North American Archaeologist* 7(2):113–36.

———. 1988. Where are the Late Woodland Villages in Eastern Massachusetts? *Bulletin of the Massachusetts Archaeological Society* 49(2):58–65.

McBride, Kevin. 1984. Prehistory of the Lower Connecticut River Valley. Ph.D. diss., Department of Anthropology, University of Connecticut.

———. 1984a. The Development of the Household As an Economic Unit in the Lower Connecticut River Valley. *Man in the Northeast* 28:39–49.

———. 1990. Archaeology of the Mashantucket Pequots. Pp. 96–116 in *The Pequots in Southern New England: The Fall and Rise of an American Indian Nation*, edited by Laurence M. Hauptman and James D. Wherry. Norman: University of Oklahoma Press.

———. 1992. Prehistoric and Historic Patterns of Wetland Use in Eastern Connecticut. *Man in the Northeast* 43:10–24.

———. 1993. Dutch Exploration and Trade in Eastern Long Island Sound and the Connecticut River Valley. Paper presented at the annual meeting of the Northeastern Anthropological Association, Danbury, Conn., 27 March.

———. 1993a. The Archaeology of Conflict and Ritual. Paper presented at the Second Mashantucket History conferece, Mystic Conn., 17 October.

McBride, Kevin, and Nicholas F. Bellantoni. 1982. The Utility of Ethnohistoric Models for Understanding Late Woodland-Contact Change in Southern New England. *Bulletin of the Connecticut Archaeological Society* 45:51–64.

McBride, Kevin, and Robert Dewar. 1981. Prehistoric Settlement in the Lower Connecticut River Valley. *Man in the Northeast* 22:37–66.

———. 1987. Agriculture and Cultural Evolution: Causes and Effects in the Lower Connecticut Valley. Pp. 305–28 in *Emergent Horticultural Economies of the Eastern Woodlands*, edited by William F. Keegan. Southern Illinois University at Carbondale Center for Archaeological Investigations Occasional Paper No. 7.

McGaw, Judith. 1989. No Passive Victims, No Separate Spheres: A Feminist Perspective on Technology's history. Pp. 172–91 in *History and the History of Technology, Essays in Honor of Melvin Kranzberg*, edited by Stephen H. Cutcliffe and Robert C. Post. Bethlehem, Pa.: Lehigh University Press.

McManamon, Francis P. 1982. Prehistoric Land Use on Outer Cape Cod. *Journal of Field Archaeology* 9:1–20.

McManamon, Francis P., and James W. Bradley. 1986. The Indian Neck Ossuary and Late Woodland Prehistory in Southern New England. In McManamon, Bradley, and Magennis, eds., *Indian Neck Ossuary, Chapters in the Archaeology of Cape Cod V*, pp. 3–47.

———. 1988. The Indian Neck Ossuary. *Scientific American* 256(5): 98–104.

McManamon, Francis P., James W. Bradley, and Ann L. Magennis. 1986. *The Indian Neck Ossuary: Chapters in the Archeology of Cape Cod, V.* Cultural Resources Management Study No. 17. Division of Cultural Resources, North Atlantic Regional Office, U.S. Department of the Interior, Boston, Mass.

McManis, Douglas R. 1975. *Colonial New England: An Historical Geography.* New York: Oxford University Press.

Magennis, Ann L. 1986. The Physical Anthropology of the Indian Neck Ossuary. In McManamon, Bradley, Magennis, eds., *The Indian Neck Ossuary: Chapters in the Archaeology of Cape Cod, V*, pp. 50–183.

Malinowski, Bronislaw. 1984 [1922]. *Argonauts of the Western Pacific: An Account of Native Enterprise and Adventure in the Archipelagoes of Melanesian New Guinea*. Reprint, Prospect Heights, Ill.: Waveland Press.

Malone, Patrick. 1991. *The Skulking Way of War: Technology and Tactics among the New England Indians*. Lanham, Md.: Madison Books.

Marten, Catherine. 1970. The Wampanoags in the Seventeenth Century: An Ethnohistorical Survey. *Occasional Papers in Old Colony Studies*, December No. 2. Plymouth: Plimoth Plantation Incorporated.

Martin, Calvin. 1975. Four Lives of a Micmac Copper Pot. *Ethnohistory* 22(2):111–33.

Marx, Karl, and Friederick Engels. The Eighteenth Brumaire of Louis Bonaparte. Pp. 97–108 in *Selected Works*. New York: International Publishers.

Massachusetts Historical Commission. 1991. *Bibliography of Archaeological Survey and Mitigation Reports: Massachusetts*. Boston: Massachusetts Historical Commission.

Mather, Cotton. 1977 [1702]. *Magnalia Christi Americana: Or, the Ecclesiastical History of New-England; from its First Planting, in the Year 1620, unto the Year of Our Lord 1698*. London: T. Parkhurst, edited by Kenneth B. Murdock. Reprint. Cambridge: Harvard University Press.

Matthiessen, Peter. 1986. *Men's Lives: The Surfmen and Baymen of the South Fork*. New York: Random House.

Mayhew, Experience. 1709. *Massachuset Psalter*. Boston: Nathaniel Green.

———. 1727. *Indian Converts, or Some Account of the Lives and Dying Speeches of a Considerable Number of Christianized Indians of Martha's Vineyard*. London: J. Osborn.

Mayhew, Matthew. 1940 [1694]. A Brief Narrative of the Success Which the Gospel Had Among the Indians of Martha's Vineyard. Reprint, *The Massachusetts Historical Society*, 2nd ser., No. 119.

Medaglia, Christian C., Elizabeth A. Little, and Margaret J. Schoeninger. 1990. Late Woodland Diet on Nantucket Island: A Study Using Stable Isotope Ratios. *Bulletin of the Massachusetts Archaeological Society* 51(2):49–82.

Merleau-Ponty, Maurice. 1962. *Phenomenology of Perception*. London: Routledge and Kegan Paul.

Metcalf, P. Richard. 1974. Who Should Rule at Home? Native American Politics and Indian-White Relations. *The Journal of American History* 61(3):651–65.

MHS = Massachusetts Historical Society. 1630-present. Collections. Boston, Massachusetts.

Miller, Daniel, and Christopher Tilley, eds. 1984. Ideology, Power and Prehistory: An Introduction. Pp. 1–16 in *Ideology, Power and Prehistory*, edited by Miller and Tilley. Cambridge: Cambridge University Press.

———. 1984. Ideology, Power, Material Culture and Long-term Change. Pp. 147–52 in *Ideology, Power and Prehistory*, edited by Miller and Tilley. Cambridge: Cambridge University Press.

Miller, Jay. 1974. The Delaware as Women: A symbolic solution. *American Ethnologist* 1(3):507–14.

Miller, Perry. 1953. *Roger Williams: His Contribution to the American Tradition*. Indianapolis: Bobbs-Merrill.

———. 1964. *Errand Into the Wilderness*. New York: Harper and Row.

Mills, Peter. 1991. The Pursuit of a Regional Context: Understanding an Indian Burial near Steam Mill Road, Deerfield, Massachusetts. *Bulletin of the Massachusetts Archaeological Society* 52(2):50–58.

Moffett, Ross. 1957. A Review of Cape Cod Archaeology. *Bulletin of the Massachusetts Archaeological Society* 19(1):1–19.

Morenon, Pierre. 1986. *Archaeological Assessment at an Ecotone: Route 4 Extension. East Greenwich and North Kingstown, Rhode Island*. The Public Archaeology Program. Occasional Papers No. 14. Rhode Island College, Providence, R.I.

Morgan, Lewis Henry. 1871. *Systems of Consanguinity and Affinity of the Human Family. Smithsonian Institution Contributions to Knowledge* 17. Washington, D.C.

———. 1959. *Lewis Henry Morgan: The Indian Journals, 1859–1862*. Leslie A. White, ed. Ann Arbor: University of Michigan Press.

Morton, Nathaniel. 1910 [1669]. New-Englands Memorial. Pp. 1–225 in *Chronicles of the Pilgrim Fathers*. Edited by John Masefield. New York: E.P. Dutton.

Morton, Thomas. 1947 [1637]. New English Canaan. Reprinted in *Tracts and Other Papers, Relating Principally to the Origin, Settlement, and Progress of the Colonies of North America, from the Discovery of the Country to the Year 1776*, edited by Peter Force, vol. 2. New York: Peter Smith.

Mourt, G. 1963 [1622]. *A Journal of the Pilgrims at Plymouth: Mourt's Relation.* Edited by Dwight Heath. New York: Corinth Books.

Mrozowski, Stephen A. 1992. A Preliminary Report on the Discovery of a Late Prehistoric/Early Historic Period Horticultural Settlement on Cape Cod. Paper presented at the annual meeting of the Northeastern Anthropological Association, Bridgewater, Mass., 11–14 March.

Mrozowski, Stephen A., and Kathleen J. Bragdon. 1993. Feast or Famine? Native Agriculture and Population Stress on Seventeenth Century Cape Cod. Paper presented at the annual meeting of the Northeastern Anthropological Association, Danbury, Conn. 25–28 March 1993.

Mukhopadhyay, Carol C., and Patricia J. Higgins. 1988. Anthropological Studies of Women's Status Revisited: 1977–1987. *Annual Reviews in Anthropology* 17:461–95.

Mulholland, Mitchell Tyler. 1985. Patterns of Change in Prehistoric Southern New England: A Regional Approach. Ph.D. diss., Deptartment of Anthropology, University of Massachusetts.

Mundkur, Balaji. 1983. *The Cult of the Serpent: An Interdisciplinary Survey of Its Manifestations and Origins.* Albany: State University of New York Press.

Munson, Patrick. 1973. The Origins and Antiquity of Maize-bean-squash Agriculture in Eastern North America; Some Linguistic evidence. Pp. 107–35 in *Variations in Anthropology*, edited by D. W. Lathrap and Jody Douglas. Urbana: Illinois Archaeological Survey.

Murdock, George Peter. 1949. *Social Structure.* New York: MacMillan.

MVD = Martha's Vineyard Deeds. 1960-present. Court House, Edgarton, Mass.

Nanepashemet. 1993. Smells Fishy to Me: An Argument Supporting the Use of Fish Fertilizer by the Native People of Southern New England. Pp. 42–50 in *Algonkians of New England: Past and Present*, edited by Peter Benes. The Dublin Seminar for New England Folklife, Annual Proceedings, Boston University.

———. 1993a. Hobbomock: A Special Instrument Sent of Massasoit for Their Good Beyond Their Expectation. Paper presented at the annual meeting of the Northeastern Anthropological Association, Danbury Conn., 26 March.

Nassaney, Michael S. 1989. An Epistemological Enquiry into Some Archaeological and Historical Interpretations of 17th Century Native American-European Relations. Pp. 76–93 in *Archaeological Approaches to Cultural Identity*, edited by S. J. Shennan. London: Unwin Hyman.

NCR = Nantucket Court Records. 1650-present. Court House, Nantucket, Mass.

Nerlove, Sara, and A. Kimball Romney. 1967. Sibling Terminology and Cross-Sex Behavior. *American Anthropologist* 69:179–87.

Netting, Robert McC. 1990. Population, Permanent Agriculture, and Polities: Unpacking the Evolutionary Portmanteau. In Upham, ed., *The Evolution of Political Systems: Sociopolitics in Small-Scale Sedentary Societies*, pp. 21–61.

Nicholas, George P. 1991. Places and Spaces: Changing Patterns of Wetland Use in Southern New England. *Man in the Northeast* 42:75–98.

Niering, W., and R. Warren. 1980. Vegetation Patterns and Processes in New England Salt Marshes. *Bioscience* 30:301–307.

Nixon, S. W., and C. A. Oviatt. 1973. Ecology of a New England Salt Marsh. *Ecological Monographs* 43:463–98.

Odum, E. P. 1971. *Fundamentals of Ecology*. 3rd edition. Philadelphia: Saunders Press.

Ortner, Sherry. 1984. Theory in Anthropology Since the Sixties. *The Comparative Study of Society and History* 10:126–66.

Ortner, Sherry, and Harriet Whitehead. 1981. Introduction: Accounting for Sexual Meanings. Pp. 1–27 in *Sexual Meanings: The Cultural Construction of Gender and Sexuality*, edited by Ortner and Whitehead. Cambridge: Cambridge University Press.

Pagoulatos, Peter. 1990. Late Woodland and Contact Period Land-Use Patterns in Rhode Island: Continuity and Change. *Bulletin of the Massachusetts Archaeological Society* 51(2):69–82.

Peña, Elizabeth Shapiro. 1990. Wampum Production in New Netherland and Colonial New York: The Historical and Archaeological Context. Ph.D. diss., Department of Archaeology. Boston University: University Microfilms.

Petersen, James B. 1990. Evidence of the Saint Lawrence Iroquoians in Northern New England: Population Movement, Trade, or Stylistic Borrowing? *Man in the Northeast* 40:31–39.

Peterson, Nicolas. 1993. Demand Sharing: Reciprocity and the Pressure for Generosity among Foragers. *American Anthropologist* 95(4): 860–74.

Plane, Ann Marie. 1990. Childbirth Practices among Native American Women of New England and Canada, 1600–1800. Pp. 13–24 in *Medicine and Healing*, edited by Peter Benes. Dublin Seminar for New England Folklife, Annual Proceedings, Boston University.

———. 1991. New England's Logboats: Four Centuries of Watercraft. *Bulletin of the Massachusetts Archaeological Society* 52(1):8–17.

Poewe, Karla. 1981. *Matrilineal Ideology: Male-Female Dynamics in Luapula, Zambia*. New York: Academic Press.

Potter, Steven. 1993. *Commoners, Tribes and Chiefs: The Development of Algonquian Cultures in the Potomac Valley*. Charlottesville: University of Virginia Press.

Pratt, Mary Louise. 1986. Fieldword in Common Places. Pp. 27–50 in *Writing Culture: The Poetics and Politics of Ethnography*, edited by James Clifford and George E. Marcus. Berkeley: University of California Press.

Prentice, Guy. 1986. Origins of Plant Domestication in the Eastern United States: Promoting the Individual in Archaeological Theory. *Southeastern Archaeology* 5:103–19.

Pretola, John. 1986. The Springfield Fort Hill Site: A New Look. *Bulletin of the Archaeological Society of Connecticut* 48:35–44.

Pretola, John, and Elizabeth A. Little. 1988. Nantucket: An Archaeological Record from the Far Island. *Bulletin of the Archaeological Society of Connecticut* 51:47–68.

Pring, Martin. 1906 [1603]. *A Voyage Set Out from the Citie of Bristoll with a Small Ship and a Barke for the Discoverie of the North Part of Virginia*. Reprinted in *Early English and French Voyages Chiefly from Hakluyt 1534–1608*, edited by Henry S. Burrage, pp. 341–52. New York: Charles Scribner's Sons.

Pritchard, P. 1967. What Is an Estuary? Physical Viewpoint. Pp. 3–5 in *Estuaries*, edited by G. Lauff. Washington, D.C.: American Association for the Advancement of Science.

Pynchon, John. 1652-1701. Account Books. 6 vols. Connecticut Valley Historical Museum, Springfield, Mass.

Pynchon, William. 1645-1650. Account Books. Forbes Library, Northampton, Mass.

Quinn, David B. 1975. *North America from Earliest Discovery to First Settlements: The Norse Voyages to 1612*. New York: Harper and Row.

Rainey, Froelich G. 1936. A Compilation of Historical Data Contributing to the Ethnography of Connecticut and Southern New England Indians. *Bulletin of the Archaeological Society of Connecticut* 3:1–89.

Redfield, A. C. 1972. Development of a New England Salt Marsh. *Ecological Monographs* 42:201–37.

Rhoades, R. E. 1978. Archaeological Use and Abuse of Ecological Concepts and Studies: The Ecotone Example. *American Antiquity* 43:608–14.

Riley, Thomas J., Richard Edging, and Jack Rossen. 1990. Cultigens in Prehistoric Eastern North America: Changing Paradigms. *Current Anthropology* 31(5):525–41.

Ritchie, William A. 1969. *The Archaeology of Martha's Vineyard, A Framework for the Prehistory of Southern New England*. Garden City, N.Y.: The Natural History Press.

Robinson, Paul. 1987. The Indian Use of the Salt Pond Region between 4000 B.P. and 1750 A.D. National Register of Historic Places, U.S. Department of the Interior, National Park Service. Copy on file, Historical Preservation Commission, Providence, R.I.

———. 1990. The Struggle Within: The Indian Debate in Seventeenth-Century Narragansett Country. Ph.D. diss., Department of Anthropology, State University of New York at Binghamton.

Robinson, Paul, Marc Kelley, and Patricia E. Rubertone. 1985. Preliminary Biocultural Interpretations from a Seventeenth-Century Narragansett Indian Cemetery in Rhode Island. In Fitzhugh, ed., *Cultures in Contact: The European Impact on Native Cultural Institutions in Eastern North America, A.D. 1000–1800*, pp. 107–30.

Ronda, James. 1981. Generations of Faith: The Christian Indians of Martha's Vineyard. *William and Mary Quarterly*, 3rd ser., 38(3): 369–94.

Rosaldo, Michelle Z. 1974. Woman, Culture, and Society: A Theoretical Overview. Pp. 17–42 in *Woman, Culture, and Society*, edited by Michelle Z. Rosaldo and Louise Lamphere. Stanford: Stanford University Press.

Rosaldo, Renato. 1980. *Ilongot Headhunting 1883–1974: A Study in Society and History*. Stanford: Stanford University Press.

Rosier, James. 1930 [1605]. *A True Relation of the voyage of Captaine George Waymouth*. Reprinted in *Early English and French Voyages chiefly from Hakluyt 1534–1608*, edited by Henry S. Burrage, pp. 353–94. New York: Charles Scribner's Sons.

Rountree, Helen C. 1989. *The Powhatan Indians of Virginia: Their Traditional Culture*. Norman: University of Oklahoma Press.

Rowlandson, Mary. 1913 [1682]. *Narrative of the Captivity of Mrs. Mary Rowlandson*. Reprinted in *Narratives of the Indian Wars 1675–1699*, edited by Charles H. Lincoln, pp. 107–67. New York: Charles Scribner's Sons.

Russell, Howard S. 1980. *Indian New England Before the Mayflower*. Hanover: University Press of New England.

Sacks, Karen. 1974. Engels Revisited: Women, the Organization of Production, and Private Property. Pp. 207–22 in *Woman, Culture, and Society*, edited by Michelle Z. Rosaldo and Louise Lamphere. Stanford: Stanford University Press.

Sahlins, Marshall. 1963. Poor Man, Rich Man, Big Man, Chief: Political Types in Melanesia and Polynesia. *American Ethnological Society Monograph* 29. Seattle: University of Washington Press.

———. 1972. *Stone Age Economics*. Chicago: University of Chicago Press.

———. 1985. *Islands of History*. Chicago: University of Chicago Press.

Salisbury, Neal. 1974. Red Puritans: The "Praying Indians" of Massachusetts Bay and John Eliot. *William and Mary Quarterly*, 3rd ser., 31(1):27–54.

———. 1981. Squanto: Last of the Patuxets. Pp. 241–43 in *Survival and Struggle in Colonial America*, edited by David Sweet and Gary B. Nash. Berkeley: University of California Press.

———. 1982. *Manitou and Providence: Indians, Europeans, and the Making of New England, 1500–1634*. New York: Oxford University Press.

———. 1987. Toward the Covenant Chain: Iroquois and Southern New England Algonquians, 1637–1684. Pp. 61–74 in *Beyond the Covenant Chain: The Iroquois and Their Neighbors In Indian North America 1600–1800*, edited by Daniel K. Richter and James H. Merrell. Syracuse: Syracuse University Press.

Salwen, Bert. 1968. Muskeeta Cove 2: A Stratified Woodland Site on Long Island. *American Antiquity* 33(3):322–40.

———. 1978. Indians of Southern New England and Long Island: Early Period. In Trigger, ed., *Northeast*, pp. 160–76, *Handbook of North American Indians*, vol. 15.

Salwen, Bert, and Susan N. Mayer. 1978. Indian Archaeology in Rhode Island. *Archaeology* 31:57–58.

Schindler, Debra L., George J. Armelagos, and M. Pamela Bumsted. 1981. Biocultural Adaptation: New Directions in Northeastern Anthropology. Pp. 229–50 in *Foundations of Northeast Archaeology*, edited by Dean R. Snow. New York: Academic Press.

Schneider, David. 1984. *A Critique of the Study of Kinship*. Ann Arbor: University of Michigan Press.

Schoolcraft, Henry Rowe. 1853–1857. *Information Respecting the History, Condition and Prospects of the Indian Tribes of the United States*. Philadelphia: Lippincott, Grambo.

Seaver, J. E. 1961 [1824]. *A Narrative of the Life of Mrs. Mary Jemison*. Reprint, New York: Corinth Books.

Service, Elman R. 1962. *Primitive Social Organization: An Evolutionary Perspective*. New York: Random House.

Sewall, Samuel. 1973. *The Diary of Samuel Sewall 1674–1729*. Edited by M. Halsey Thomas. 2 vols. Reprint, New York: Farrar, Straus, and Giroux.

Shaw, Leslie. 1992. The Willowbend Site: Cold-Weather Adaptations to Southern Cape Cod, Massachusetts. Paper presented at the fifty-seventh annual meeting of the Society for American Archaeology, Pittsburgh, Pa., 8–12 April.

Shuffelton, Frank. 1976. Indian Devils and Pilgrim Fathers: Squanto, Hobomok, and the English Conception of Indian Religion. *The New England Quarterly* 49:108–16.

Silver, Annette. 1981. Comments on Maize Cultivation in Coastal New York. *North American Archaeologist* 2(2):117–30.

Simon, Brona. 1991. Prehistoric Land Use and Changing Paleoecological Conditions at Titicut Swamp in Southeastern Massachusetts. *Man in the Northeast* 42:63–74.

Simmons, William Scranton. 1970. *Cautantowwit's House, An Indian Burial Ground on the Island of Conanicut in Narragansett Bay*. Providence: Brown University Press.

———. 1976. Southern New England Shamanism: An Ethnographic Reconstruction. Pp. 217–56 in *Papers of the Seventh Algonquian Conference*, edited by William Cowan. Ottawa: Carleton University.

———. 1978. Narragansett. In Trigger, ed., *Northeast*, pp. 190–97, *Handbook of North American Indians*, vol. 15.

———. 1979. Conversion from Indian to Puritan. *New England Quarterly* 52(2):197–218.
———. 1986. *Spirit of the New England Tribes: Indian History and Folklore, 1620–1984*. Hanover and London: University Press of New England.
Simmons, William, and George Aubin. 1975. Narragansett Kinship. *Man in the Northeast* 9:21–31.
Smith, Bruce. 1989. Origins of Agriculture in Eastern North America. *Science* 246:1566–71.
Smith, John. 1912 [1624]. The Generalle Historie of Virginia, New-England and the Summer Isles. The Sixth Booke: The Generall History of New England. Pp. 650–753 in vol 2 of *Forerunners and Competitors of the Pilgrims and Puritans*, edited by Charles H. Levermore. Brooklyn, N.Y.: Published for the New England Society of Brooklyn.
Snow, Dean R. 1976. The Solon Petroglyphs and Eastern Abnaki Shamanism. Pp. 281–88 in *Papers of the Seventh Algonquian Conference*, edited by William Cowan. Ottawa: Carleton University.
———. 1978. Eastern Abenaki. In Trigger, ed., *Northeast*, pp. 137–47, *Handbook of North American Indians*, vol. 15.
———. 1980. *The Archaeology of New England*. New York: Academic Press.
Snow, Dean, and Kim M. Lanphear. 1988. European Contact and Indian Depopulation in the Northeast: The Timing of the First Epidemics. *Ethnohistory* 35(1):15–33.
Solecki, R. S. 1950. The Archaeological Position of Historic Fort Corchaug, Long Island and Its Relation to Contemporary Forts. *Archaeological Society of Connecticut Bulletin* 24:3–40.
Speck, Frank. 1909. Notes on the Mohegan and Niantic Indians. Pp. 181–210 in *The Indians of Greater New York and the Lower Hudson*, edited by Clark Wissler. Anthropological Papers, vol. 3. New York: American Museum of Natural History.
———. 1919. Penobscot Shamanism. *Memoirs of the American Anthropological Association* 6:237–38.
———. 1928. Native Tribes and Dialects of Connecticut: A Mohegan-Pequot Diary. *43rd Annual Report of the Bureau of American Ethnology 1925–1926*. Washington, D.C.: U.S. Government Printing Office.
———. 1928a. *Territorial Subdivisions and Boundaries of the Wampanoag, Massachusett, and Nauset Indians*. Indian Notes and Monographs, no. 7. Museum of the American Indian, Heye Foundation.

———. 1964 [1919]. The Functions of Wampum among the Eastern Algonkian. *Memoirs of the American Anthropological Association* 6:3–74. Reprint, New York: Krauss Reprint.

Spiess, Arthur E., and Bruce D. Spiess. 1987. New England Pandemic of 1616-1622: Cause and Archaeological Implication. *Man in the Northeast* 34:71–83.

Springer, J. W. 1984. An Ethnohistoric Study of the Smoking Complex in Eastern North America. *Ethnohistory* 28(3):217–35.

Starna, William A. 1992. The Biological Encounter: Disease and the Ideological Domain. *The American Indian Quarterly* 16(4):511–19.

Stiles, Ezra. 1916. *Extracts from the Itineraries and Other Miscellanies of Ezra Stiles, D.D., LL.D., 1755–1794.* Edited by Franklin Bowditch Dexter. New Haven: Yale University Press.

Sturtevant, William C. 1975. Two 1761 Wigwams at Niantic, Connecticut. *American Antiquity* 40(4):437–44.

———. 1983. Tribe and State in the Sixteenth and Twentieth Centuries. Pp. 3–16 in *The Development of Political Organization in Native North America*, edited by Elisabeth Tooker. Philadelphia: American Ethnological Society.

Tanner, Helen. 1989. The Land and Water Communication Systems of the Southeastern Indians. Pp. 6–20 in *Powhatan's Mantle: Indians in the Colonial Southeast*, edited by Peter Wood, Gregory Waselkov, and M. Thomas Hatley. Lincoln: University of Nebraska Press.

Tantaquidgeon, Gladys. 1930. Notes on the Gay Head Indians of Massachusetts. *Indian Notes* 7(1):1–26. Museum of the American Indian, Heye Foundation.

Taylor, William. 1976. The Fort Hill Bluff Site. *Bulletin of the Massachusetts Archaeological Society* 38(1, 2):7–12.

Thomas, Peter A. 1976. Contrastive Subsistence Strategies and Land Use as Factors for Understanding Indian-White Relations in New England. *Ethnohistory* 23(1):1–18.

———. 1979. In the Maelstrom of Change: The Indian Trade and Cultural Process in the Middle Connecticut River Valley 1635–1665. Ph.D. diss., Department of Anthropology, University of Massachusetts.

———. 1985. Cultural Change on the Southern New England Frontier, 1630–1665. in Fitzhugh, ed., *Cultures in Contact: The European Impact on Native Cultural Institutions in Eastern North America,* A.D. *1000–1800*, pp. 131–62.

Thomson, Betty Flanders. 1958. *The Changing Face of New England*. New York: Macmillan.

Thorbahn, Peter F. 1984. Socioeconomic Complexity in Prehistoric Hunter-Gatherer Land Use Systems. *Man in the Northeast* 28:12–25.

———. 1988. Where Are the Late Woodland Villages in Southern New England? *Bulletin of the Massachusetts Archaeological Society* 49(2):46–57.

Trent, Robert. 1982. Coastal Algonkian Culture 1500–1680. Pp. 66–94 in *Introduction, Migration and Settlement*, edited by Johnathan L. Fairbanks and Robert Trent. Vol. 1 of *New England Begins: The Seventeenth Century*. Boston: Museum of Fine Arts.

Trigger, Bruce G., ed. 1978. Vol. 15 of *Handbook of North American Indians*, edited by William Sturtevant. Washington, D.C.: Smithsonian Institution.

———. 1987. Introduction to Papers on the Beginnings of the Fur Trade. *Man in the Northeast* 33:27–30.

———. 1992. Constraint and Freedom—A New Synthesis for Archaeological Explanation. *American Anthropologist* 93(3):551–69.

Trumbull, James Hammond. 1903. *Natick Dictionary*. Bureau of American Ethnology Bulletin 25, Washington, D.C.

Tuma, Stuart John Jr. 1985. Contact Period (1500–1675) Burials in Southeast New England. M.A. thesis, Department of History and Historical Archaeology, University of Massachusetts.

Turnbaugh, William. 1976. The Survival of a Native Craft in Colonial Rhode Island. *Man in the Northeast* 11:74–79.

Turner, Victor. 1967. *The Forest of Symbols: Aspect of Ndembu Ritual*. Ithaca: Cornell University Press.

———. 1969. *The Ritual Process*. Chicago: Aldine.

Ubelaker, Douglas H. 1981. Approaches to Demographic Problems in the Northeast. Pp. 175–94 in *Foundations of Northeast Archaeology*, edited by Dean R. Snow. New York: Academic Press.

Underhill, Ruth. 1965. *Red Man's Religion: Beliefs and Practices of the Indians North of Mexico*. Chicago: University of Chicago Press.

Upham, Steadman, ed. 1990. *The Evolution of Political Systems, Sociopolitics in Small-Scale Sedentary Societies*. Cambridge: Cambridge University Press.

Van Gennep, Arnold. 1960. *The Rites of Passage*. Edited by Solon T. Kimball and translated by Monika B. Vizedom and Gabrielle L. Caffee. Chicago: University of Chicago Press.

Vastokas, Joan M., and Roman K. Vastokas. 1973. *Sacred Art of the Algonkians.* Peterborough, Ontario: Mansard Press.

Vaughan, Alden. 1979. *New England Frontier: Puritans and Indians, 1620–1675.* Boston: Little, Brown.

Verrazzano, Giovanni da. 1968. Voyages. Pp. 1–24 in *Sailors' Narratives of Voyages along the New England Coast 1524–1624,* edited by George Parker Winship. New York: B. Franklin.

———. 1970 [1524]. *The Voyages of Giovanni da Verrazzano 1524–1528.* Edited by Lawrence C. Wroth. New Haven: Yale University Press.

Von Gernet, Alexander, and Peter Timmons. 1987. Pipes and Parakeets: Constructing Meaning in an Early Iroquoian Context. Pp. 31–42 in *Archaeology as Long-Term History,* edited by Ian Hodder. Cambridge: Cambridge University Press.

Von Lonkhuyzen, Harold W. 1989. A Reappraisal of the Praying Indians: Acculturation, Conversion, and Identity at Natick, Massachusetts, 1646–1730. *New England Quarterly* 62:396–428.

Wallace, Anthony F. C. 1957. Political Organization and Land Tenure Among the Northeastern Indians, 1600–1830. *Southwestern Journal of Anthropology* 13:301–21.

Wallerstein, Immanuel. 1974. *The Modern World-System.* 3 vols. New York: Academic Press.

Ward, Edward. 1970 [1905]. A Trip to New England in 1699. Reprinted, New York: Burt Franklin.

Warner, Robert Austin. 1935. *The Southern New England Indians to 1725: A Study in Culture Contact.* Ph.D. Diss., Department of History, Yale University, New Haven.

Washburn, Wilcomb E. 1978. Seventeenth-Century Indian Wars. In Trigger, ed., *Northeast,* pp. 89–100, *Handbook of North American Indians,* vol. 15.

Wassenaer, Nicholaes van. 1909. From the *"Historisch Verhael" [1624–1630].* Pp. 61–96 in *Narratives of New Netherland, 1609–1664,* edited by J. Franklin Jameson. Original Narratives in Early American History. New York: Charles Scribner's Sons.

Waters, Joseph H. 1962. Animals Used as Food by Late Archaic and Woodland Cultural Groups in New England. *Science* 137(3526): 283–84.

Waters, Thomas Franklin. 1905. *Ipswich in the Massachusetts Bay Colony.* Ipswich, Mass.: The Ipswich Historical Society.

Watson, Patty Jo, and Mary C. Kennedy. 1991. The Development of Horticulture in the Eastern Woodlands of North America: Women's Role. Pp. 255–75 in *Engendering Archaeology*, edited by Gero and Conkey. London: Basil Blackwell.

Weiner, Annette B. 1992. *Inalienable Possessions: The Paradox of Keeping-While-Giving*. Berkeley: University of California Press.

Weiner, James F. 1991. *The Empty Place: Poetry, Space, and Being among the Foi of Papua New Guinea*. Bloomington: Indiana University Press.

Weinstein, Laurie Lee. 1983. Indian vs. Colonist: Land Competition in 17th Century Plymouth Colony. Ph.D. Diss., Department of Anthropology, Southern Methodist University, Dallas.

———. 1985. The Dynamics of Seventeenth Century Wampanoag Land Relations: The Ethnohistorical Evidence for Locational Change. *Bulletin of the Massachusetts Archaeological Society* 46(1):19–35.

White, Richard. 1991. *The Middle Ground: Indians, Empires, and Republics in the Great Lakes Region, 1650–1815*. Cambridge: Cambridge University Press.

Whitfield, Henry. 1834. Strength out of Weakness; Or a Glorious Manifestation of the Further Progresse of the Gospel among the Indians in New England. Reprint, *Collections of the Massachusetts Historical Society* 35(4):149–96.

Whitlach, R. B. 1982. *The Ecology of New England Tidal Flats: A Community Profile*. Washington, D.C.: United States Fish and Wildlife Service, Biological Services Program.

Whorf, Benjamin Lee. 1956. *Language, Thought, and Reality: Selected Writings of Benjamin Lee Whorf.* Edited by J. B. Carroll. Cambridge, Mass.: M.I.T. Press.

Williams, Lorraine E. 1972. A Study of Seventeenth-Century Culture Contact in the Long Island Sound Area. Ph.D. diss., New York University.

Williams, Roger. 1936 [1643]. *A Key into the Language of America*. Reprint, Providence: The Roger Williams Press.

Williamson, Margaret Holmes. 1979. Powhatan Hair. *Man*, n.s. 14:392–413.

———. 1993. Negotiating Life and Death in Aboriginal Virginia. Paper presented at the annual meeting of the American Anthropological Association, San Francisco, Ca., 17–21 November.

Willoughby, Charles. 1935. *Antiquities of the New England Indians, with Notes on the Ancient Cultures of Adjacent Territories.* Cambridge, Mass.: Peabody Museum.

Winship, George Parker. 1968. *Sailors' Narratives of the Voyages along the New England Coast 1524–1624.* New York: B. Franklin.

Winslow, Edward. 1910 [1624]. Relation. Reprinted in *Chronicles of the Pilgrim Fathers*, edited by Ernest Rhys, pp. 267–356. London: J.M. Dent & Sons.

———. 1834 [1649]. The Glorious Progress of the Gospel amongst the Indians in New England. Reprint, *Collections of the Massachusetts Historical Society*, 3rd ser., 4:69–99.

Winslow, Ola Elizabeth. 1968. *John Eliot Apostle to the Indians.* Boston: Houghton Mifflin.

Winthrop, John. 1908 [1630-1649]. *Journal: "History of New England."* Edited by James Kendall Hosmer. Original Narratives in Early American History. 2 vols. New York: Charles Scribner's Sons.

Winthrop, John, Jr. 1889 [1678]. The Description, Culture and Use of Maiz. Reprint, *Proceedings of the Royal Society* 14:1065–71.

Witthoft, John. 1949. Green Corn Ceremonialism in the Eastern Woodlands. *Occasional Contributions from the Museum of Anthropology of the University of Michigan* 13:31–77.

Wojciechowski, Franz L. 1985. The Paugussett Tribes: An Ethnohistorical Study of the Tribal Interrelationships of the Indians in the Lower Housatonic River Area. Catholic University of Nijmegen, Department of Cultural and Social Anthropology, Nijmegen, The Netherlands.

Wolf, Eric. 1982. Europe and the People without History. Berkeley: University of California Press.

Wood, William. 1634. *Nevv England's Prospect: A True, Lively, and Experimental Description of That Part of America, Commonly Called Nevv England*[. . .] London: Tho.Cotes.

———. 1977 [1634]. *New England's Prospect.* Edited by Alden Vaughan. Amherst: University of Massachusetts Press.

Wright, Rita P. 1991. Women's Labor and Pottery Production in Prehistory. Pp. 194–223 in *Engendering Archaeology*, edited by Gero and Conkey. London: Basil Blackwell.

Wroth, Lawrence C. 1970. *The Voyages of Giovanni da Verrazzano, 1524–1528.* New Haven: Yale University Press.

Yentsch, Anne E., Melbourne R. Carriker, Robert H. Parker, and Victor A. Zullo. 1966. *Marine and Estuarine Environments, Organisms and Geology of the Cape Cod Region.* Marine Biological Laboratory, Woods Hole, Mass.

Yesner, David R. 1980. Maritime Hunter-Gatherers: Ecology and Prehistory, *Current Anthropology* 21(6):727–50.

Young, Alexander. 1970 [1846]. *Chronicles of the First Planters of the Colony of Massachusetts Bay 1623–1636.* Reprint, New York: De Capo Press.

Index

Index